Strategic Marketing in Practice
2008–2009

Strategic Marketing in Practice 2008–2009

Ashok Ranchhod and Ebi Marandi

AMSTERDAM • BOSTON • HEIDELBERG • LONDON • NEW YORK • OXFORD
PARIS • SAN DIEGO • SAN FRANCISCO • SINGAPORE • SYDNEY • TOKYO

Butterworth-Heinemann is an imprint of Elsevier

Butterworth-Heinemann is an imprint of Elsevier
Linacre House, Jordan Hill, Oxford OX2 8DP, UK
30 Corporate Drive, Suite 400, Burlington, MA 01803, USA

First edition 2008

Copyright © 2008 Elsevier Ltd. All rights reserved.

No part of this publication may be reproduced, stored in a retrieval system or transmitted in any form or by any means electronic, mechanical, photocopying, recording or otherwise without the prior written permission of the publisher.

Permissions may be sought directly from Elsevier's Science & Technology Rights Department in Oxford, UK: phone (+44) (0) 1865 843830; fax (+44) (0) 1865 853333; e-mail: permissions@elsevier.com. Alternatively, you can submit your request online. Visit the Elsevier website at http://elsevier.com/locate/permissions, and select *Obtaining permission to use Elsevier material*.

Notice
No responsibility is assumed by the publisher for any injury and/or damage to persons or property as a matter of products liability, negligence or otherwise, or from any use or operation of any methods, products, instructions or ideas contained in the material herein.

British Library Cataloguing in Publication Data
A catalogue record for this book is available from the British Library

Library of Congress Cataloguing in Publication Data
A catalogue record for this book is available from the Library of Congress

ISBN: 978 0 7506 8961 8

For information on all Butterworth-Heinemann publications
visit our website at http://www.elsevierdirect.com

Designed by P.K. McBride

Typeset by Butford Technical Publishing Ltd, Birlingham, Worcs.

Printed and bound in Italy
08 09 10 11 12   10 9 8 7 6 5 4 3 2 1

Working together to grow
libraries in developing countries

www.elsevier.com | www.bookaid.org | www.sabre.org

ELSEVIER   BOOK AID International   Sabre Foundation

Contents

Unit 1	**Introduction**	**1**
	Introduction	1
	Marketing drives the business agenda	2
	'Models' of marketing	3
	Marketing contexts	4
	Strategic marketing activities	5
	Plans and planning processes	5
	The role of strategic marketing	6
	Aims and outcomes for Strategic Marketing in Practice	9
Unit 2	**What is meant by case study analysis?**	**19**
	A brief overview	19
	Analysing a case study	20
	The analyses	20
	Space analysis	23
	Key issues	28
	Example analysis of the mini-case	32
Unit 3	**Understanding the direction and management of marketing activities**	**37**
	Introduction	37
	Business intelligence	38
	The role of information technology	47
	The learning organization and market-based learning	48
	The internationalization process of firms	53
	Globalization	56
Unit 4	**Contemporary issues in marketing**	**61**
	Introduction	61
	Customer loyalty	62
	What is loyalty?	64
	Relationship marketing	68
	Key account management (KAM)	75
	Introduction	75
	What is key account management?	75
	The key account development cycle	78
	Identifying key accounts	79

Contents

Serving key accounts: KAM activities	82
Servicing key accounts: developing a KAM infrastructure	84
The relevance of KAM to relationship marketing	88
Sustainability and strategy	91
Introduction	91
Understanding environmental marketing	93
The Life Cycle Analysis (LCA) concept – life cycle thinking	104
Green marketing strategies	120
Corporate identity	132
Branding	135
Segmentation, targeting and buyer behaviour	140
Internal marketing	148
Social marketing utilizing Internet marketing campaigns	150
Introduction	150
Previous studies	150
Theories and models of social change	151
Adopting an ecological perspective on social marketing	151
Cognitive behavioural models	152
The 'Stages of Change' model	153
The 'Health Belief' model	154
Research methodology	155
Online social marketing – a theoretical framework	158
Concluding remarks	161

Unit 5 Effective customer orientation 165

Introduction	165
Valuing customers	169
Financial analysis and marketing measures	172

Unit 6 The examination 185

The examination	185
Extending knowledge	189
An examiner's point of view	192

Index 195

Unit 1 Introduction

Introduction

The Strategic Marketing in Practice module is part of the new Professional Postgraduate Diploma in Marketing that has been developed at the Chartered Institute of Marketing (CIM). It replaces the old Analysis and Decision paper. It carries many of the same hallmarks, but the format is now slightly different and students are expected to prepare analyses before the examination. The examination will also be a *closed-book examination* now. It is likely that this will be the final paper that students studying for CIM qualifications undertake. The paper requires students to have a good knowledge of all the subjects covered at all levels. It is particularly important that candidates have a good knowledge of subject areas at Certificate, Professional Diploma and Professional Postgraduate Diploma levels. The assessment constitutes questions based on a major case study. For this reason, there is no specific syllabus for this paper, and much of the rationale for this module lies in developing suitable outcomes for candidates considering a career in marketing. It is expected that candidates will have passed the other Professional Postgraduate Diploma modules: Marketing Analysis and Evaluation, Strategic Marketing Decisions and Managing Marketing Performance. Each of these modules covers a wide array of marketing topics that are important for a thorough understanding of marketing at higher levels. The paper requires the application of all the marketing knowledge and experience that students would have gained over several years.

As the title of the paper, 'Strategic Marketing in Practice' (SMIP), suggests, candidates need to be able to *apply* their marketing knowledge and skills to a real-life case study. Also, as in real life, candidates are expected to analyse the case study before the examination and to utilize this analysis in their answers. The case study may take a number of formats. It may be a long case study divided into sections or themes, or it may be in the form of a number of mini cases with a common theme running through them. Comparative mini cases may also be set where students would be required to analyse and comment on different approaches to the same business issues and aims. This type of flexibility allows the examiner to test the candidate's ability to be flexible, creative and innovative when asked to tackle a range of differing types of marketing problems and issues. For this reason, good analytical and implementation skills within a marketing context are required. Strategic marketing plans also may not always feature in the examination questions, but the students' knowledge of key marketing issues will always be tested. Marketers always need to have good analytical capabilities to develop marketing strategies. Once these strategies have been developed, clear and sensible decisions need to be made. Candidates need to be conversant with all aspects of marketing, especially contemporary issues. Cases are by their very nature set in different sectors, have different contexts and require knowledge from different

Unit 1: Introduction

areas of marketing. Marketing problems are rarely neatly packaged. Candidates, therefore, have to have the capability to draw from their wealth of experience and knowledge and also to demonstrate flexibility and creativity by being able to tackle problems in various contexts set in various sectors in different areas of the globe. At present, marketing is undergoing many changes and marketers need to be able to develop a range of skills. The module sits within the overall Professional Postgraduate Diploma scheme as outlined below.

	Entry modules	Research and analysis	Planning	Implementation	Management of marketing
Professional Postgraduate Diploma	Entry Module – Professional Postgraduate Diploma	Analysis and Evaluation	Strategic Marketing Decisions	Managing Marketing Performance	**Strategic Marketing in Practice**
Professional Diploma	Entry Module – Professional Diploma	Marketing Research and Information	Marketing Planning	Marketing Communications	Marketing Management in Practice
Professional Certificate		Marketing Environment	Marketing Fundamentals	Customer Communications	Marketing in Practice
Introductory Certificate		Supporting Marketing Processes (research and analysis, planning and implementation)			

Marketing drives the business agenda

Marketing is a set of activities concerned with creating value for shareholders and other stakeholders by creating and capturing exceptional value for customers. Marketers are the people – business as well as marketing professionals – who make decisions about marketing. Organizations expect professional marketers to take increasing ownership of the whole customer experience. This requires them to become more aware of the operational business agenda, more commercial, more strategic and more innovative. They have to develop an even deeper understanding of customers and take a more integrated approach to marketing, both internal and external. This syllabus is an early step in equipping strategic marketers of the future to fulfil these expectations. Professional marketers in publicly quoted or limited companies have to:

◆ **Focus on the long term** – The focus for marketing is the generation of economic profit (operating profit adjusted for the cost of capital invested in a business or activity), which is how shareholders measure value. Although other business functions can maximize economic profit through efficiency, marketing is the only way to create value.

◆ **Create and capture value for customers** – Marketers create value by increasing the value perceived by customers in an organization's products and services. The key is positioning, which, in today's competitive markets, requires deeper insights (into customers' needs and behaviours) and innovation. By increasing perceived value, marketers create the opportunity for premium pricing through which economic profit is increased.

◆ **Take charge of the business agenda** – Marketing uses its activities and assets (such as brands and relationships) to create customer value. At the same time, these activities and the use of the marketing assets generate results that are consolidated with other financial results and reported. Shareholders measure the value that the business has created for them as the sum of dividends paid and the increase in price of the shares they own. Marketing has to take charge of investment in marketing assets and all the marketing activities that create value. In short, they must take charge of the business agenda.

◆ **Understand the role that technology plays in developing marketing** – Marketing is increasingly becoming technologically-led. Marketers have to understand the key role that technology plays in managing the supply chain, in developing customer relationships and in communicating offers and services through multimedia channels. It is clear that the marketing paradigm is changing swiftly and surely because of the Internet and search engines such as Google, offering companies ready presence on world markets.

'Models' of marketing

The type, or 'model', of marketing practised in any organization depends on a number of factors, not least of which are the nature of the business context and the organization's dominant orientation. Marketing activities in organizations can be grouped broadly into four models:

1 **Sales support** – The emphasis in this model is essentially reactive: marketing supports the direct sales force. It may include activities such as telesales or telemarketing, responding to inquiries, co-ordinating diaries, customer database management, organizing exhibitions or other sales promotions and administering agents. These activities usually come under a sales and marketing director or manager. This form of marketing is common in small and medium enterprises (SMEs) and some organizations operating in a business-to-business (B2B) context.

2 **Marketing communications** – The emphasis in this model is more proactive: marketing promotes the organization and its product/service at a tactical level, either to customers (pull) or to channel members (push). It typically includes activities such as providing brochures and catalogues to support the sales force. Some business-to-consumer (B2C) organizations may use marketing to perform the 'selling' role using direct marketing techniques and to manage campaigns based on a mix of media to raise awareness, generate leads and even take orders. In B2B markets, larger organizations may have marketing communications departments and specialists to make efficient use of marketing expenditures and to co-ordinate communications between business units.

3 **Operational marketing** – The emphasis in this model is for marketing to support the organization with a co-ordinated range of marketing activities including market research, brand management, product development and management, corporate and marketing communications, and customer relationship management (CRM). Given this breadth of activities, planning is also a function usually performed in this role but at an operational or functional level. Typically part of fast-moving consumer goods (FMCG) or B2C organizations, the operational marketing role is increasingly used in B2B organizations.

4   Strategic marketing – The emphasis in this model is for marketing to contribute to the creation of value and competitive customer strategy. Strategic marketing also encompasses positioning strategies for companies both large and small. Strategic marketing is the envelope within which a company's long-term positioning with regard to the opportunities present and resources available is determined. For larger companies, the larger envelope would take in strategic business units as well. In a large or diversified organization, it may also be responsible for the co-ordination of marketing departments or activities in separate business units.

Professional marketers are likely to be responsible for strategic marketing only in those organizations with a strong market, or customer orientation, or with separate marketing departments in business units that require co-ordination. Organizations vary in their need for professional marketers, depending on their size and growth trajectories. Suffice to say that most organizations, whether small or large, for profit or not-for-profit, generally need strategic marketing input, whether in-house or through consultants.

Marketing contexts

Organizations operating in various contexts use different marketing activities. There is no 'one size fits all' approach. Organizations and their marketers have to select and use techniques appropriate to their specific context. Typically, marketing contexts are summarized as follows:

Context	Characteristics
FMCG	Used in organizations with a strong market orientation, the 'standard' model of marketing is based on identification of customers' needs and techniques of segmentation, targeting and positioning supported by branding and customer communications.
B2B	The model of marketing adopted depends on factors such as the importance of face-to-face selling, the dominant orientation and power of buyers. Markets are often less information-rich than FMCG markets, which constrains marketing decisions.
Capital projects	A variant of the B2B model where opportunities for positioning are few and the value of any single order constitutes a significant proportion of turnover in a period.
Not-for-profit	The organization is not driven by shareholder value but by value that can be given to the recipients of charity or environmental benefits. Although competition may not be a significant factor in strategy, positioning may well be very important.
SMEs	Operating in any of the above sectors, SMEs may be limited in their scope of marketing, either because of a lack of resources or lack of full knowledge of marketing techniques. Such organizations may have a rudimentary marketing section or the marketing work may be carried out by the Managing Director. Many SMEs that succeed in the market-place have a strong sense of strategic marketing.

Not-for-profit organizations are driven not by shareholders but by other stakeholders, such as government (public sector), beneficiaries (charities) and volunteers (voluntary sector). The concept of shareholder value may not be relevant in these organizations where, instead, concepts such as 'best value' (public sector) and the level of disbursements to beneficiaries operate. The element of competition may not be explicit in the strategy of these organizations, whose strategies may be more collaborative. However, even such organizations need to be answerable to their stakeholders, and many of the marketing techniques needed are variants of those required for the profit-oriented companies. In fact, some strategies are coming closer together because of the development of Corporate Social Responsibility. The Stock Exchange, for instance, now has a sector FTSE4Good. The *FTSE4Good Index Series* has been designed to measure the performance of companies that meet globally recognized corporate responsibility standards and to facilitate investment in those companies (http://www.ftse.com).

Given the range of different possibilities for practising strategic marketing, it is important, therefore, that those students studying the SMiP paper can explore the application of marketing in a range of different contexts, utilizing the syllabi from the various linked modules and also drawing from current contemporary issues in marketing.

Strategic marketing activities

The full spectrum of strategic marketing activities is illustrated in the statements of marketing practice on which the syllabi of the three modules link to the summative SMiP exam. They include:

- Research and analysis
- Strategic marketing and planning
- Brand management
- Implementing marketing programmes
- Measuring effectiveness
- Managing marketing teams

It goes without saying that strategic marketing operates in a global context. This is not to say that the syllabus has nothing to offer the organization pursuing a domestic strategy or entering its first foreign market. Even if an organization is not operating across borders, it is likely to be working in a market in which competitors based in other countries are operating – in other words, a global context. Throughout this syllabus, the term 'global context' embraces domestic and international activities as well as true global activities of the largest organizations.

Plans and planning processes

The planning processes used in organizations are typically geared to the annual operating and financial reporting cycle. In those organizations in which annual or longer term plans are produced, these plans are usually at three levels:

1   Corporate level

2 Business level

3 Functional level

Marketing contributes to corporate and business plans and develops its own functional plan at an operational level. In organizations with strong strategic management practices (often those with a strong customer orientation), plans are likely to contain the strategies of the organization or business. In organizations where plans are effectively 'budgets', strategy is unlikely to be explicit. It is therefore important to recognize that:

- The terms 'strategy' and 'plan' may not be the same.
- Strategy making and planning may be different processes in organizations.
- Organizations approach strategy formulation in a range of formal and informal ways.

What is sometimes referred to as the 'strategic marketing plan' can take different forms in different organizations. For example:

- It may be the name given to the plans that co-ordinate the marketing activities of the different businesses or units throughout an organization.
- It may be synonymous with the term 'business plan' or 'corporate plan' in an organization with a strong customer focus or responsibility only for marketing products made elsewhere and bought in.
- It may simply be the name given to the marketing plan, which specifies the objectives or targets, activities, resources and budgets of the marketing function.

However, it should be recognized that the majority of organizations do not produce a strategic marketing plan. The major plans that specify and control the organization's strategy are corporate or business plans, into which strategic marketing should have an input.

The role of strategic marketing

In organizations where strategic marketing does not exist as a function, the process or decisions are still undertaken by senior managers or business leaders. Where it is an explicit function, the strategic marketing role will usually be performed by a marketing function in a business unit and by a corporate-level marketing function, which may also have responsibility for co-ordinating the activities of marketing departments in business units.

The primary role of strategic marketing is to identify and create value for the business through strongly differentiated positioning. It achieves this by influencing the strategy and culture of the organization to ensure that both have a strong customer focus. When this role is carried out by a marketing specialist, the role is called 'marketing director' or 'strategic marketing manager', sometimes based in a department called 'marketing' rather than 'strategic marketing'. Strategic marketers should champion the customer experience and exert a strong influence on the organization to adopt a customer orientation, contribute along with other directors and senior managers to its competitive strategy, align the organization's activities to the customer and manage the organization's marketing activities.

During strategy formulation, strategic marketing is about choices that customer-focused organizations make on where and how to compete and with what assets. It is also about developing a specific competitive position using tools from the marketing armoury including brands, innovation, customer relationships and service, alliances, channels and communications, and increasing price. Strategic marketing does not own the business strategy but, like other departments and functions, should contribute to it and control the operational levers that make a strategy effective. However, marketing has an exceptional contribution to make in identifying opportunities and determining ways to create value for customers and shareholders.

During implementation, strategic marketing is the 'glue' that connects many aspects of the business. It will often manage one brand or a portfolio of brands. Increasingly, it works with HR to ensure that the culture and values in the organization are consistent with the brand and to ensure that marketing competencies are part of the overall framework for staff development across the business. Strategic marketing also has responsibility for directing the implementation of marketing activities needed to execute the organization's strategy. Other key tasks of strategic marketing in today's organizations are:

- Contributing to strategic initiatives being undertaken by the organization, for example marketing input to a 'due diligence' evaluation of a prospective merger or acquisition. In some cases, strategic marketers will be managing multi-disciplinary teams.
- Co-ordinating and managing customer information across the organization within the data protection and privacy legislation. This involves close relationships with the IT function.
- Developing and driving the business case for investment in brands, new products and services.
- Championing and developing innovation and entrepreneurship within the organization.
- Ensuring that the marketing function is appropriately skilled and resourced.
- Providing input with finance on the valuation of brands for reporting and disclosure.

This concept of strategic marketing draws heavily on the theory and practice of strategic management, not just of marketing. This is an important distinction because strategic marketing is as much a part of directing how the organization competes as it is a part of marketing itself. Professional marketers engage in relationships with most functions within the organization and are 'business people' rather than 'technical marketers'. This is particularly so at the strategic level. It requires participants at this level to embrace a wider range of management theory and practice than has been the case in the past. In addition to traditional marketing theory, **strategic marketing also embraces:**

- Business and corporate strategy
- Investment decisions
- Culture and change management
- Quality management
- Programme and project management

Unit 1: Introduction

Marketers still have an essential role to play in contributing their specialist marketing skills to the formulation, implementation and control of strategy. These specialist marketing skills are of vital importance to organizations.

The syllabus at Professional Postgraduate Diploma has been divided into four modules:

1. **Analysis and Evaluation** – Covers the concepts, techniques and models involved in developing a detailed understanding of the market, customers and competitive environment externally and internally in the organization, its capabilities and assets, the opportunities available to it and its current performance.

2. **Strategic Marketing Decisions** – Covers the concepts, techniques and models involved in formulating a customer-focused competitive business or corporate strategy and developing a specific and differentiated competitive position. It includes investment decisions affecting marketing assets.

3. **Managing Marketing Performance** – Covers the implementation stage of the strategy. This encompasses managing marketing teams, managing change, implementing strategy through marketing activities and working with other departments, and using measurement as the basis for improvement.

4. **Strategic Marketing in Practice** – Provides the opportunity to explore strategic marketing in a practical setting. It also incorporates the latest trends and innovations in marketing. This module will draw on all the preceding modules and their syllabi.

Figure 1.1 Strategic Marketing in Practice and links with the other modules at Professional Postgraduate Diploma

Unit 1: Introduction

Aims and outcomes for Strategic Marketing in Practice

To understand the range of outcomes that are defined for SMiP, it is useful to consider the range of skills that students will be expected to exhibit in this module. This is indicated in Table 1.1.

Table 1.1 Personal skills development

Key skill unit: Personal Skills Development	Analysis and Evaluation	Strategic Marketing Decisions	Managing Marketing Performance	Strategic Marketing in Practice
Communication				
Interpret and evaluate information	✓	✓		✓
Synthesize and structure information	✓	✓		✓
Present information	✓	✓		✓
Problem solving				
Select and use strategies to solve problems		✓		✓
Establish what is needed to get results		✓		✓
Monitor progress		✓	✓	✓
Working with others				
Gain commitment			✓	✓
Brief others			✓	✓
Lead implementation			✓	✓

Aim

Marketing has to be firmly rooted in both theory and practice. Practice informs theory and vice versa. The SMiP module is designed to allow participants to put strategic marketing into practice. As the final module at Professional Postgraduate Diploma level, it not only builds on the knowledge and skills developed in all the preceding modules but also looks for an overall competence in marketing that encompasses all the various subject areas covered at Certificate and Professional Certificate level. As marketing is constantly evolving,

Unit 1: Introduction

continuously informed by both academic and business research, one of the aims of this module is to explore the latest trends and innovations relevant to marketers who are operating at a strategic level within organizations. One of the other aims is to understand marketing as an activity, which is important in all contexts (profit, not-for-profit, societal, global). It is expected that participants undertaking this module will be able to add value to both their marketing experience and marketing knowledge. This module therefore does not have a specific syllabus and draws from all the preceding modules and syllabi.

Related statements of practice

This module relates to the statements of practice:

Ad.1 Define intelligence requirements and lead the intelligence gathering process.

Ad.2 Develop a detailed understanding of the organization and its environment.

Bd.1 Promote a strong market orientation and influence/contribute to strategy formulation and investment decisions.

Bd.2 Specify and direct the marketing planning process.

Cd.1 Promote organization-wide innovation and co-operation in the development of brands.

Cd.2 Distil the essence of brands and direct/co-ordinate a portfolio of brands.

Dd.1 Develop and direct an integrated marketing communications strategy.

Dd.2 Lead the implementation of the integrated marketing communications strategy.

Ed.1 Promote corporate-wide innovation and co-operation in the development of products and services.

Ed.2 Direct and maintain competitive product/service portfolios.

Fd.1 Promote the strategic and creative use of pricing.

Fd.2 Lead the implementation of the strategic and creative use of pricing.

Gd.1 Select and monitor channel criteria to meet the organization's needs in a changing environment.

Gd.2 Direct and control support to channel members.

Hd.1 Promote and create a customer orientation and infrastructure for customer relationships.

Hd.2 Direct and control information and activities that deliver customer relationships and service.

Jd.1 Establish and maintain a project management framework in line with strategic objectives.

Jd.2 Direct and control the delivery of programmes and projects.

Kd.1 Establish and promote the use of metrics to improve marketing effectiveness.

Unit 1: Introduction

Kd.2 Create a system of critical review and appraisal to inform future marketing activity.

Ld.1 Provide professional leadership and develop a co-operative environment to enhance performance.

Ld.2 Promote effective cross-functional working linked to brands and the integration of marketing activities.

Ld.3 Promote and create an environment for career and self-development.

Ld.4 Contribute to organizational change and define and communicate the need for change within the department.

Learning objectives

Participants will be able to:

9.64.1 Identify and critically evaluate marketing issues within various environments, utilizing a wide variety of marketing techniques, concepts and models.

9.64.2 Assess the relevance of, and opportunities presented by, contemporary marketing issues within any given scenario including innovations in marketing.

9.64.3 Identify and critically evaluate various options available within given constraints and apply competitive positioning strategies, justifying any decisions taken.

9.64.4 Formulate and present a creative, customer-focused and innovative competitive strategy for any given context, incorporating relevant investment decisions, appropriate control aspects and contingency plans.

9.64.5 Demonstrate an understanding of the direction and management of marketing activities as part of the implementation of strategic direction, taking into account business intelligence requirements, marketing processes, resources, markets and the company vision.

9.64.6 Promote and facilitate the adoption and maintenance of a strong market and customer orientation with measurable marketing metrics.

9.64.7 Synthesize various strands of knowledge and skills from the different syllabus modules effectively in developing an effective solution for any given context.

Knowledge and skill requirements

There is no formal specification of knowledge and skills requirements for this module. Participants are required to demonstrate a full understanding of, and to satisfy the knowledge and skills requirements specified in, the syllabus modules at Certificate, Professional Diploma and Professional Postgraduate Diploma levels. The emphasis in this module is more on applying the knowledge and practical skills acquired in the previous modules. The essential skills assessed as part of this module are:

Unit 1: Introduction

- Analysis, interpretation, evaluation and synthesis of information, including the ability to draw conclusions
- Identification, exploration and evaluation of strategic options
- Selection and justification of an appropriate option using decision criteria
- Establishing the activities, resources and schedule needed to implement the chosen strategy
- Working with others to implement and control the strategy

Participants will be expected to demonstrate their awareness of current issues and an ability to make recommendations for a given context. From time to time, CIM will publish a list of trends and innovations to guide tutors and participants in their preparation for assessment. Participants will be expected to read widely in the area of strategic marketing as part of their studies at this level.

The links with other syllabi

The syllabus aims of the other three modules within Professional Postgraduate Diploma level are as listed below. They provide a link with key skills and show the linkage between the learning outcomes for each module and the Statements of Marketing Practice. All these are linked to the outcomes for SMiP as indicated:

1 Contribute research and insights to inform strategic marketing decisions. This encompasses:

   a Identifying the organization's business intelligence requirements

   b Understanding organizational culture and its consequences for strategy

   c Developing and synthesizing a detailed understanding of an organization's customers, internal and external environments and its current business performance from the relevant stakeholders' perspectives

2 Influence strategic decisions in an organization to create value for customers and other stakeholders. This encompasses:

   a Contributing specialist marketing input to strategic decisions to achieve competitive advantage and customer preference

   b Influencing decisions within the organization concerning priorities for marketing activities and investment in marketing assets

   c Promoting a strong market orientation and consistency with the values of the brand

3 Manage and measure marketing activities undertaken as part of the implementation of a customer-focused strategy. This encompasses:

   a Evaluating the techniques available to organizations for integrating teams and activities across the organization

   b Identifying the barriers to effective implementation of strategies and plans and developing measures to prevent or overcome them and effect change

c   Explaining techniques for managing a marketing team, including assessing the organization's need for marketing skills and resources and developing strategies for acquiring, developing and retaining them

d   Initiating and critically evaluating systems for control of marketing activities

4   Formulate, present and justify a creative, customer-focused and innovative strategy for any given context. This encompasses:

a   Identifying and critically evaluating relevant marketing issues and opportunities, including trends and innovations in marketing and business

b   Identifying and critically evaluating the various options available to achieve the desired goal(s)

Points to ponder

- Marketing as a subject area is undergoing major changes. These changes are taking place because of dramatic shifts in technology, demographics, globalization, systems of production, logistics and ecological issues. The papers, therefore, are designed to reflect more of these contemporary issues in addition to the knowledge base mentioned above.

- The case studies will also be designed to develop strategic marketing issues that can be operationalized and implemented within realistic constraints. It is often forgotten that marketing is not just about positioning and growth but also about effectiveness within given constraints within most organizations. These constraints mean that strategies have to be sensibly evaluated and chosen with hard decisions being made. When particular strategies are chosen, it is clear that the constraints could be many and varied. Constraints, for instance, could be financial, organizational (both employee and culture related), marketing (image, size of markets, branding, distribution systems, networks) and, if the organization is a division of a larger entity, headquarter-imposed constraints.

- Strategy development and strategic management are looked at differently by different authors and practitioners. Most adopt the so called 'Classical', 'Deliberate' or 'Prescriptive' approach. Lynch (2006) defines the prescriptive approach to strategy as one whose 'objective has been defined in advance, and whose main elements have been developed before the strategy commences'. Such an approach normally follows a sequential approach where a strategic analysis is followed by strategy development and then strategy implementation. On the other hand, there are those who believe strategy emerges over time, developing incrementally and continuously and, as such, it is not recommended that strategy should be summarised in a plan and then implemented. This approach is often referred to as 'Emergent Strategy' and is one 'whose final objective is unclear and whose elements are developed during the course of its life, as strategy proceeds' (Lynch, 2006). In this approach, while it is accepted that analysis may be carried out as a first step, strategy is nevertheless developed through a trial and error process and there is not a clear distinction between developing strategy and implementing it. It ought to be pointed out here, for the benefit of those taking the SMiP exam, that in the past any questions requiring a strategic marketing plan have normally required a classical approach in the answer and this will continue. However, students answering the question from an emergent perspective will not be penalized in anyway.

Globalization

- The rapid changes in technology are far reaching as they are changing the normal paradigms of marketing. The four Ps cannot now be discussed with certainty. The nature and direction of marketing strategies necessarily have to take into account the massive computing power available and the new developments on the Web. Many multinationals have operated globally for decades, but technology is changing the patterns of production and consumption.

- For instance, global brands are available anywhere, and production facilities may be located in a myriad of different countries. For smaller companies, locked into local markets, the Internet holds the promises and pitfalls of operating in a global arena.

- The introduction of the Euro means that pan-European marketing strategies have to be thought through in a different manner. The changing nature and the growth of South Asian markets has an enormous impact on the marketing strategies of organizations. The nature and strength of the American market is often forgotten. The case studies will reflect these changes and will embrace many different sectors of industry.

Organizational issues

- When developing marketing strategies, it is important that the culture and nature of the organization be taken into account. Marketing strategies often succeed and fail because of inappropriate personnel, inappropriate structures or climates within organizations. Success or failure of strategies can be defined by utilizing a number of different performance measures such as market share growth, return on investment, brand awareness and sales growth. Organizations are, therefore, always striving to create the appropriate structures and develop appropriate cultures to meet the demands of the market-place.

- The customer is king, and marketing strategists have to place the level of market orientation at the centre of their thinking.

Sustainability

- With the growing problems related to the general environmental deterioration and the increasing concern over climatic changes, the issues surrounding sustainability are of critical importance to marketers. Marketing literature has for long been concerned with growth and market share. It is important that issues surrounding the constraints imposed by the environment are taken into account. The world is facing an enormous challenge in terms of the availability of resources and the needs of the population.

Constraints

- In some respects, a challenge posed to marketing strategists is the need to consider constraints and responsibility. Constraints can be financial or related to the human resource capabilities of an organization. In many instances, constraints can be imposed by the external environment, and these are particularly important for the growth of a company's markets.

Financial issues

◆ Financial issues will always play a key role in developing strategies. A good knowledge of basic financial statements, such as profit and loss accounts, balance sheets and cash-flow statements, is required.

Knowledge of contemporary marketing issues

◆ Each case is different and will therefore test some knowledge of contemporary issues. Students therefore need to be encouraged to read journal articles pertaining to the case study.

Application of previous knowledge

◆ The need to apply models for analysis will continue. However, a more critical approach in applying these techniques will be needed. The paper will reflect the need for both academic and practical knowledge, as true marketers need to have experience in both areas for developing sensible strategies.

Issues of implementation and control

◆ An awareness of the clear decision-making and implementation strategies will be tested, as will be strategic positioning, innovation and branding in the context of implementation and control.

◆ Formulating an appropriate strategy, incorporating investment decisions, control aspects and contingency plans.

Assessment methodology for the module

◆ Students will receive a case study – normally between 30 and 60 pages (including company/industry data) four weeks before the examination date.

◆ The examination on the case study will be a closed book examination; however, students will be allowed to bring in six sides of A4 prepared analysis and a copy of their case study, which may also be annotated. The examination questions will remain unseen until the start of the examination.

◆ The marking scheme will allocate 25 per cent of marks for the six pages of prepared analysis as follows:

- 10 per cent awarded for originality and appropriateness of analysis in the context given
- 15 per cent awarded for appropriate application of analysis within the questions

Guidelines for pre-prepared work

Candidates should be given the following advice:

1. Write or print pre-prepared analysis on *six single-sided* pages. Examiners will be looking for tables, diagrams and key issues. Tables such as SWOT, although helpful, do not show deep analytical thought.
2. If candidates use the available sheets for writing 'crib' material, such as models or plans, they will penalize themselves as there will be less space for good analysis that counts towards the final marks.
3. The diagrams should be clearly visible, and the writing should be clearly legible. Typing should be no less than font size 11.
4. Data given within the case should be analysed clearly and effectively.
5. Please note that it will be totally unacceptable for students to present standardized group analysis/appendices, and they will therefore be penalized accordingly.

During the examination

1. The answers should reflect the use of the pre-prepared material as necessary. Candidates, when writing answers, should cross-reference the work to guide the Examiner to a particular table or chart or piece of analysis.
2. Examiners do not expect students to use *all* the pre-prepared material to augment their answers. Obviously, they should only use whatever is necessary for answering the questions as set.
3. Candidates should attach the pre-prepared work as an appendix. All papers must be hole-punched and include the student registration and centre number.
4. Please note that 15 marks are allocated *for the application* of the pre-prepared work.
5. Only the pre-prepared analysis can be taken into the examination room; therefore no textbooks, journals or other pre-prepared work will be allowed.

Summary

This chapter gives you an idea of the marketing skills that the SMiP module aims to develop and test. It also shows that learning outcomes are more important than specific syllabus regurgitation. To reach the desired outcomes, students need to be able to critically assess and absorb the key concepts in the other areas of the Professional Postgraduate Diploma and their applications to real marketing problems. Students also need to consider the context in which an organization will be operating, especially the type of company and also the environment in which it does business. When studying previous cases, students should attempt to list the key outcomes that they have achieved, together with some of the key skills that they have used to reach a satisfactory level of competence.

References

Lynch, R. (2006) *Corporate Strategy, 4th edition*, Harlow: Prentice Hall.

http://www.ftse.com

Unit 2
What is meant by case study analysis?

Learning objectives

In this unit you will:

- Identify and critically evaluate marketing issues within various environments, utilizing a wide variety of marketing techniques, concepts and models.

- Identify and critically evaluate various options available within constraints and apply competitive positioning strategies, justifying any decisions taken.

Candidates should also be familiar with the Analysis and Evaluation module, and the Strategic Marketing Decisions and Managing Marketing Performance syllabi.

A brief overview

A case study is an account of the major events taking place in a business within an industry sector over a number of years. A case usually features many of the key events in that it chronicles the events that have been dealt with and have to be dealt with by marketing managers. Issues pertaining to the competitive environment, changes in the business definition and the main areas of the served market segments have to be dealt with by marketing managers.

Cases give students a chance to understand some of the problems faced by organizations and be able to analyse them in detail.

Cases allow students to utilize their understanding of key concepts. Their meaning is made clearer when applied to case studies. Theory and concepts help to analyse a company's situation. Analysing a case requires great powers of deduction. Facts and figures are often hidden in the different areas of the case. The conceptual tools help to probe the case and gather evidence of events. In the real world, it is important to understand that there are no right answers. For most companies, strategic marketing management is difficult. Developing strategies is generally an uncertain game, making it more important to develop a careful diagnosis. All that managers can do is to make the best guess.

As different individuals have differing ideas, case studies provide students with the opportunity to participate in class and to learn from others. Tutors often act as facilitators in this

Unit 2: What is meant by case study analysis?

process of enquiry and analysis. In actual businesses, this is exactly the way decisions are made. It is important, therefore, that students can analyse the situation and be confident of their solutions.

Analysing a case study

One of the purposes of the case study is to let you analyse the situation that the company finds itself in. In doing this, you will need to apply many of the key concepts that you would have learnt in the other modules. A case study has to be read several times before a clear idea of the key issues can be established. This enables you to establish a picture of the environment in which the company is operating as well as the company's position within it. Eventually, based on this analysis, you will make a series of decisions to take the company forward into the future. A detailed and effective analysis of a case should include the following:

- The key historical events that have contributed to the development of the company.
- A PESTLE analysis, which looks at Political, Economic, Social, Technological, Legal and Environmental issues surrounding the case.
- A SWOT analysis, which evaluates the organization's internal strengths and weaknesses, as well as the external threats and opportunities it faces.
- Product market analyses and the links to strategic marketing.
- Analyses of a range of issues that pertain to the particular case study. Often, case studies are not straightforward and different types of analyses are required. These may be more contemporary in nature.
- Any constraints that the company faces from a resource point of view. These could be human, financial, technical or environmental.
- Any structural features or control systems.
- A list of key issues that emanate from the above.

The analyses

The key historical events that have contributed to the development of the company or sector

Cases often contain a history of the company. It is important to analyse this history and to list the key critical events that helped to shape the company's development. At the same time, an analysis of the history will also offer insights into the evolution of a particular industry. Historical analysis and charting can help in understanding product market decisions and any development and diversification decisions that have been made by the company.

A PESTLE analysis

A PESTLE analysis looks at Political, Economic, Social, Technological, Legal and Environmental issues surrounding the case.

Cases will contain some or all of the key PESTLE factors. This type of analysis allows you to understand the macro-environment facing the industry sector that the company is immersed in. The Porter Five Forces framework allows a structured analysis of the environment and the competitive pressures on companies within the industry sector. The PESTLE factors also help to highlight key trends within the markets. Amongst others, these could be demographic profile trends, sociological issues, branding trends in different markets or ethics and sustainability issues (as in the December 2004 case). Some of the technological factors may show up the life-cycle stages and any special factors affecting the life-cycle model. Analysing each of the factors gives some idea of the opportunities and threats facing a company.

A SWOT analysis and its evaluation

In addition to the PESTLE analysis, a review of the company's strengths and weaknesses is required. This is an internal audit of the company set against the environmental and competitive forces within which it is operating and allows you to examine each function in which the company is currently strong and weak. Companies could have a weakness in their branding strategies or new product development, yet may have current products that are well positioned in the market. Is a company in an overall strong position? Can it operate profitably in its current market sectors? How can the company minimize the threats to its position and expand on its opportunities? Can the company turn its weaknesses into strengths? A good SWOT analysis helps you to understand, in a clear and succinct manner, how the company is positioned. As part of this analysis, you may want to use the Porter Five Forces framework (Figure 2.1) plus other analyses: for example, financial and human resource competencies,

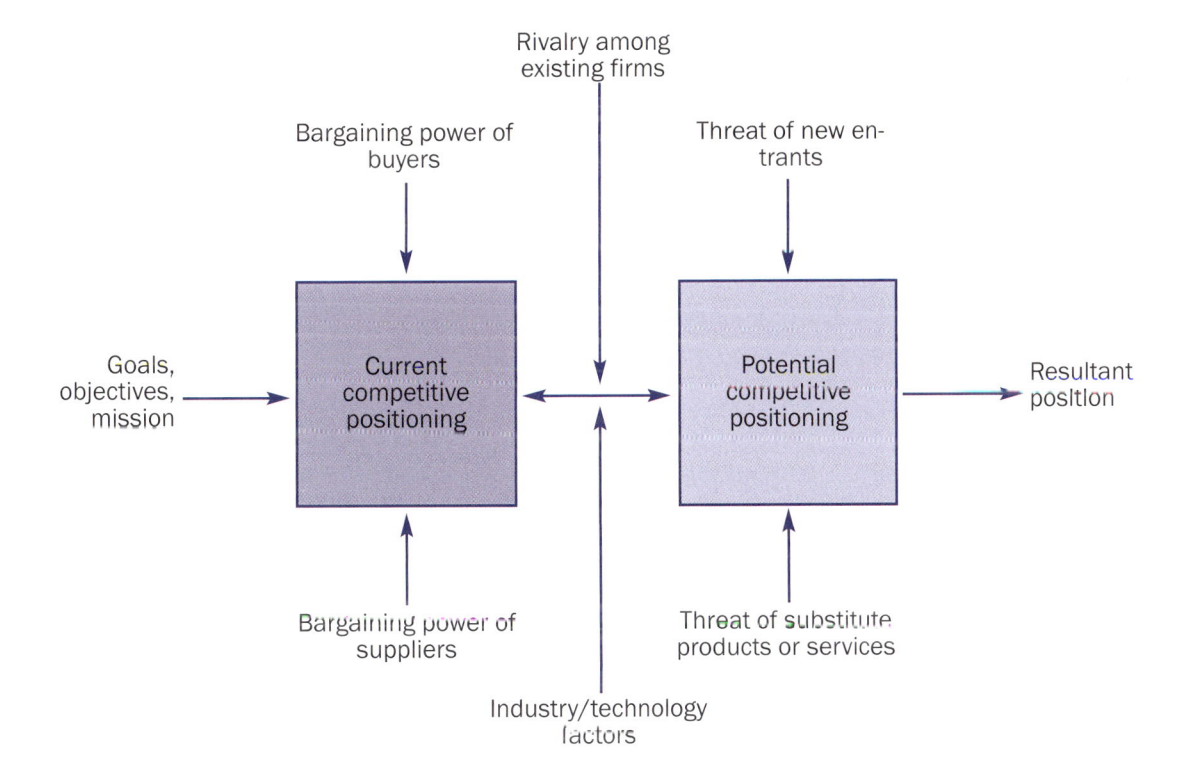

Figure 2.1 Porter Five Forces framework

Unit 2: What is meant by case study analysis?

product portfolio, product range and lifecycle, degree of innovation, brands and patents. The SWOT analysis is an important background against which a company's objectives and strategies are set. Candidates are recommended to pay great attention to SWOT analysis in the SMiP examination.

Product market analyses and the links to strategic marketing

Following on from the SWOT analysis, an analysis of the products and the markets within which the products and services are sold should be undertaken. This type of analysis will require you to be familiar with the various portfolio models such as the GE Matrix, the BCG Matrix, the Ansoff Matrix and various other relevant matrices. Below is an example of the expanded Ansoff Matrix (Figure 2.2), and Figure 2.3 shows the Directional Policy Matrix.

Product alternatives

	Present products	Improved products	New products
Existing market	Market penetration	Product variants, imitations	Product line extension
Expanded market	Agressive promotion	Market segmentation product	Vertical diversification
New market	Market development	Market extension	Conglomerate diversification

Options (vertical axis label)

Figure 2.2 Growth vector analyses

Market potential

	Unattractive	Average	Attractive
High	Diversification	Market segmentation	Market leadership innovation
Medium	Saved withdrawal; merger	Maintenance of position; market penetration	Expansion product differentiation
Low	Divestment	Imitation; phased withdrawal	Cash generation

Company capability (vertical axis label)

Figure 2.3 Directional Policy Matrix

In addition to these, you may wish to utilize perceptual maps and consider product positioning from a competitive point of view. Linked to the product/market analysis should be a review of any gaps that the organization faces. These gaps could be:

- **Product line gap** – Closing this gap entails completion of a product line, either in width or in depth, by introducing new or improved products.
- **Distribution gap** – This gap can be reduced by expanding the coverage, intensity and exposure of distribution.
- **Usage gap** – To increase usage, a firm needs to induce current non-users to try the product and encourage current users to increase their usage.
- **Competitive gap** – This gap can be closed by making inroads into the market position of direct competitors as well as those who market substitute products.
- **Internationalization gap** – This gap can be shortened through exporting, joint venture arrangements and strategic alliances.
- **Communications gap** – This gap can be shortened through advertising strategies, PR or proactive use of the Web.

SPACE analysis

All these analyses can be tied together by using SPACE analysis as discussed by the BCG group. SPACE stands for Strategic Position and Action Evaluation. This analysis is based on the following:

1. The company's financial strength (FS)
2. The company's competitive advantage (CA)
3. The industry strength – the strength of the industry sector in which the company operates (IS)
4. The stability of the environment in which the company operates (ES)

This analysis is based on your ability to analyse key aspects of the case study pertaining to the company. The analysis depends on answering a range of questions and then taking an average.

Step one analyses each aspect as shown above.

Unit 2: What is meant by case study analysis?

Financial strength (FS)

Factors determining financial strength

Return on investment	Low	0	1	2	3	4	5	6	High
Leverage (debt to equity ratio)	Low	0	1	2	3	4	5	6	High
Liquidity (cash held)	Low	0	1	2	3	4	5	6	High
Capital required/capital available	High	0	1	2	3	4	5	6	Low
Cash flow	Weak	0	1	2	3	4	5	6	Strong
Ease of exit from the market	Difficult	0	1	2	3	4	5	6	Easy
Risk involved in the business	Low	0	1	2	3	4	5	6	High
Other (your own factor)	Low	0	1	2	3	4	5	6	High

Average

Critical factors and your assessment of this area of the organization

Competitive advantage (CA)

Factors determining competitive advantage

Market share	Low	0	1	2	3	4	5	6	High
Product/service quality (compared to competitors)	Low	0	1	2	3	4	5	6	High
Product life-cycles stages (for range of products/services)	Similar	0	1	2	3	4	5	6	Different
Product/service replacement cycle	Variable	0	1	2	3	4	5	6	Fixed
Customer loyalty	Low	0	1	2	3	4	5	6	High
General utilization of capacity by the competition	Low	0	1	2	3	4	5	6	High
Technological knowledge and competence	Low	0	1	2	3	4	5	6	High
The degree of vertical integration of the company	Low	0	1	2	3	4	5	6	High
Other (your own factor)	Low	0	1	2	3	4	5	6	High

Average – 6   =

Suppose the total score comes to 36. This divided by 8 factors = 4.5. Take away 6 = –1.5. (So you will get a negative score for this factor.)

Critical factors and your assessment of this area of the organization

Unit 2: What is meant by case study analysis?

Industry strength (IS)

Factors determining industry strength

Growth potential	Low	0	1	2	3	4	5	6	High
Profit potential	Low	0	1	2	3	4	5	6	High
Financial stability (within the sector)	Low	0	1	2	3	4	5	6	High
Technological know-how (needed to operate within the sector)	Simple	0	1	2	3	4	5	6	Complex
Resource utilization (generally within the sector)	Poor	0	1	2	3	4	5	6	Good
Capital intensity (requisite capital for operating in the sector)	High	0	1	2	3	4	5	6	Low
Ease of entry into the market	Easy	0	1	2	3	4	5	6	Difficult
Level of productivity and capacity utilization	Low	0	1	2	3	4	5	6	High
Other (your choice of factor)	Low	0	1	2	3	4	5	6	High

Average:

Critical factors determining industry strength

Environmental stability (ES)

Factors determining environmental stability

Technological changes	Many	0	1	2	3	4	5	6	Few
Rate of inflation	High	0	1	2	3	4	5	6	Low
Variability of demand	High	0	1	2	3	4	5	6	Low
Price range of competing products	Wide	0	1	2	3	4	5	6	Narrow
Barriers to entry into the market	Few	0	1	2	3	4	5	6	Many
Competitive pressure	High	0	1	2	3	4	5	6	Low
Price elasticity of demand	Elastic	0	1	2	3	4	5	6	Inelastic

Other (a factor of your own choice)

Average – 6   =

Again for this assessment, suppose the average is 40. This divided by 8 = 5. Then 5 – 6 = –1 (a negative figure).

The key critical factors that determine environmental stability

Unit 2: What is meant by case study analysis?

Your analysis should then be plotted on the following axes in order to determine the strategic position of the company under question (Figure 2.4).

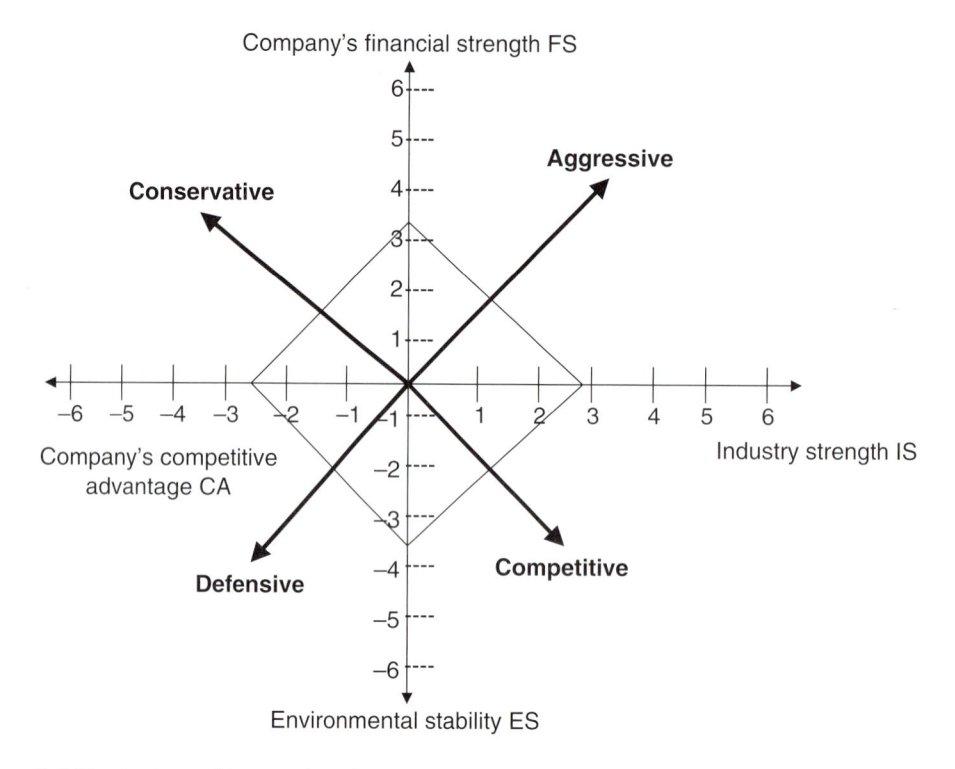

Figure 2.4 Strategic position and action evaluation SPACE matrix

Once this analysis is done, you can plot the actual position of the company by just getting two points (one for the X-axis and one for the Y-axis). This can be easily obtained by adding CA and IS (you will either get a negative point or a positive point) and adding FS and ES (you will get either a negative point or a positive point). These two points will then determine the overall quadrant in which the company will fall.

Always remember that this exercise should be quite objective and be based on as much real information that you can obtain as possible. Like any other real-life analysis you may also have to make certain assumptions (for all the examples, it is assumed that the company positions are in the middle of each quadrant).

The implications for falling within particular sectors are these:

1. **Aggressive posture** – In this quadrant, a company is set within an attractive industry that faces little environmental turbulence. The company enjoys a good competitive advantage, which it can protect with good financial strength. As this sector is attractive, it is likely to attract new entrants. The company needs to protect its position through acquisitions, by increasing market share or by extending its lead in specific products and services in which it is the market leader. Companies in this sector have the potential to be cost leaders if they are in an FMCG market.

2. **Competitive posture** – In this quadrant, the industry is attractive and the company enjoys competitive advantage within a turbulent environment. The company needs

to acquire financial strength. It needs to do this to improve its marketing and its product lines. It may also need to reduce costs and protect competitive advantage in a declining market. In such a quadrant, a company may need to look for cash resources either through merger or through being acquired. Companies in this area need to differentiate their product offerings and utilize their marketing skills as much as possible.

3. **Conservative posture** – If a company is positioned within this quadrant, it has a focus on financial stability within a stable market. The chances are that the growth is fairly low. Under such circumstances, a company will need to become competitive in its product or service offering. It may also need to consider investing its cash in entering new attractive markets or offering new competitive products. It may also need to consider pruning its product lines. Companies located in this sector would benefit from a more focused product or service. They may be able to do well in niche markets, organized along geographic lines, product lines or buyer groups.

4. **Defensive posture** – A company set within this quadrant lacks a competitive product or service. It also has low financial strength and is situated in an unattractive industry sector. Competitiveness is crucial, and the company will have to consider retrenchment by pruning its product lines, reducing costs dramatically, cutting capacity and slowing down on any investment. Companies located within this sector are often ripe for turnaround strategies. They can also be relatively defenceless, making them easy targets for takeovers. Product strategies probably need to consider 'harvesting' cash cows.

Note: It is important to realize that the SPACE analysis should be used *judiciously* as it may only be *appropriate* for many private sector companies. It may be *inappropriate* for public sector or non-profit sector analysis. Parts of the analysis could be modified for use in different sectors. This, however, will need sound knowledge, creativity and an ability to sensibly translate the basic premise of SPACE to a new sector.

Any constraints that the company faces from a resource point of view

Companies face various constraints when developing their strategies. These constraints could be market constraints (size and growth potential of a market), financial constraints (the ability to finance marketing campaigns, foster new product development, cash flow, ability to raise money, etc.), technical (the ability to develop new products, to market products, manage information systems, Web capability) and finally environmental (these could be pollution management capability or public concerns, as in the case of marketing Genetically Modified foods in Biocatalysts).

Any structural features or control systems

Analyses should include an understanding of the present structural pattern of the organization and the way in which this contributes to or detracts from developing its marketing strategies. For instance, is there a defined marketing structure? Are there systems for monitoring marketing effectiveness or orientation? Are the systems rigid or flexible?

Unit 2: What is meant by case study analysis?

Key issues

Because of these analyses, you should be able to list a number of key issues that are facing the company described in the case study. These key issues form a valuable resource when answering the questions set in the examination.

These type of analyses can then be linked to any *strategic plan* that you may have considered developing.

A generalized approach to formulating strategies would probably contain the following:

1. **Statement of the problem** – This will contain a situation analysis of the company, its problem areas and its general capability.

2. **Analysis of data:**

   a. **Industry** – This would cover an analysis of the growth potential, SWOT, market structure and competitive pressures.

   b. **Product/service analysis** – This would consider areas such as market share, pricing, promotion, new product development, distribution, branding and level of market orientation of the company.

   c. **Financial analysis** – The financial performance of a company gives guidelines on its profitability, return on investment, shareholder value, liquidity, inventory levels and possible resource requirements for growth (see section on Financial Analysis in Unit 5).

   d. **Management** – If organization charts are available, any gaps in the marketing structure should be ascertained. Also, issues such as mission, values and objectives should be taken into account.

3. **Generation of options and an evaluation of these** – In this section, the options regarding entry into different product/market sectors, strategic alliances, branding strategies, R&D, internationalization, joint ventures, diversification, vertical or horizontal integration.

4. **Recommendations (decisions) and strategies** – This should be the crucial element of the plan, encompassing key decisions that may be taken, giving reasons for choosing these, understanding the possible reactions to these by competitors and the justifications for these. Resource implications also need to be considered. Clear and decisive objectives must be set.

5. **Implementation, contingency and control** – This section should look at how easily the recommendations could be adopted, taking into account resource allocation, cost implications, budgets and timetables. This section should also envisage contingency requirements in case of difficulties regarding implementation strategies. When considering implementation, it is also important to develop monitoring systems for ascertaining the success of the recommended strategy.

Unit 2: What is meant by case study analysis?

Case study: World Class International

World Class International (WCI) is an interesting company that deals in supplying services to different business sectors. It operates in the business-to-business (B2B) market and has built a strong client base in this area. Figure 2.5 shows the company structure. It has a turnover of £60 million.

```
                    World Class International
                         Holdings Ltd.
         ┌───────────────────┼───────────────────┐
World Class International   World Class International   WCI Technology Ltd.
    Consulting Ltd.            Technology Ltd.          formerly Counterpoint Ltd.
                            formerly 2GL Computing Ltd.
```

Figure 2.5 Company structure

There are four legal operating entities, managed within two distinct divisions within WCI. These operate cohesively and provide a seamless comprehensive service to clients. This is shown in Figure 2.6. General services, such as finance, marketing, communications, HR and sales, are provided centrally to the two key operating units.

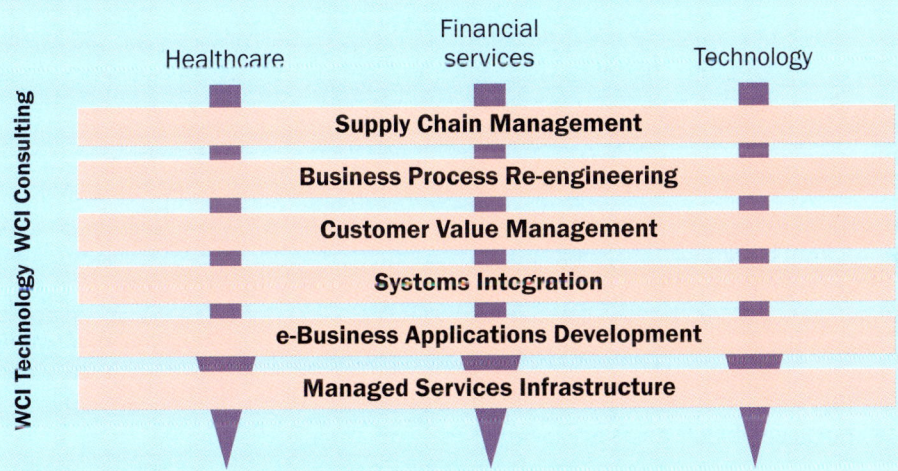

```
                        Financial
        Healthcare       services        Technology
            │               │               │
    ┌───────▼───────────────▼───────────────▼───────┐
    │         Supply Chain Management               │
    ├───────────────────────────────────────────────┤
    │       Business Process Re-engineering         │
    ├───────────────────────────────────────────────┤
    │         Customer Value Management             │
    ├───────────────────────────────────────────────┤
    │            Systems Integration                │
    ├───────────────────────────────────────────────┤
    │       e-Business Applications Development     │
    ├───────────────────────────────────────────────┤
    │        Managed Services Infrastructure        │
    └───────▼───────────────▼───────────────▼───────┘
 WCI Technology  WCI Consulting
```

Figure 2.6 Key business areas and integrating structures

The markets and the main aspects of each of the key businesses are now discussed.

WCI Technology

WCI Technology was 2GL Computer Services before the merger with WCI.

The company expanded its sales force in the 1990s and also developed Novell networking expertise. It soon became a dominant player in the education market, in the South of England, by providing Administrative Schools networks. This was extended to curriculum development through a product called Classlink. The intellectual property

Unit 2: What is meant by case study analysis?

rights for this software were eventually sold to Viglen plc, which continued to develop and refine this award-winning school software.

In 1991, 2GL Healthcare was formed as a subsidiary to enable staff from former health authorities to continue their relationship with the National Health Service by providing IT infrastructure and tailored software solutions. Initially, Ashton Tate products were being used, but then a strong relationship began developing with Microsoft. In 2000, the company won a multi-million pound NHS Direct infrastructure and managed service contract as a partner of AXA Assistance.

By 1992, 2GL's corporate business to large enterprises needed its own focus and started to strengthen relationships with major IT companies. These relationships are shown in Figure 2.7.

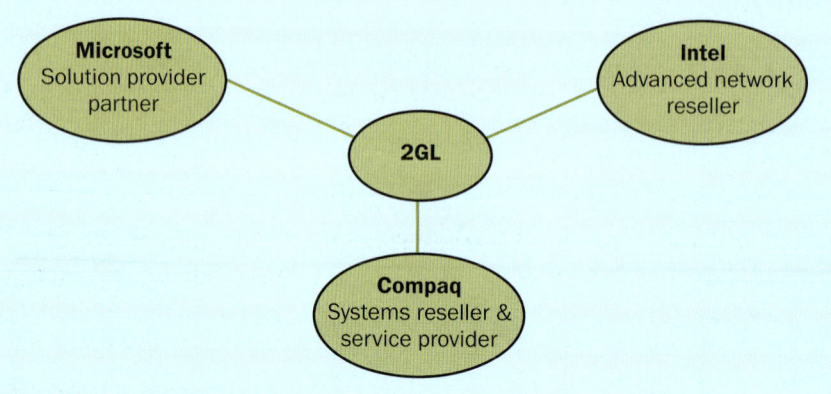

Figure 2.7 2GL business relationships

WCI's services

WCI offers a range of services to its clients. It combines expertise in process design, Internet technology and managed service capabilities. Businesses can therefore benefit from 'Building Better Businesses' on the web.

- ◆ **E-business strategy** – This aspect of the company's offering concentrates on assisting companies to re-evaluate their business strategies in the web age. It enables them to look at new channels to market and the impact on their businesses through leveraging new technology. This type of strategic development focus may lead to:

    a   Integrating applications

    b   Web-enabling legacy systems

    c   Web-enabling processes that support the supply chain

    d   Developing new routes to market and augmenting the current ones

    The market growth in this area is high, and the company has a low market share.

- ◆ **Selling systems** – WCI's combined experience in global supply chains, IT and Internet technology enables the promise of e-commerce to be achieved. This experience allows products to be ordered online and delivered efficiently and speedily utilizing integrated processes. E-CRM utilization allows direct contact with customers and an understanding of their needs. The company has a low market share in a high-growth area.

- **Internal systems** – WCI offers waste-free high-performance processes, which incorporate Internet technology, linking IT platforms and legacy systems together to ensure that integration is achieved throughout a business. The company has a good market share in a low-growth area.

- **Purchasing** – The company offers integration of all parts of the supply chain to provide web-enabled advanced planning systems, working with manufacturing processes and suppliers. This helps to manage and get closer to real demand for products and services. In this high-growth area, the company has a low market share.

- **Lean compliance** – It takes about 6–8 years, with the final phases taking 4–5 years, to obtain compliance for new drugs. About 80 per cent of drugs fail to get through clinical trials. These facts demonstrate the need for complex and sophisticated information systems within the Biotechnology and Pharmaceutical sectors. This is a high-growth area with the company having a low market share.

- **E-software** – This service offering includes a full range of software development services to create a digital business. Solutions often require a complex design to incorporate issues of security, non-repudiation, scalability and application integration. This is a high-growth area and the company's market share is low.

- **Infrastructure** – The company offers a range of consulting expertise in networking systems infrastructure combined with the ability to procure systems, install the software and add to a client's new or existing networks. To improve implementation of infrastructures, WCI provides both support and training. A 24-hour, 7-day support service and accredited training facilities are also available. This is a low-growth area with the company taking a good share of the market.

- **Managed services** – This range of services offers solutions tailored to meet a customer's individual needs. These can vary from isolated services to complete IT operations, enabling clients to concentrate on their core business. The lease/purchase of hardware is also part of this service. This is a high-growth market area with the company taking a reasonable slice of the market. WCI currently manages IT resources for organizations such as the NHS, Volvo Cars, WH Smith and Hutchison 3G.

- **Business process outsourcing** – These are solutions developed to manage the non-core processes for clients. WCI can offer cost effectiveness because of economies of scale and the increased process expertise on offer. Examples of process expertise offered are Supply Chain Management, Pharmaceutical Drug Safety and Clinical Trials. Again, this is a high-growth area, and the company's share is also growing rapidly.

Question

Recommend and justify a strategic direction for the company for the next five years.

Unit 2: What is meant by case study analysis?

Example analysis of the mini-case

Key issues

With the recent merger, the company has to establish a clear brand image:

- The company has grown on the back of a range of consultants who are linked to the company; so, marketing instead of selling becomes an important priority.
- The company must move steadily towards m-commerce platforms.
- The company needs to develop the outsourcing market substantially.
- The company must develop focused and targeted marketing for local/national/international clientele.
- The company is essentially an SME, and it needs to grow to a reasonable size to challenge its main competitors.
- The nature of the IT service market is constantly changing.
- Challenges are being posed by the growth of e-commerce and m-commerce.
- The company is heavily dependent on the pharmaceutical sector.
- Companies are getting more sophisticated in their needs, demanding more value added services.
- The company needs to globalize as quickly as its clients globalize.

Figures 2.8–2.10 illustrate how a basic analysis of the case study could be carried out.

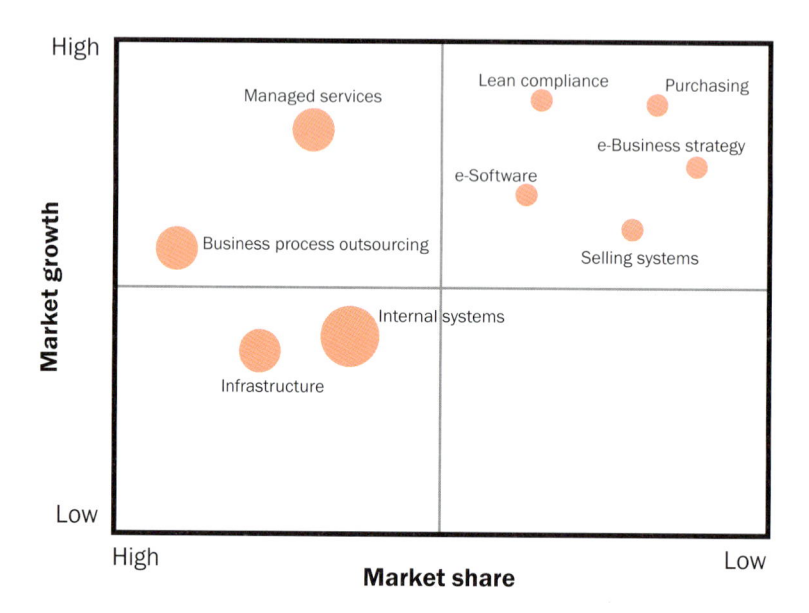

Figure 2.8 Portfolio analysis of business areas

Unit 2: What is meant by case study analysis?

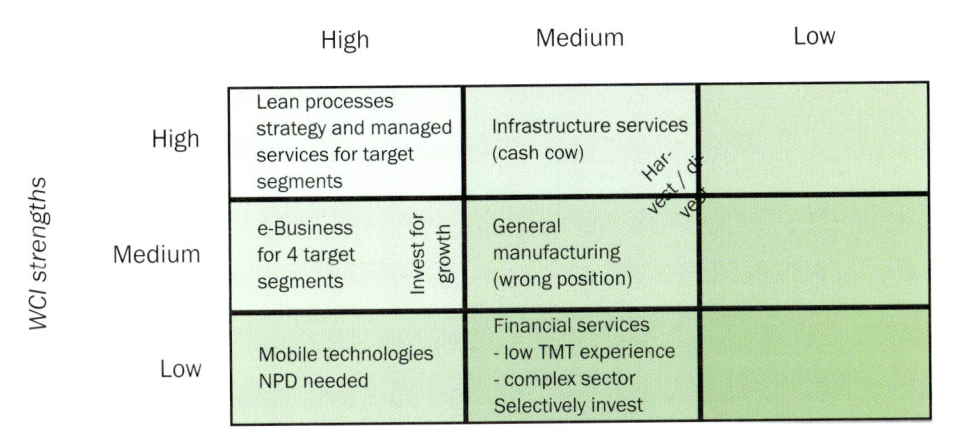

	High	Medium	Low
High	Lean processes strategy and managed services for target segments	Infrastructure services (cash cow)	Harvest / divest
Medium	e-Business for 4 target segments — Invest for growth	General manufacturing (wrong position)	
Low	Mobile technologies NPD needed	Financial services - low TMT experience - complex sector Selectively invest	

WCI strengths (vertical axis)

Figure 2.9 GE matrix

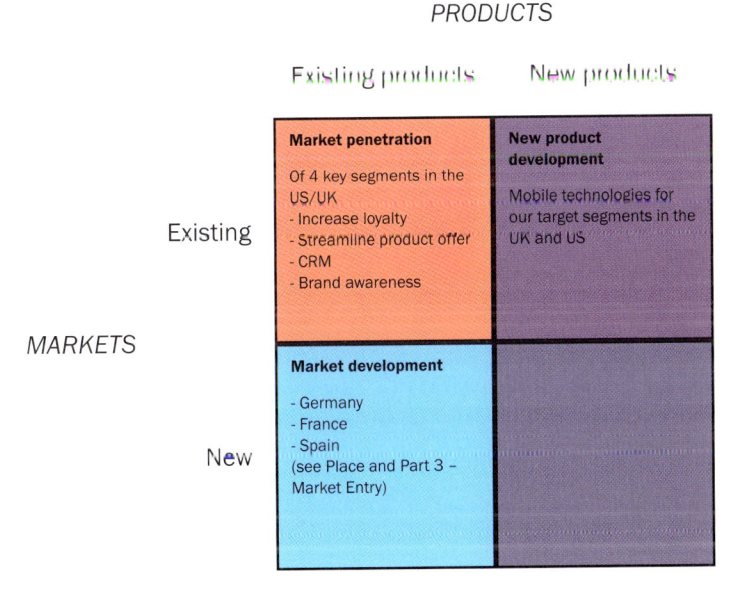

PRODUCTS

	Existing products	New products
Existing	**Market penetration** Of 4 key segments in the US/UK - Increase loyalty - Streamline product offer - CRM - Brand awareness	**New product development** Mobile technologies for our target segments in the UK and US
New	**Market development** - Germany - France - Spain (see Place and Part 3 – Market Entry)	

MARKETS

Figure 2.10 Ansoff matrix

In terms of the client connection, the key points to consider are:

- The importance of sharing knowledge
- Addressing the needs of different customers sensibly
- Incentivization
- Key account management
- A well-configured company has a seamless interaction with its clients
- A configuration needs to be aligned according to metrics (measuring effectiveness), incentives and structures

33

Unit 2: What is meant by case study analysis?

- Utilizing the Internet effectively within the organization
- Customer-service connections and measurement of success
- CRM is not just about databases but about a complete reorientation towards the customer

The other main analyses to consider are shown below.

Potential strategies emanating from portfolio analysis

- Building relationships with clients where the businesses are classified in the Question Marks section as High Growth but Low Market Share. *There is potential to gain share through repeat orders and market development. New and old clients need to be nurtured.*

- Key Account Management where businesses are in the Star and Cash Cow areas of the Portfolio Matrix. *Key Account Management will allow the company to concentrate on high value clients and build according to the 80/20 Pareto principle.*

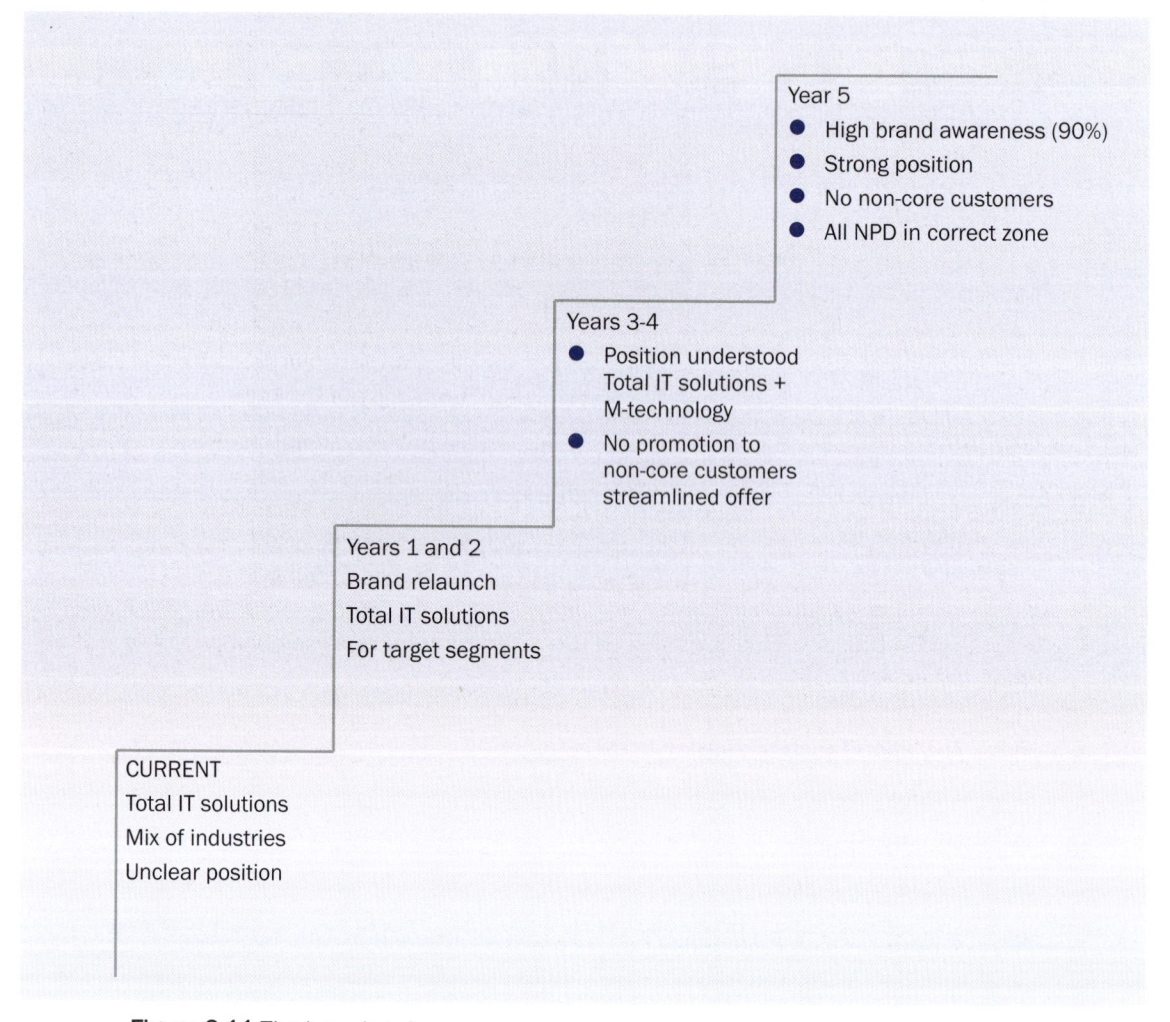

Year 5
- High brand awareness (90%)
- Strong position
- No non-core customers
- All NPD in correct zone

Years 3-4
- Position understood Total IT solutions + M-technology
- No promotion to non-core customers streamlined offer

Years 1 and 2
Brand relaunch
Total IT solutions
For target segments

CURRENT
Total IT solutions
Mix of industries
Unclear position

Figure 2.11 The brand staircase

The analyses shown above indicate the way in which new case studies could be analysed for the purpose of the examination. It is important to consider what you wish to concentrate on and the angle that you wish to take. The examiners find that most students are quite innovative and creative in the way they undertake case study analysis. Some aspects of financial analysis may well be generic, and mathematical calculations such as ratios are not likely to vary from one analysis to another.

Summary

When evaluating a case, it is important to be systematic. Analyse the case in a logical fashion, beginning with the identification of operating and financial strengths and weaknesses and environmental opportunities and threats. Move on to assess the value of a company's current strategies only when you are fully conversant with the SWOT analysis of the company. Ask yourself whether the company's current strategies make sense, given its SWOT analysis. If they do not, then what changes need to be made? What are your recommendations? Above all, link any strategic recommendations you may make to the SWOT and GAP analyses. State explicitly how the strategies you identify take advantage of the company's strengths to exploit environmental opportunities, how they rectify the company's weaknesses, and how they counter any of the threats from the PESTLE factors.

It is also important that you consider the strategic options that may be available to the organization. Some of the options may not be feasible, suitable or acceptable in the light of the points you will have covered above. Make sure that you outline the strategies that need to be adopted to implement any recommendations that you make. Many company strategies fail because of poor implementation or unrealistic expectations of market growth and demand. You therefore have to be aware that your recommendations are sensible and fit the existing resource base and capability of the firm.

Remember that this unit only gives you an indicative and not a comprehensive range of analytical tools. You need to read widely and use other new analytical tools that may be available, including your own ideas. In the first SMiP case, candidates needed to utilize new types of analyses to bolster their arguments, and examples of these are incorporated in the book. You must also be familiar with all aspects of the syllabi in the other Professional Postgraduate Diploma modules. Further ideas are given in Unit 4. Finally, remember that for the SMiP syllabus, you have to prepare analyses *before the examination* (as explained in Unit 1).

Unit 3: Understanding the direction and management of marketing activities

Learning objectives

In this unit you will:

- Demonstrate an understanding of the direction and management of marketing activities as part of the implementation of strategic direction, taking into account business intelligence requirements, marketing processes, resources, markets and the company vision.

Introduction

This outcome knits together a range of different areas of marketing. Marketing is a complex area of business, and for successful implementation, it is important for marketers to develop strategic direction for an organization, taking into account marketing intelligence in conjunction with company resources and processes. The importance of developing a vision is also very important when developing a strategic focus. This helps an organization to develop a clear direction. Strategy in marketing involves harnessing a company's resources to meet customer needs through market analysis – an understanding of competitor actions, governmental actions and globalization, together with consideration of technological and other environmental changes.

Unit 3: Understanding the direction and management of marketing activities

Business intelligence

The development and organization of marketing intelligence systems has always been an important aspect of marketing. Market intelligence can be gathered in several ways. Companies can gather information from secondary sources and reports produced by companies such as Mintel and AC Neilson or commission primary research. An example of primary research is provided by the following mini-case (taken from a previous CIM case study – Titan).

Case study: Titan's brand image in India

Over the last five years, consumers have consistently regarded Titan as one of the top brands in India. In 1998, Titan was regarded as the most admired consumer goods company in a survey carried out by Advertising Marketing in India. Titan's history in the polls has been outstanding, as Tables 3.1 and 3.2 indicate.

In 1999, the Advertising and Marketing Survey was carried out by IMRB, along the same lines as in the previous seven years, to maintain continuity and establish the survey's validity in enabling comparisons with previous years. The surveys were carried out exclusively among professional marketers in companies marketing FMCG and durables. Respondents were drawn from all levels and conducted in the major cities of Delhi,

Table 3.1 Company rankings over 6 years in India 1993–1999

Company	1999	1998	1997	1996	1995	1994	1993
FMCG companies							
HLL	1	1	1	1	1	1	1
Coca-Cola	2	7	9	11	13	16	–
Cadbury	3	8	3	3	6	7	6
Pepsi foods	4	3	5	4	7	6	11
Colgate	5	9	6	5	4	5	5
Durables companies							
Titan	1	1	2	1	1	1	1
BPL	2	2	1	5	3	3	5
Maruti	3	4	5	2	–	–	–
Intel	–	–	–	–	–	–	–
LG Electronics	5	11	–	–	–	–	–

Source: Advertising, Marketing, e-commerce, India

Unit 3: Understanding the direction and management of marketing activities

Table 3.2 Most admired durable brands in India 1998/1999

Rank 1999	Rank 1998	Company	Score	Rank 1999	Rank 1998	Company	Score
1	1	Titan	7.96	19	26	Compaq	6.62
2	2	BPL	7.76	20	21	Eureka Forbes	6.6
3	4	Maruti	7.55	21	24	Carrier Aircon	6.51
4	–	Intel	7.47	22	9	Ericsson	6.5
5	11	LG Electronics	7.39	23	12	Philips	6.5
6	7	Godrej-GE	7.13	24	15	Modi Xerox	6.43
7	3	MRF	7.07	25	29	Videocon	6.41
8	13	Bajaj Auto	7.05	26	23	Chloride India (Exide)	6.38
9	13	Hero Honda	6.96	27	20	HCL Infosystems	6.22
10	5	Asian Paints	6.95	28	21	LML	6.16
11	24	Hewlett-Packard	6.9	29	27	Mahindra and Mahindra	6.1
12	18	Samsung	6.82	30	31	Hero Cycles	6.07
13	18	Whirlpool	6.81	31	33	Onida	5.93
14	15	TVS Suzuki	6.79	32	17	Bausch and Lomb	5.92
15	6	Nokia	6.78	33	30	Goodlass Nerolac	5.86
16	–	Telco	6.67	34	9	Motorola	5.85
17	–	Infosys	6.63	35	8	Baron International	5.82
17	28	Wipro Infotech	6.63	36	32	Blow Past	5.61

Source: Advertising, Marketing, e-commerce, India

Calcutta, Chennai and Bangalore. The company received top positions when the following questions were asked (figures in brackets are scores out of 10):

1. Products are designed to meet customer needs (7.88).
2. Products are different from competitors (7.25).
3. Better than average at new product launches (7.59).
4. Brands provide long-term stability (7.52).
5. Products are market leaders (7.91).
6. Products are innovative (number 2 slot) (7.32).
7. Products are consistently superior to competitors (7.51).
8. Products offer value for money (7.66).

39

Unit 3: Understanding the direction and management of marketing activities

9 Company's marketing personnel are of high calibre (7.20).

10 Company's advertising is consistently superior (number 2 slot) (7.53).

11 Company keeps in touch with market constantly (7.4).

12 Company has a superior distribution network (7.78).

13 Provides good after-sales service (number 2 slot) (7.43).

As can be seen, Titan retained its leadership position. Working in its favour was its product launches into new segments, including the Dash! range for children. In 2000, an Economic Times survey of top Indian companies revealed that Titan was regarded as the top brand in India, ahead of all FMCG companies. A consumer brand is much more than a bundle of tangible and intangible benefits. For this particular survey, seven attributes were considered:

1 The quality of the brand

2 Value for money

3 The future of the brand

4 Distinctiveness

5 Uniqueness

6 The feelings that the brand evokes amongst the consumer

7 How inclined the consumers were to purchase the brand

The target audience for the survey were chief wage earners, housewives and young adults between the ages of 15 and 45 years belonging to the A/B/C households in urban India (Figures 3.1-3.3). In general, the brands are less well known in rural India. A ten-point scale was applied and 3164 interviews were conducted in the following locations: Mumbai (537), Delhi (520), Calcutta (423), Chennai (409), Rajkot (345), Allahabad (300), Cuttack (300) and Vijayawada (330). The brand received such success because it appeals to the youth segment and is aspirational. Titan, in India, is also known for its classy elegance, while being a popular mass-market brand with a strong presence at the

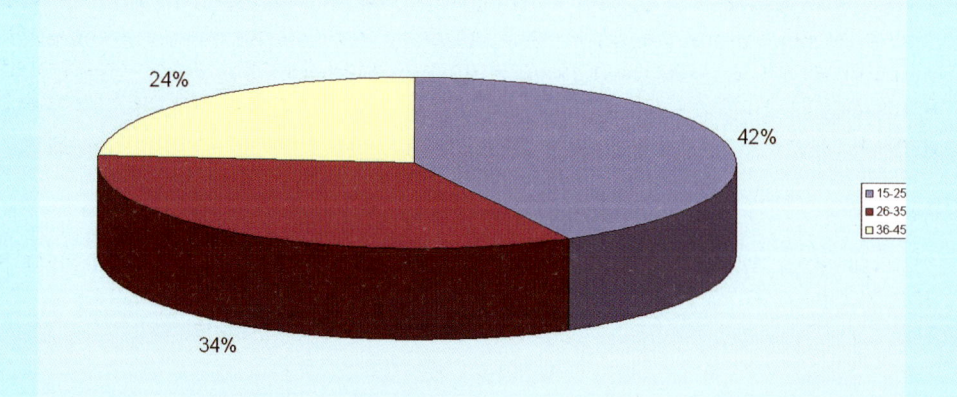

Figure 3.1 Respondent profile by age
Source: Economic Times, India

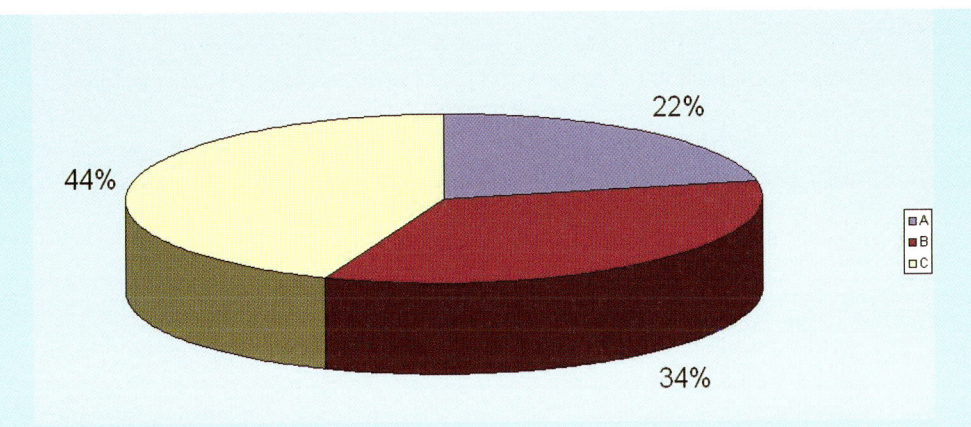

Unit 3: Understanding the direction and management of marketing activities

Figure 3.2 Socio-economic classes surveyed

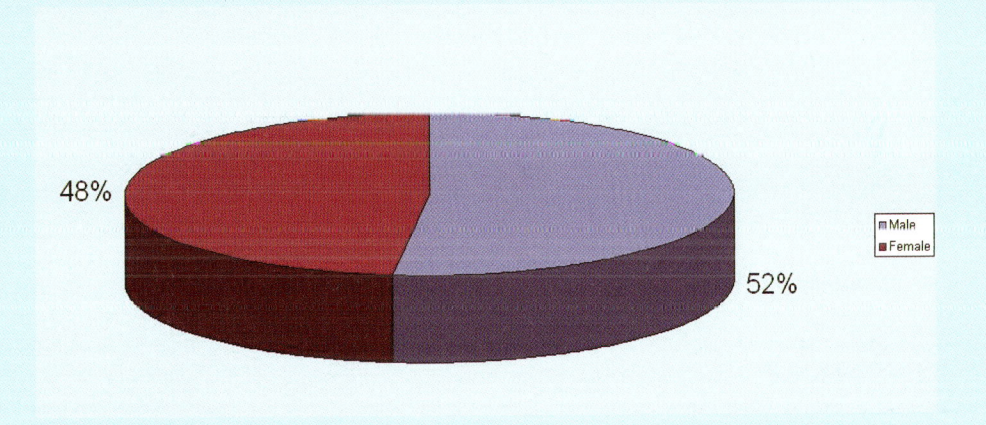

- A: 22%
- B: 34%
- C: 44%

Figure 3.3 Gender breakdown or respondents
Source: Economic Times, India

- Male: 48%
- Female: 52%

lower end. The brand is regarded as 'mass with class' by brand consultants. It is a brand that is also equally popular with both men and women. The company is consistent in its brand expenditure and spends, on average, around Rs 25–30 crore on brand building. Although this is small compared with others within the top ten, the amount spent appears to be highly effective.

Question

Highlight and evaluate the different uses of marketing intelligence to a business organization with reference to the above case and other companies that you know.

The above excerpt shows the usefulness to Titan of primary research carried out by various agencies. The company could also carry out its own primary research by commissioning agencies to carry out work on customer satisfaction or design of the watches.

41

Primary research

Good market research provides a good foundation in formulating successful marketing strategy. Conducted carefully, qualitative primary market research studies can yield insights on issues such as product usage patterns, unmet needs, product positioning and pricing – all of which are central to strategy formulation and decision-making.

Effective qualitative primary market research

The effectiveness of qualitative primary market research depends on how it is carried out, and it can be improved by concentrating on the following issues:

- **Focus on strategic marketing decisions** – All aspects of the research study, from questionnaire design to recruitment and analysis, should fit together and be focused clearly on developing information, insights and understanding for strategic decision-making.

- **Quality of respondents** – Data collected in any primary research are only as good as the respondents interviewed. In this respect, respondents should be identified and screened carefully to ensure that each interview increases confidence in the findings.

- **Building confidence** – In all market research studies, it is important to develop confidence in the study's findings. In qualitative research such confidence is achieved, as data accumulate to build a believable 'picture' of the study area and findings from different respondents are in substantial agreement. It may be advisable to conduct both quantitative and qualitative research so that each area complements the other. Figure 3.4 illustrates the key points that need to be understood when researching customers.

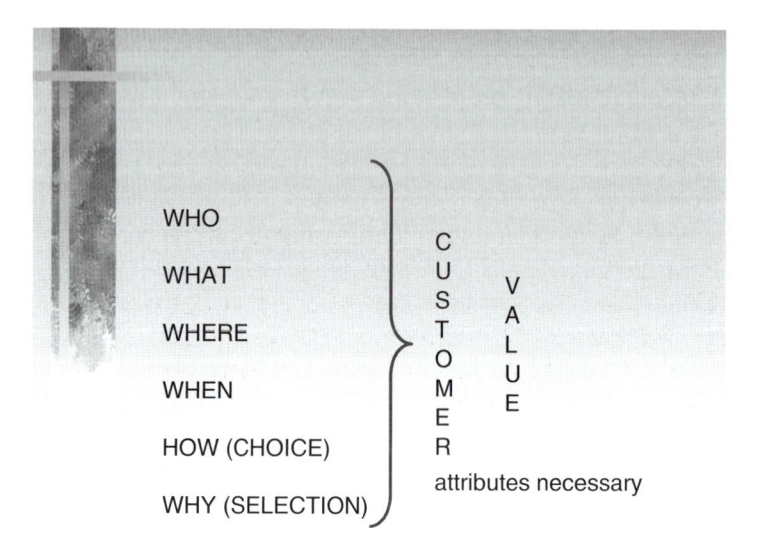

```
WHO         ⎫
WHAT        ⎪   C
WHERE       ⎬   U   V
WHEN        ⎪   S   A
HOW (CHOICE)⎪   T   L
WHY (SELECTION)⎭ O   U
                M   E
                E
                R
                attributes necessary
```

Figure 3.4 Customer analysis

At the same time, an organization needs to take a comprehensive view of all its research areas. This is illustrated in Figure 3.5. This research is necessary to understand the market potential of products and services. Market research in conjunction with market intelligence helps an organization to develop effective marketing strategies. Success depends on information about a particular market segment, a geographic area or customer preferences, enabling better targeting.

Case study: Marketing campaigns' impact on consumer habits

Andy Farquarson looks at the way partnerships between business and charities leave their mark on the consumer.

Cause-related marketing campaigns are having a significant impact on consumer habits and are bringing benefits to both the businesses and the charities they link up with, according to new research. This latest study looks for the first time at how people respond to such campaigns – rather than how they think they would.

The key finding is surprisingly high public awareness of campaigns such as Tesco's donation of computers to schools, Avon's support for breast cancer research or the Andrex puppy appeal in association with the National Canine Defence League. Almost 90 per cent of those surveyed had heard of at least one cause-related programme and almost half could spontaneously name a specific company or brand involved in a campaign. Two in three people believed more businesses should get involved. Against this, however, a small percentage felt cause-related marketing was exploitative or that it was inappropriate for business to become involved in social issues.

Until now, research into the effectiveness of cause-related marketing campaigns has focused on consumers' attitudes, rather than their actions. The new study, Profitable Partnerships, was commissioned by Business in the Community (BITC) and is based on a survey of 2000 adults by the British Market Research Bureau. Although previous work has established that a majority of people support the concept of cause-related marketing, and would probably express that support in their purchasing choices, the fresh research indicates that this broad approval is affecting consumers' choices.

More than 65 per cent of respondents said they had participated in a cause-related marketing campaign. Of them, three-quarters had switched brand, tried out a product or increased their usage, and four in five had felt more positive about certain purchases, more loyal to a company or brand and more inclined to look out for further cause-related campaigns. Although 30 per cent of respondents were regular Internet users, comparatively few had found cause-related marketing campaigns on the Web. Old media predominated, with awareness of campaigns garnered through in-store promotion (23 per cent), television commercials (18 per cent) and advertisements in print media (11 per cent).

Cause-related marketing is defined as any partnership between business and charity, which markets an image, product or service for mutual benefit. 'This is not about corporate philanthropy,' says Sue Adkins, BITC's director of marketing. 'It's about commercial benefit for both cause and company. Any business which tries to project this sort of campaign as strings-free giving is heading for a fall; the public is not gullible.' A good match between partners is also vital, says Adkins. Unless campaigns are properly managed, and based on integrity and transparency, they can be counter-productive.

The new report does not specify what constitutes a 'good' campaign. Among a wide variety of factors cited by those surveyed were schemes that supported local community activity, a high level of donation or support for the project or charity and clearly communicated, unambiguous benefits. Tesco's 'computers for schools' initiative is a good example of such clarity, argues Adkins. It has delivered more than £30 million of computer equipment to schools, raised Tesco's profile (more than 40 per cent of adults know about the initiative) and bolstered public perception of the company as a good corporate citizen.

Unsurprisingly, Tim Mason, Tesco's marketing director, welcomes the BITC findings. 'Successful marketing is all about meeting customer needs and most consumers expect companies to be socially responsible,' he says. 'That's what is driving the rapid growth of cause-related marketing and I am sure that growth will continue for the foreseeable future.' Marketing departments may formulate corporate strategies, but it is the advertising industry that gets the messages across to consumers. So, it is hardly surprising that advertising agencies are establishing specialist teams to provide cause-related marketing expertise to their clients.

One of the longest established is Saatchi & Saatchi's 'cause connection' set up in 1997 by Marjorie Thompson (who worked both in the public and in the voluntary sectors before joining Saatchis). 'There are huge opportunities to develop cause-related marketing in the UK,' says Thompson. 'For instance, government could provide much more in the way of match-funding and tax breaks to encourage good corporate citizenship. That would help charities gain long-term funding and exploit the expertise of the communications profession to promote their missions and messages.'

Note: Profitable Partnerships is available at £75, or £50 to registered charities, from BITC, 44 Baker St, London W1M 1DH. Further information at www.bitc.org.uk.

Source: The Guardian, Wednesday, 15 November 2000.

Question

There is a degree of scepticism about the cause-related marketing efforts of most companies, at least by some consumers. Where does this scepticism originate from and how would you advise a company to overcome public scepticism and establish an ethical and caring image for itself?

This article indicates the way in which market research can be utilized by companies to boost their corporate image.

Unit 3: Understanding the direction and management of marketing activities

Case study: The life cycle of a dinosaur

Michael Crichton's novel *Jurassic Park* was published in 1985 and remained on the best seller list for three years before it was made into a film. If you look at the concept of *Jurassic Park*, the brand, it soon becomes apparent that it was a real marketing success story: in terms of segmentation, branding, merchandising and associated themed products. Below is a selected timetable of events relating to the *Jurassic Park* phenomenon.

1986   Michael Crichton Publishes *Jurassic Park*.

1988   Deal struck with Steven Spielberg and Universal Studios. (N.B. Universal is owned by Matsuhita, the Japanese Kieratsu, which also controls UCI cinemas, Technics and Panasonic.)

1991   Trailers and tasters released to cinemas in USA.

1992   Limited release of premiers to build interest.

1992   General release for 8-month period.

The film cost $60 million to make, $65 million to market. It grossed $200 million at the box office. It was specifically targeted at the under-25 segment of the market, representing 87% of the cinema-going public.

Total revenue from over 1000 lines of associated merchandise, sweat shirts, baseball caps etc. > $1 billion.

1993   *Jurassic Park* video game launched, grossed $800 million (total market worth $8 billion).

1993   *Jurassic Park* video released.

1995   Rights sold to cable and satellite channels.

1996   Film rights sold to network TV.

1997   *The Lost World* (sequel) launched.

Questions

1   What was the segmentation policy adopted by Universal; how was it affected by demographics and time-scales?

2   What does the life cycle for *Jurassic Park: The Brand* look like? Where is it now? Does it conform to the classic model?

3   Why was *Jurassic Park* so much more successful than, say, ET or Last Action Hero?

Source: George W. Downie

Unit 3: Understanding the direction and management of marketing activities

Secondary research

This type of research is based on information gleaned from studies previously performed by government agencies, chambers of commerce, trade associations and other organizations. This includes Census Bureau information and Nielsen ratings. Such information is now readily available through the Web. In some instances, detailed reports are produced for industry sectors by major agencies such as the Gartner group. However, these are quite expensive to purchase.

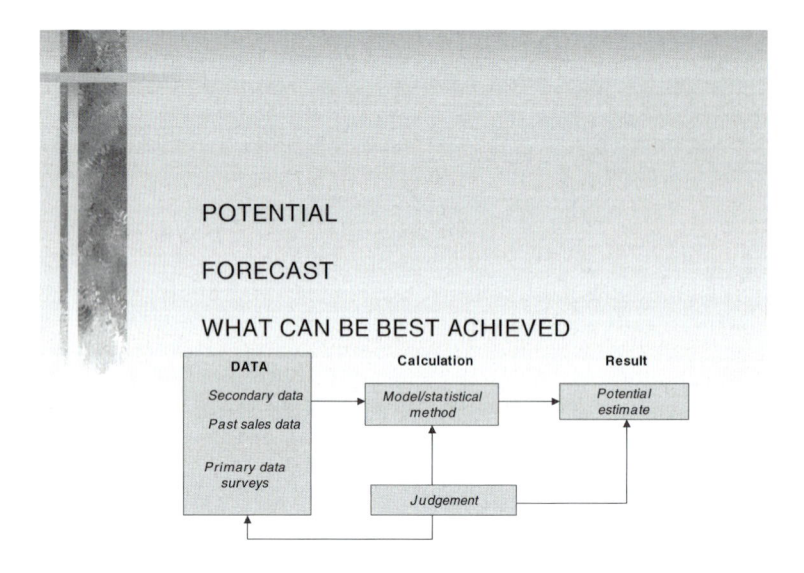

Figure 3.5 Marketing potential and forecasting

Although secondary research is less expensive than primary research, it is not as accurate, or as useful, as specific, customized research. For instance, secondary research may help a shoe manufacturer to understand the number of shoes sold within a country. However, pricing data, the impact of shoe design or how well the brand is accepted may not be available. This is where primary research can be used to obtain more specific information. Organizations rely on information systems, and this aspect is summarized in Figure 3.6. An organization, as it develops and grows, has much historical information that it can draw from its archives. Often, interesting information lies hidden until it is analysed. Market intelligence is drawn from company sources, customers, sales force, secondary information, commissioned research and the Internet. All the information has to be drawn together to form a Marketing Decision Support System.

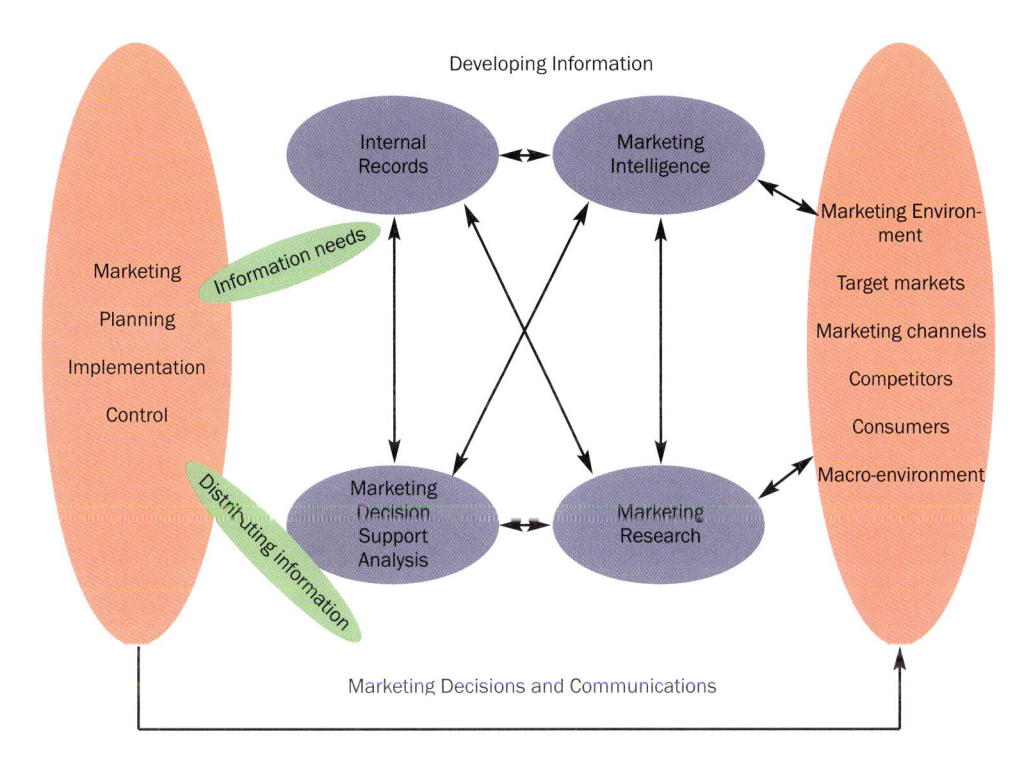

Unit 3: Understanding the direction and management of marketing activities

Figure 3.6 Marketing information system
Source: Adapted from Kotler (1992)

The role of information technology

In the last decade, information technology has become a very important part of a marketer's armoury. There is little in marketing that does not incorporate information technology. Market intelligence can therefore be gathered in many ways (Ranchhod, 2004):

1. Salesmen, on the road, can be updated on customer requirements as necessary. This information can be used for enhancing CRM and logistics.

2. As mobile devices become more sophisticated, customers will be able to access inventories of their suppliers. This means that they can place orders and specify delivery times. This can be done through links to an intranet or the Internet. Well-organized companies can gather and store this information.

3. Individuals, apart from talking to others, will also be able to communicate with machines. This is already a reality, with consumers being able to buy soft drinks, chocolates and car washes through mobile devices. Data on consumption patterns can be stored.

4. Consumers will be able to pay for meals in restaurants through secure transactions through a mobile device.

5   The 'bluetooth' devices can enable retailers to market special offers to customers on their mobile devices if they are within a 20m radius. This will also allow customers to undertake transactions with shops and restaurants.

6   Radio will become an integral part of the mobile device, allowing an individual access to a myriad of radio stations. This also has implications for advertising and branding.

7   The incorporation of ground positioning systems (GPS, through satellite) into mobile devices means that individuals will be able to easily locate their positions and also the nearest outlets or services that they need.

As customers become fluid in the way they contact and interact with companies, companies in turn need to be fluid in their approach. Often, the IT/Marketing link is not good. The marketing function, often, does not understand what happens in IT with regard to service provision and prices. There is often a cultural gap between marketing and IT, and therefore, there is a need to integrate data and for computer experts to work side by side with marketers.

There is a need to share experiences. It is important that for good CRM, IT and marketing work together, with IT being able to understand what the internal customer needs are. A change of management philosophy is required, where IT shifts from 'building solutions' to defining requirements from the front end with business and customers in building the best solutions. The one-to-one relationship means that a customer is known to the enterprise and interacts with the enterprise, with the enterprise flexing and changing to meet his/her needs. The enterprise can then have a unified view of a single customer across the entire enterprise, linking other functional and geographical units together.

As the relationship develops across boundaries, it is clear that the organization truly becomes a learning organization with the customer finding that he/she is investing in a continuing relationship with it. At every given opportunity, the organization can 'tailor' and refit its behaviour to suit the customer. In the end, the way the relationship is maintained, grown and nurtured means that a customer is less likely to invest time in building such a relationship with a competitor. This relationship-building needs to be regarded as a business process rather than a technology suite. The technology needs to be able to support and enable this process. With the growth of the Internet fuelling online purchases, websites are now very sophisticated and techniques for advertising are now increasingly becoming technologically based. For instance, AdSense allows businesses with websites to run key word text or image advertisements through a system managed by Google. This allows companies to position themselves cleverly on the search engine, enabling customers to locate them easily. Of course, it also generates massive revenues for Google.

The learning organization and market-based learning

The learning organization can 'learn' in different ways. An organization can be adaptive to its environment, thereby learning from the subtle changes taking place in the marketplace. In other instances, an organization can become efficient in the way it utilizes information, developing information-processing patterns that can enable it 'read' the changes taking place in the market-place, and can change its behaviour patterns accordingly. Authors such as Senge (1990) view a learning organization as a continuously creative, innovative organization, where each member is an active participant within the learning process. This allows for continuous learning and flexibility.

Learning is often constrained (single-loop learning) at a low level or it is of a higher, creative order where cognitive learning takes place (double-loop learning).

Single-loop learning

It is easy for organizations to be conditioned by single-loop learning. In many instances, companies have to adjust to specific demands in the market, and often they will have well-developed strategies to cope with this. Single-loop learning is also prevalent within functional areas of businesses as bureaucratic systems are in place to deal with orders and demands. These are routine patterns and are triggered by particular stimuli within the environment. The marketing function in a chocolate company, for instance, will respond to low demand by spending more on advertising. In general, short-term tactical issues are dealt with efficiently. Single-loop learning does not stretch to questioning the phenomena that create the response (i.e. Why are the chocolate sales low?), it merely sets in motion patterned responses to external pressures.

Single-loop learning is often constrained by a learning 'boundary'. This is not unusual or undesirable. In many instances, companies serve particular markets, and they have to focus on these markets to deal with them efficiently and to give customers satisfaction. This efficiency in the market-place can create rigid adherence to organized approaches and leave little to the imagination. The way in which the business is conceptualized guides core capabilities. However, in many instances these could become 'core rigidities' and can just concentrate on the served market, fostering quite a narrow perspective. Therefore, an adaptive approach (single-loop) is usually sequential, incremental and focused on issues or opportunities within the traditional scope of the organization's activities. This leaves little room for imagination and for any moves towards more interesting and potentially lucrative areas of business.

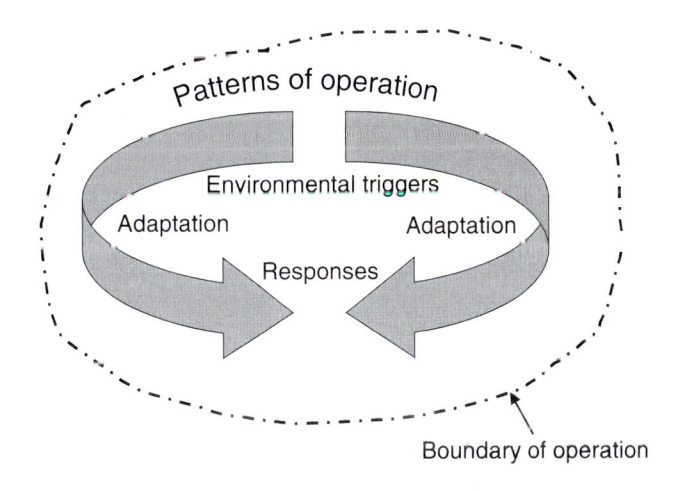

Figure 3.7 Single-loop learning

Double-loop learning

This higher level of learning affects the whole organization and is rarely contained within functional areas. It entails a deeper challenge to routine practices and rules. This type of generative learning shows a willingness to question long-held assumptions about mission, customers, capabilities or strategy. Often, this is based on systems theory and works through existing relationships, linking key issues and events. When an organization begins to embrace double-loop learning, interrelationships and dynamic processes of change are important. Often, a learning organization adept at double-loop learning can take advantage of 'windows' of opportunity that may be available to organizations. Often, slower-moving organizations that have 'fixed' views of markets and their role within them may fail to take advantage of these opportunities.

Higher-level learning usually occurs during some types of crisis, for example, new strategy, new leader, and significant changes in the market. It corresponds to the development of a new frame of reference(s). One of the consequences of a double-loop learning organization is the necessity to 'unlearn' an old process, as old frames are no longer efficient in coping with the new reality.

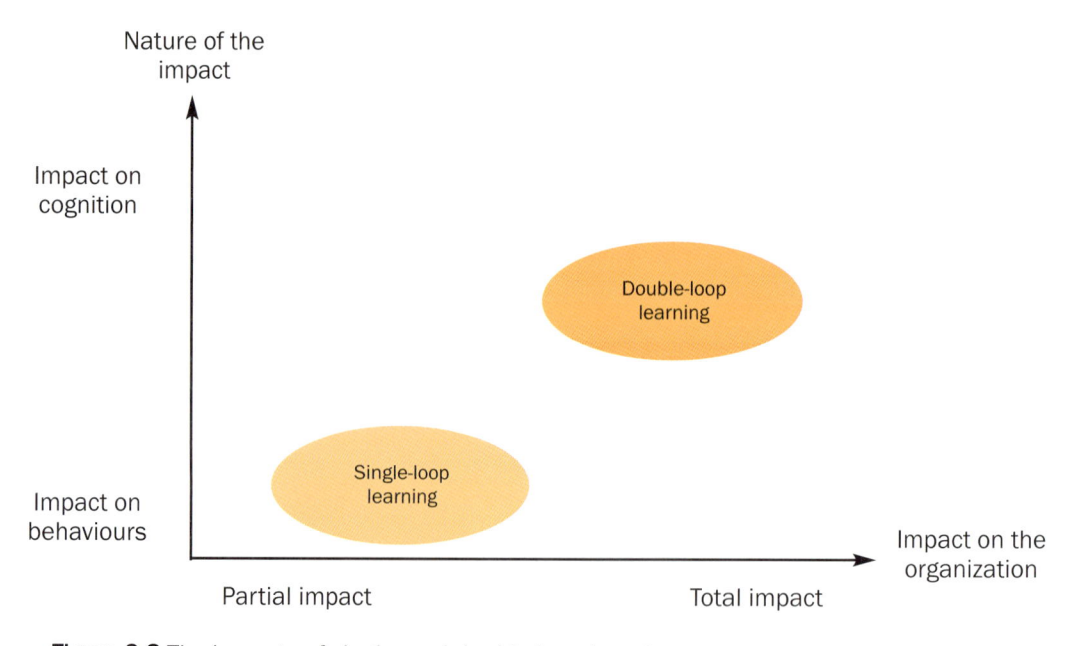

Figure 3.8 The impacts of single- and double-loop learning

For instance, the advent of the Internet has profoundly changed the way in which music and entertainment are delivered. The record industry was essentially stuck in its old paradigm of selling records or CDs through retailers. It generally failed to grasp the opportunities offered by the new medium. Records and movies are at the end of the day essentially bits of information. The Internet made it possible to transmit this information globally. Individuals began to freely exchange information and music. Although illegal, this still occurs regularly and vast amounts of pirated music changes hands on a daily basis. Artists now have their own websites and in some instances are distributing music through these sites. The music companies, in general, were very good at responding to fluctuating demands in the marketplace, but the single-loop response pattern created a situation where they failed to see the changes beyond their own self-made 'boundaries'. No sensible Internet strategies were therefore developed. This has led to much heartache and refocusing within the sector. Music can now be stored on CDs, mobiles, Mpeg players, memory sticks and computer hard disks, making the one-dimensional approach to music sales obsolete. The same is true for television programmes and films.

A company's intelligence-gathering system needs to be flexible and wide ranging so that old paradigms are constantly challenged. A true learning organization, therefore, will place great value on information transmission contributing to general learning. This will depend on the following:

- **Knowledge acquisition** – Converting data into knowledge that can be understood and assimilated.
- **Information distribution** – Distributing information and knowledge throughout the organization.
- **Information interpretation** – Understanding the information and interpreting it so that sensible opinions can be formed.
- **Organizational memory** – Understanding the new knowledge and embedding it in the organization's memory.

Organizations need to learn from the markets that they operate in so that the organizational memory consists of market-based learning (Figure 3.9).

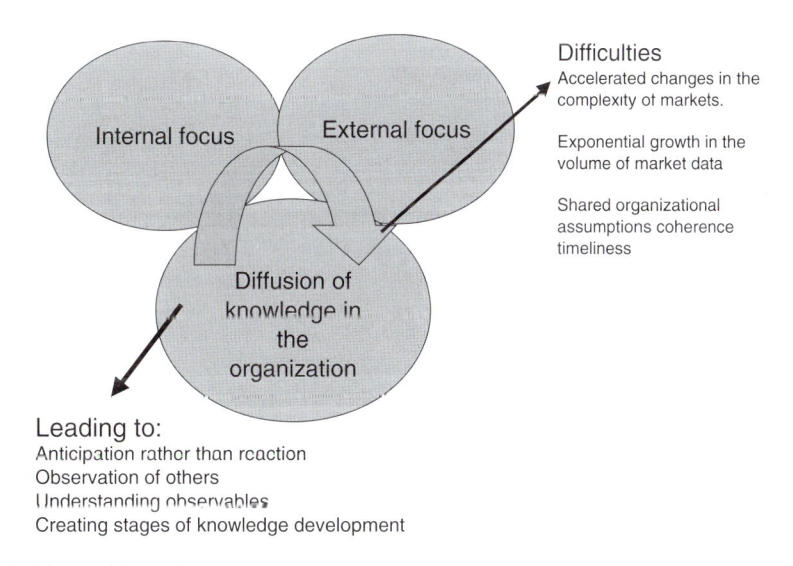

Figure 3.9 Market-based learning

To achieve some sort of shared purpose so that organizations benefit from learning, a mission statement can be of benefit, provided its scope is not too narrow and constricting. Pearce and David (1987) suggested that a mission statement should contain the following aspects:

1. Customers (the target market)
2. Products/services (offerings and value provided to customers)

Unit 3: Understanding the direction and management of marketing activities

3	Geographic markets (where the firm seeks customers)
4	Technology (the technology used to produce and market products)
5	Concern for survival/growth/profits (the firm's concern for being financially sound)
6	Philosophy (the firm's values, ethics, beliefs)
7	Public image (contributions the firm makes to communities)
8	Employees (the importance of managers and employees)
9	Distinctive competence (how the firm is better or different compared with its competitors)

Each of these points covers aspects of the organization where information and learning are important. A broad encompassing statement can, therefore, be quite helpful to an organization.

Some examples of mission statements

The Co-operative Bank has this as its ecological statement:

However, we undertake to continually assess all our activities and implement a programme of ecological improvement based on the pursuit of the following scientific principles:

- *Nature cannot withstand a progressive build-up of waste derived from the Earth's crust.*

- *Nature cannot withstand a progressive build-up of society's waste, particularly artificial persistent substances which it cannot degrade into harmless materials.*

- *The productive area of nature must not be diminished in quality (diversity) or quantity (volume) and must be enabled to grow.*

Society must utilize energy and resources in a sustainable, equitable and efficient manner.

We consider that the pursuit of these principles constitutes a path of ecological excellence and will secure future prosperity for society by sustainable economic activity.

The Co-operative Bank will not only pursue the above path itself but endeavour to help and encourage all its partners to do likewise.

From the Unilever company report we have this statement:

Our founders had strong values and a clear commitment to corporate social responsibility (it wasn't called that then, but that is what it was). It was William Lever who famously built a 'garden village' for his workers at Port Sunlight near Liverpool. He introduced such pioneering initiatives as a shorter working week, sickness benefits, holiday pay and pensions. He felt so strongly about broadening the experience of his employees that he regularly took them all to London for the day to see exhibitions and even built them an art gallery.

William Lever was living at a time when the fabric of society and the forces in society were very different from today. When the Church and Christian values played a dominant role in people's lives, when there was little or no state-funded social provision and when businesses operated in often appalling conditions. He had clear moral views and believed he had a moral responsibility to help, both through business and his personal actions.

Indeed, his very visionary mission statement was itself an expression of his values:

> To make cleanliness commonplace; to lessen work for women; to foster health and contribute to personal attractiveness, that life may be more enjoyable and rewarding for the people who use our products.

From Cadbury's we have the following:

- Promote social housing of good quality that enhances the environment
- Manage all their housing and estates to the highest standards for all residents
- Encourage residents to share in decisions affecting their communities

Each of the above examples are very good examples of mission statements where corporate social responsibility is taken into account. Mission statements can be quite varied and address different issues. Often, all the issues discussed by Pearce and Webb are rarely addressed.

The internationalization process of firms

The SMiP paper is frequently international in nature, and the candidates need to be conversant with international constraints under which marketing managers operate. This section provides the reader with a reminder of some of the relevant issues.

Trade has been taking place between nations for dozens of centuries and is not a new phenomenon. The volume of international trade however is increasing rapidly with the membership of the World Trade Organization and various trading blocs expanding and the tariff and non-tariff trade barriers being dismantled or reduced periodically. The European Union, for example, is now a reality for European firms, enabling them to compete freely in a market of hundreds of millions of consumers. This is set to increase as the new members take up their seats and full membership status within the Union.

Most companies are now faced with international competition in their domestic markets and look to international marketing as the way forward if they are to secure their future and remain competitive. Indeed, there are various reasons for which companies, particularly SMEs, may engage in international marketing, for example to offload excess production at home, to find new markets for products that have reached their decline stage in the domestic market, to benefit from cheaper factors of production, and to remain competitive in the face of foreign competition in their domestic markets. The current political and economic pressures towards trade liberalization and the consequently increasing competition from around the world has made internationalization a relevant issue for the majority of SMEs in both manufacturing and service sectors.

Several definitions of the process of internationalization exist. Most of these treat internationalization as the step-by-step process of business development whereby a firm increasingly commits itself to in international operations through specific products in selected markets. The decision to operate internationally is of course a strategic decision, and many studies and theories attempt to explain the process of internationalization of firms.

One of the earlier attempts at theorizing about the process is Vernon's (1966) International Product Life Cycle theory (IPLC). Originally based on research into US firms, the suggestion is that manufacturing by the innovator was normally for the domestic market in its initial phase and then for export purposes. This was later followed by production overseas because of growing overseas markets, increase in competition and the standardization of products. Subsequently, foreign products became competitive, and imports into the USA began to offer serious competition. Hence, firms relocated to developing countries from where they shipped products back to the home country.

Focusing on the experiences of Swedish firms, Johanson and Wiedersheim-Paul (1975) highlighted four stages in the internationalization process, starting with exporting through independent representatives to a final phase of overseas production. The Uppsala Internationalization Model (Johanson and Vahlne, 1977) assumes a process made up of stages too. The firm begins with less risky ventures in physically close markets and gradually increases its commitment and its geographical reach through a process of experiential learning.

Vatne (1995) suggested that SMEs, which are engaged in manufacturing, are influenced by their internal resources in terms of their business territory. That is, social networking and entrepreneurial quality may influence a firm's ability to identify and acquire external resources, as well as its ability to utilize such resources for its operations and marketing mix. The internationalization process of SMEs engaged in the service sector has been examined by O'Farrell *et al.* (1998) who have extended the above model and highlighted the importance of client-supplier interaction. They have suggested that the ability to internationalize depends on the availability of suitably educated and experienced individuals with various skills who help the SME to sell specialized and innovative services internationally.

From the above discussion, it can be seen that most internationalization theories are process models which assert that an SME's lack of experiential knowledge leads to a gradual, or incremental, process of internationalization. For example, the Uppsala model of internationalization process is a model that is based on the implicit assumption of incremental and continuous growth. There is, however, an alternative approach represented by the entrepreneurial models, which are based on identifying opportunities that arise in response to external demand or the availability of new resources.

Lack of knowledge of international markets at the start of the internationalization process seems to be common to most theories. Whereas some of these theories emphasize individual learning and improvement in management understanding of international markets as crucial in the incremental process, others recognize the importance of networks in fuelling the process, for example Johanson and Vahlne (1990).

It ought to be noted that not every firm will follow an incremental process in its internationalization. For example, an exception is the so-called born-global company. Such companies from the outset view the world as one market. These are often small, technologically-based firms who strive for innovations and breakthroughs. According to Freeman and Cavusgil (2007) these young entrepreneurial firms, which take on internationalization early in their evolution, are now found in large numbers in smaller, open economies such as Finland and Denmark. Such firms require rapid internationalization to make the most of their innovation and to gain first-mover advantage. Freeman and Cavusgil (2007) argue that recent deregulation, advances in technology and broader effects of globalization may be the drivers for the continued steeply rising medium of smaller born-global. Some have suggested that born-global companies may be more common than it is generally assumed. Others have questioned that such companies do not follow the incremental process of internationalization, in that while the companies may be set up as global the entrepreneurs behind them often have many years' experience of international business.

Foreign market entry strategies

The process of internationalization involves decisions regarding foreign market entry strategies. The mode of entry is often at least a medium-term decision, if not a long-term one, and has therefore strategic implications for the firm. Although exporting is the first option for most firms other options, particularly as the firm grows, need to be evaluated too. Important factors to consider, as well as the firm's experience in international marketing, are:

◆ Market accessibility in terms of the ease, and cost, of entry

◆ Market size, in terms of current and potential value

◆ Profitability of the target market and costs of operating in that market, including logistics, promotion and channel management

◆ The firm's desire to exercise control over its overseas operations

The entry-level mode, as discussed above, is often that of exporting.

In this case, the firm produces domestically and sells overseas. There are two main choices for exporting. The firm can either use a domestic intermediary (in the exporter's country) or one located in the foreign market.

As an *indirect* exporter, the firm commits few resources to international marketing and chooses the low-cost option of having its products sold overseas by others on its behalf. A common method of doing so is called 'piggybacking', where an established international distribution network of one producer may be approached to distribute the products of another producer as well.

As a *direct* exporter the company becomes more active in, and devoted to, marketing overseas. The company may make use of many different intermediaries, including agents and distributors. Direct exporting gives the firm more control over both market selection and its marketing mix, but is costlier and is more risky than indirect exporting.

A firm also has a choice of different methods of overseas production with varying degrees of involvement, control, risk and profit potential. These are:

◆ **Licensing** the firm's offering, for a fee, its expertise or other assets, such as brand name or production methods, to a foreign company. This method of entry helps avoid paying tariffs, is relatively quick, saves on market research costs and does not require much capital. In practice, licensing often involves some kind of technology transfer, and this is regarded by many as its weakness, in that the foreign company may learn and copy the licensor's technology. Carefully negotiated contracts are important in eliminating or reducing risk.

◆ **Franchising** is a form of licensing. In this case, the agreement includes more than simple licensing. The franchiser grants the franchisee the right to conduct business in a specified and agreed manner, for example using the franchiser's products or name, and production and marketing techniques. As with licensing, this is a quick way of entering foreign markets and is potentially highly profitable with little capital investment required by the franchiser. Problems however may arise. The most important is probably the need to standardize the name, the business format, production and services processes to create and enhance the franchiser's reputation so the business can expand and more franchises can be sold. This requires careful monitoring and training of all franchisees.

- An international **strategic alliance** and a **joint venture** are both collaborative arrangement between two firms, but increasingly, an alliance is regarded as a non-equity-based agreement whereas a joint venture is regarded as one that is based on equity.

    Firms engage in strategic alliances, share information, assets and technology. Such firms may even be competitors in practice but feel they can save costs and increase their competitiveness against those outside the alliance. The airline industry has seen many strategic alliances with partners sharing routes, check-in desks and so on.

    Joint ventures normally require the transfer of one or more of the following from the foreign partner to a local firm: capital, management know-how, workforce and technology. The local firm in return offers local knowledge and possibly land and/or labour. Some companies are reluctant to select this method for fear of sharing technology and seeing it copied by the partner and the venture being dissolved. In some cases, government regulations make this the only option available for overseas production.

- **Foreign Direct Investment** (FDI) or **wholly owned production subsidiary overseas** is normally an option for the larger companies as it requires substantial financial investment and involves a high degree of risk. The decision ought to be based on an evaluation of the risks against the benefits of being closer to the sources of raw materials, cheaper labour or the strategic position of the overseas country in terms of logistics and distribution.

Globalization

Globalization, in marketing, refers to the growing convergence of demand and supply across the world. Driven by changes in consumer expectations, technological change, deregulation and regional forces, globalization is a reality to be faced by most companies and nations. The process is most apparent in the areas of consumption, business and finance. Supporters claim that these trends encourage competition and therefore offer better choice, better quality and lower prices for consumers. They additionally argue that the removal of trade barriers and increase in trade results in the transfer of technology, management know-how and more employment.

Opponents of globalization, on the contrary, claim that multinational/global companies are running the economies of the poorer nations and that as a consequence of globalization the gap between the poor and the rich is getting bigger–as is the gap in education levels and health care between the poor and the rich, with the former pushed into increasingly bigger amounts of debt in pursuance of the consumer lust triggered by globalization and the spread of capitalism.

Unit 3: Understanding the direction and management of marketing activities

Responses to globalization

Whatever the personal views of international marketing managers about globalization, they have to respond to the growing trend. The various ways that firms can respond are summarized below.

- **Ethnocentric orientation** assumes the home country (where the company is headquartered) is superior to the rest of the world. Sometimes associated with national arrogance, ethnocentric orientation sees only similarities in markets and assumes that products or practices that succeed in the home country/domestic market will be successful everywhere. Ethnocentric orientation tends to ignore many of the opportunities outside the domestic market whereas those that venture outside tend to operate on the basis of 'standardized' or 'extension approach' marketing and do not engage in adaptation to any noticeable degree.

- **Polycentric orientation** is the opposite of ethnocentric orientation and refers to a management belief that each country is unique. Companies in this case allow subsidiaries to develop their own strategies and marketing mix based on localized or adaptation approach. Such companies are known as multinationals.

- **Regiocentric orientation** focuses on a region as the unit of geographic relevance and attempts to cater for regional similarities through regional strategies.

- **Geocentric orientation** is adopted by global or transnational companies. Building on the similarities across the world, they view the world as a potential market and develop standardized marketing strategies and, more or less, standardized marketing mix.

In practice, it is difficult to categorize companies as purely multinational or global, but examples would possibly include Unilever as a multinational and Coke as a global company.

Case: Martin Allen Soccer Schools

Most sports stars, including footballers, dread the day that they have to finish as a professional competitor through either injury or age. Very few, even in the present environment of inflated wages, can afford to retire completely. Many endeavour to remain within their sport, in some capacity, as it is often perceived to be a comfort zone that they are familiar with. Obviously, there are only a limited number of employment positions within each sport and certainly not enough to provide all interested parties with an income. Recent data from the English Sports Council have suggested that about 3400 sports personnel retire each year, which is indeed a high figure to cater for.

Professional football is perhaps slightly different from other sports in that it employs players for 12 months of the year and that the players have large periods of free time to pursue other interests, including business ventures. This allows them, in some cases, to become experienced in business while still a player. Some take advantage of this, whereas others delay making such a decision until forced to do so at the end of their careers.

After the abolition of the footballers' maximum wage, in 1961, players started to think about investing some of their earnings ready for their non-playing years. On retirement,

Unit 3: Understanding the direction and management of marketing activities

running public houses, hotels, guest houses and sports shops seemed to be a popular choice for some ex-pros. In more recent times, owning racehorses, restaurants and working in the media are popular alternatives. Another area that has become popular with footballers is that of soccer schools. There are now a number of these throughout the country, and some of them are well established and have been in operation for a considerable time. They are usually scheduled to coincide with school holidays at a time when the football season has ended and are often for a duration of 3 or 4 days. Some are owned by well-known footballers, whereas others are set up and managed by the football clubs themselves, who employ local physical education teachers with coaching badges. The largest of the schools and the most established in terms of how long they have been operating is the Martin Allen Soccer School.

Martin has been organizing his soccer schools for well over a decade and is regarded within the industry as the market leader. He offers a well-tried and tested recipe, which includes appearances and activities from well-known international players, *Martin Allen Soccer School* tee-shirts and a signed certificate of attendance for each child attending the course. He also personally meets and talks with each class at all centres.

Martin organizes all of the operations including printing of the brochures and tee-shirts as well as the staffing and booking of all facilities. It is a complex operation that requires effective organization skills and a basic knowledge of marketing to ensure success. Allen is an open-minded person who is constantly looking for ways to make his schools even more successful and devotes much energy into this and other business ventures.

A few years ago, he even found time, with his wife, to organize the 'Mad Dog' charity ball, an all day and night event, using his football nickname, which raised over £40,000 for a cancer charity close to the Allen family's heart.

The Martin Allen Soccer Schools are well attended in all regions because Martin, now a football club manager, ensures that the customers get what they want. His wide array of networks and persuasive skills have also seen him attract major sponsors such as FujiFilm and Puma, which enable him to price the schools at a competitive and affordable level.

Martin Allen is now looking at the possibility of extending his successful brand into a 'new' country where the market might need developing. After a visit to the United States, he decided to explore the possibility of doing one, or both, of two things to expand his business. There was a possibility of exporting his current soccer schools as they were on a trial basis to a couple of centres in the United States. After all, soccer has re-emerged as a popular participation sport across the Atlantic and the time might now be ripe to profit from this. The other possibility was to re-format the existing schools into a soccer-camp style approach in the United Kingdom, as Martin had witnessed the popularity of these American summer camps during the school vacations during his last visit.

Questions

Relevant information is needed before any decision can be made. As a marketing consultant, how would you advise Martin on the following:

Unit 3: Understanding the direction and management of marketing activities

1. What key areas of market research will be needed for the United States as well as the United Kingdom? Use PESTLE analysis as an aid.
2. Are the target markets for the two countries likely to be the same?
3. What aspects of the marketing mix might need 'tweaking'?
4. Advise on mode of entry into the US market.

Source: John Cross

Summary

This unit considers the importance of having a mission for an organization and subsequently organizing for information acquisition and dissemination. It is clear that an organization with a well-developed sense of direction has the opportunity to create learning situations. Organizations have to learn and grow and base their learning on particular insights gained from the market. Technology also has an important role to play in the dissemination of knowledge and organizational learning.

The unit has also pointed out that international competition can no longer be ignored by most firms and that appropriate strategies for competing outside the domestic market ought to be part of the marketing plan of most organizations.

References

Freeman, S. and Cavusgil, S.T. (2007) Toward a Typology of Commitment States Among Managers of Born-Global Firms: A Study of Accelerated Internationalization, *Journal of International Marketing*, **15**(4): 1–40.

Johanson, J., Wiedersheim-Paul, P.E. (1975) The internationalization of the firm: Four Swedish cases, *The Journal of Management Studies*, **12**: 306–307.

Johanson, J., Vahlne, J.E. (1977) The internationalization process of the firm: A model of knowledge development and increasing foreign market commitment, *Journal of International Business Studies*, **8**: 35–40.

Johanson, J., Vahlne, J.E. (1990) The mechanism of internationalization, *International Marketing Review*, **7**(4): 11–24.

Kotler, P. (1992) *Marketing Management: Analysis, Planning and Control*, Prentice Hall.

O'Farrell, P.N., Wood, P.A., Zheng, J. (1998) Internationalisation by business service SMEs: an inter-industry analysis, *International Small Business Journal*, **16**(2): 13–33.

Pearce, J.A. II and David, F. (1987) Corporate mission statements: The bottom line, *Academy of Management Executive*, **1**(2): 109-116.

Ranchhod, A. (2004) *Marketing Strategies: A Twenty-first Century Approach*, Harlow: Pearson Education Ltd.

Senge, P.M. (1990) The leader's new work: Building learning organizations, *Strategic Management Review,* 7–23, Fall.

Vatne, E. (1995) Local resource mobilization and internationalization strategies in small and medium sized enterprises, *Environment and Planning,* **27**(1): 63–80.

Vernon, R. (1966) International investment and international trade in the product cycle, *Quarterly Journal of Economics,* **80**(2): 190–207.

www.bitc.org.uk

Unit 4 Contemporary issues in marketing

Learning objectives

In this unit you will:

◆ Assess the relevance of opportunities presented by contemporary marketing issues within any given scenario including innovations in marketing.

In attempting to look at this outcome, this unit offers an insight into several contemporary issues, such as relationship marketing, key account management, sustainability in marketing, branding and corporate identity.

Introduction

Several environmental factors are combining to bring pressure upon companies to adopt more elaborate strategies to differentiate themselves from close competitors. There are many reasons for this. The following section makes brief references to some of them.

Similarity of core products

Compared to a few decades ago, there are now numerous suppliers of goods and services offering identical or very similar products. Most consumer products, and consumer goods in particular, can now be made not just by so many companies but also by so many nations. There is a fierce competition in the market-place for customers of most products.

International trade and globalization

Barriers to international trade are constantly coming down and coupled with the adoption of free trade and business practices by most of the previously socialist/communist countries, an increasing number of companies are entering the international trade arena adding to competition in the market-place. Monopolies, state subsidies and protected industries are becoming things of the past, and almost every company must now fight for its share of customers. The work of the World Trade Organization (WTO) and also creation of trading blocs, for example the EU, are major drivers of this process.

Increasing customer awareness

Customers are now much better positioned than ever before to collect information on companies, products, prices and all that they are interested in with respect to their purchases. Today, information technology brings the world markets into consumers' homes at the touch of a button, making them more aware and more demanding.

Additionally, customers, or at least some of them, are showing increased awareness of the impact of capitalism and marketing on the environment and on consumers. Corporate social responsibility, with its many branches, for example green marketing, are contemporary issues that organizations have to deal with.

Increasing consumer protection legislation

In response to pressure groups, and consumers in general, governments are increasingly putting legal measures into place to protect consumers, as well as the environment. In many instances, such measures are international or regional, for example labelling laws emanating from the EU.

Increased mergers, alliances and takeovers

The increasing number of mergers, alliances and takeovers means that organizations are in danger of losing their identities and consequently many of their customers.

As a response to the circumstances described above, many companies are making serious attempts to differentiate themselves and to gain or maintain competitive advantage. To these companies, the issues relating to branding, relationship building, corporate social responsibility and developing a strong corporate identity are of vital importance, because these are key tools in differentiation. This unit discusses these topics.

Customer loyalty

Change of emphasis in the marketing paradigm

There is a general belief that a radical change in the marketing paradigm is taking place. For a long time, traditional marketing emphasized manipulation of the marketing mix for satisfying customers. However, as long as customers came through the door and the firm reached its target sales, it did not matter too much who those customers were. Today, emphasis has turned on relationships, and the focus is on developing loyal customers.

Wallace et al. (2004) point out that *with an increasingly competitive retail environment and decreasing customer switching costs, customer loyalty is a critical goal for merchants of all types*. Benady and Bierley (2004) add that customer loyalty/retention has become a fundamental issue both for practitioners and for researchers. They suggest that this orientation is the result of not only the shift of marketing paradigm, from transactional to relational approach, but also from a radical change in the marketing environment, which has made loyalty a 'Holy Grail' for marketers.

This radical change in the environment has been discussed by authors such as Little and Marandi (2003) who have pointed out the implications of globalization, which have resulted in a massive choice for customers around the world that, together with increasing knowledge of markets by customers, has contributed to a decline in loyalty. Suppliers are now faced with customers who are no longer content with local and/or national products as they can choose from hundreds of suppliers around the world who are available not only on the high street but on the Internet too. It may be argued that in the past, organizations have been founded on the premise that customers will stay loyal if the product or service is good enough. Recently, customers have become more 'sophisticated' and demanding, because they have more options, more channels and more power.

Benefits of customer loyalty

Many different benefits are suggested to arise from customer loyalty. Reichheld (1993, 1996), a widely quoted author on loyalty, suggests that when a company consistently delivers superior value and wins customer loyalty, market share and revenues go up, and the cost of acquiring new customers goes down. Reichheld adds that the better economics mean the company can offer its workers better pay, which sets off a whole chain of events. Increased pay boosts employee morale and commitment; as employees stay longer, their productivity goes up and training costs fall. Employees' overall job satisfaction, combined with their experience, helps them serve customers better; and customers are then more inclined to stay loyal to the company. Furthermore, Reichheld suggests that as the best customers and employees become part of the loyalty-based system, competitors are left to survive with less desirable customers and less talented employees. In a similar way, Griffin (1995) refers to *The Loyal Customer-Loyal Employee Connection* and argues, that when a company is spending less to acquire new customers, it can afford to pay its employees better. Better pay prompts a chain reaction, with a host of benefits including higher motivation levels.

Reichheld (1996) analysed the profit per customer in different service businesses categorized by the number of years that a customer had been with the firm. He found that there was a correlation between how long the customer stayed with a firm in each of these industries and the profitability of serving those customers; that is, the customers who stayed longer were usually the more profitable because of less money spent on them, cross-selling of additional product lines and so on.

Hollensen (2003) suggests that getting a new customer could cost five to six times as much as it costs to serve existing customers through sales calls, providing information about new goods and services and so on. Hollensen (2003) argues that new customers often benefit from introductory promotional discounts, whereas long-tem customers are more likely to pay regular and higher prices. The subject of premium pricing is also taken up by Garvin (1988) who argues that satisfied customers are more willing to pay for the benefits they receive and are more likely to be tolerant of increases in price.

Anderson (1994) and Reichheld and Sasser (1990) discuss positive word of mouth as a benefit of having loyal customers. Loyal and satisfied customers are generally thought to be more likely to engage in positive word of mouth and less likely to engage in damaging negative word of mouth for the company. Of course word of mouth amounts to free advertising for the company.

What is loyalty?

Handy (2004) states that:

> *Loyalty is an inner state that leads to an orientation toward the future, the willingness to continue the relationship, a commitment to the product, the brand or the supplier. To say that a customer is loyal is to confer an active role on the customer.*

Handy (2004) goes on to suggest that a retained customer is in a passive role. This means not all retained customers continue to do business with a firm out of loyalty. Loyalty implies a choice. Another difference between retention and loyalty is in the way they are measured. Loyalty is essentially measured through the duration of the relationship, retention through the churn rate.

Griffin (1995) proposes that there are two factors that are critical for loyalty to exist and to flourish:

1. An attachment to the product or service that is high compared with that to potential alternatives
2. Repeat purchase

Following on from the above discussion, it is appropriate now to establish a definition of customer loyalty.

Lovelock et al. (1999) define customer loyalty as:

> *A customer's willingness to continue patronizing a firm over the long term by purchasing and using its goods and services on a repeated and preferably exclusive basis, and voluntarily recommending the firm's products to friends and associates.*

Types of customer loyalty

It is also generally agreed that there are different types of loyalty based on customers' attachment and frequency of purchase. For example, Griffin (1995) identifies the following types of loyalty:

- **Premium loyalty** – Prevails when a high level of attachment and repeat patronage exists.
- **Inertia loyalty** – A low level of attachment coupled with high repeat purchase. The customer buys out of habit.
- **Latent loyalty** – Situational rather than attitudinal influences determine repeat purchase.
- **No loyalty** – Lack of loyalty to certain products, services and suppliers.

Customer satisfaction and customer loyalty

Traditionally, it has been assumed that customer satisfaction leads to customer loyalty. More recently, satisfaction is considered a necessary first step (Little and Marandi, 2003) but one that does not always mean loyalty. Satisfied customers may still wish to be adventurous. Hence, a long-term relationship must be built, it is suggested, with customers, which should be based on trust, value and dialogue. Such a long-term relationship leading to customer loyalty can be established in one of two main ways: relationship marketing, which applies to the customer-supplier interface and is most relevant in the service sector, and branding, which is not based on individual understanding of customers but on understanding physical and emotional requirements of a segment of customers.

Regarding trust, it seems that there is no universally agreed definition of trust. One frequently quoted definition is by Moorman et al. (1993) who define trust as 'a willingness to rely on an exchange partner in whom one has confidence'. Morgan and Hunt (1994) identify trust and commitment, in a relationship marketing context, as key because they encourage marketers to:

- Work at preserving relationship investors by co-operating with exchange partners
- Resist attractive short-term alternatives in favour of the expected long-term benefits of staying with existing partners
- View potentially high-risk actions as being prudent because of the belief that their partners will not act in an opportunistic way

The concept of relationship marketing is discussed in the next section. So here, emphasis will be placed on customer loyalty expressed through brand loyalty.

Brand loyalty and its measurement

According to Sheth et al. (1999), some authors define loyalty as *the consistent repurchase of a brand*. This is a behavioural definition that does not show whether consumers actually like a brand and buy it out of choice, necessity or habit. Therefore, others propose an attitudinal definition. For example, Sheth et al. (1999) define attitudinal brand loyalty as *the biased loyalty (i.e. non-random) behavioural response (i.e. purchase), expressed over time, by some decision making unit, with respect to one or more alternative brands out of a set of brands, and is a function of psychological (decision-making, evaluative) process*.

Owing to the inconsistent definition of brand loyalty and lack of clear differentiation between brand loyalty and repeat purchasing behaviour, 'this lack of clarity has led to a great deal of difficulty in interpreting many of the brand loyalty studies' (Knox and Walker, 2001: 113). Despite incoherent interpretations of the concept, the same authors explain that classification of brand loyalty to date can be grouped into three different types, which are 'exclusive purchase', 'brand preference' and 'brand insistence'. The concepts represent a balance of behavioural and psychological attitudes towards brands, which – assessed in combination – provide a more comprehensive picture of brand loyalty.

Despite several benchmark instruments that provide insights, brand loyalty remains difficult to establish given the complexity of influences that impact consumer perceptions and behaviour with regard to the multitude of different product or service purchases individuals engage in on a day-to-day basis. Whereas most of the measures explained above take a consumer perspective to brand loyalty, business factors can significantly impact the loyalty factor, such as for instance through distribution width or product availability factors (Knox and Walker, 2001). Building a strong brand that offers relevance and trust for a consumer may thus be a separate endeavour from ensuring brand exposure and opportunity for purchase, both of which impact brand loyalty. Nevertheless, there are several ways of measuring the degree of brand loyalty (Sheth et al., 1999):

- **Proportion of purchase** – With this method, the loyalty is measured as a percentage: the number of times the most frequently purchased brand is purchased divided by the total purchase (for example, 7 out of 10 times).

- **Sequence of purchase** – This method of measurement is based on the consistency with which the consumer switches between brands; for example, AAABAAABBB (or 60 per cent loyal to brand A).

- **Probability of purchase** – This is based on a combination of proportion and sequence measures to calculate the probability of purchase based on a consumer's long-term purchase history.

Value creation and customer loyalty

Creating value for customers is also discussed as a means of gaining customer loyalty. Naumann (1995) suggests there are seven antecedents to creating value for the consumer, which translate into customer loyalty. These include place, product, service, people, communication, image and price. Each of these elements can be weighted differently and is in itself further differentiated depending on the type of good or industry it is applied to. For instance, business buyers may place high emphasis on staff knowledge as may consumers who engage in a high-involvement purchase. On the contrary, buyers of FMCG products may be more interested in adequate staffing to reduce check-out times. In both instances, negative image perceptions of a brand may lead to loss of loyalty because of decline in trustworthiness. Within the context of research in the area of e-loyalty, Anderson and Srinivasan (2002) propose that there are eight antecedents of customer loyalty, which are customization, contact interactivity, cultivation, care, community, choice, convenience and character. Despite the specific context, it is possible to draw parallels to any goods or service provider in that the findings indicate customers' emphasis on individuality and personal experience in purchasing, both of which pose complex and emotional challenges to deal with for marketers.

The identification of the importance of each of these elements to a firm's consumer segment or target markets is vital to appeal to these perceptions in the most effective way, so that the opportunity for customer loyalty is maximized through gaining the trust of customers by giving them maximum value. Value is defined by Lasser et al. (1995) as:

> *The perceived brand utility relative to its costs, assessed by the consumer and based on simultaneous considerations of what is received and what is given up to receive it.*

What is becoming increasingly important is the need for corporations to take a holistic approach to their operations as their ability to stay close to consumers and satisfying their changing needs more precisely is dependent on collaboration with other significant entities in the market that are linked to the firm during the operational process. It is recognized that collaborations with a multitude of stakeholder groups in the business environment may create favourable conditions for innovation through inter-partner learning, allowing firms to acquire knowledge, skills and other capabilities that they lack (Dussage et al., 1999). Hence, opportunities for achieving customer value can be actively created through building and leveraging business relationships and thereby gaining collaborative advantages.

What is suggested here is that value creation for the customer and thus the ability to develop customer loyalty is dependent not just on the business orientation but also on a firm's ability to leverage network relationships. For instance, the ability to re-stock regularly is dependent on supplier relationships that allow for these conditions to be set in contractual agreements.

The limitations of customer loyalty

A number of writers (for example, Dowling and Uncles, 1997) warn of being overly optimistic in what can be achieved in loyalty terms. Although they support ongoing customer-orientated efforts, they suggest that markets and companies are equally faced by similar threats and opportunities and that simple customer loyalty programmes may be ineffective. Dowling and Uncles (1997) suggest that in many established and competitive markets, the purchasing of products and services is characterized by a number of empirical regularities. Given that these regularities are so widespread, it will be difficult to increase brand loyalty above the market 'norms' with anything as easy to replicate as an 'add-on' customer loyalty program. This is not to deny that companies *can* have a short-term 'lucky break' or that they may feel forced to act because of competitive pressures. These authors suggest that for any customer loyalty program to be as effective as possible, given the prevailing competitive conditions, it will need to provide leverage to the brand's core customer value proposition.

References

Anderson, E.W. (1994). Cross-Category Variation in Customer Satisfaction and Retention, *Marketing Letters*, **5** (Winter): 19–30.

Benady, D., Bierley, S. (2004) Few Benefits on the Cards, *Retail Loyalty*, **2** (September): 5.

Dowling, G.R., Uncles, M. (1997) Do customer loyalty programmes really work?, *Sloan Management Review*, **38**(4): 71–82.

Dussage, P., Garrete, B. and Mitchel, W. (1999), Learning from competing partners: outcomes and durations of scale and link alliances in Europe, North America and Asia, *Strategic Management Journal*, **21**.

Griffin, J. (1995) *Customer Loyalty*, San Fransisco: Jossey-Bass Publishers.

Handy, H. (2004) Loyalty, Retention and Profits, *Journal of Targeting, Measurement and Analysis for Marketing*, **2**(3).

Hollensen, S. (2003) *Marketing Management: A Relationship Approach*, Harlow: Prentice Hall.

Little, E., Marandi, E. (2003) *Relationship Marketing Management*, London: Thomson Learning.

Knox, S., Walker, D. (2001) Measuring and managing brand loyalty, *Journal of Strategic Marketing*, **9**: 111–128.

Lasser, W., Mitall, B. and Sharma, A. (1995) Measuring customer-based equity, *Journal of Consumer Marketing*, **12**(4): 11–19.

Lovelock, C.H., Vandermerwe, S. and Lewis, B. (1999). *Services Marketing: A European Perspective*, London: Prentice Hall Europe.

Moorman, C., Deshpande, R. and Zaltman, G. (1993) Factors Affecting Trust in Market Research Relationships, *Journal of Marketing*, **57**: 81–101.

Naumann, E. (1995) *Creating customer value – The path to sustainable competitive advantage*, Cincinnati, OH: Thomson Executive Press.

Reichheld, F.F. (1993) Loyalty Based Management, *Harvard Business Review*, **71** (March/April): 64–73.

Reichheld, F.F. (1996). *The Loyalty Effects: The hidden force behind growth, profits and lasting values*, Boston, MA: Harvard Business School Press.

Reichheld, F.F., Sasser, W.E. (1990) Zero Defections: Quality Comes to Services, *Harvard Business Review*, **68**: 105–111.

Wallace, D.W., Giese, J.L. and Johnson, J.L. (2004) Customer retailer loyalty in the context of multiple channel strategies, *Journal of Retailing*, **80**(Summer): 249–263.

Sheth, J.N., Banwari M. and Newman, B. (1999). *Customer Behaviour: Consumer Behavior and Beyond*, New York: Dryden.

Relationship marketing

The last couple of decades witnessed the growing importance of relationship marketing within both the academic and the practitioner fields. Numerous authors enthusiastically sang the praises of the so-called 'new approach' to marketing, some even calling it a new paradigm. The 1990s, in particular, saw the adoption of the term, if not the real practice, by many organizations. In the early years, there were many different interpretations of the concept, and it meant different things to different people. While the plethora of different definitions still exist and it cannot be claimed that there is unanimous agreement about the concept, there is slowly a form of consensus appearing. Authors and practitioners are finding common ground as to what relationship marketing is and what it is not.

Misconceptions about relationship marketing

Many of the practitioners who attempted to adopt relationship marketing, particularly those in the fields of database and direct marketing, now realize that putting a customer's name on a communication does not mean you are in a relationship with that customer. Nor does holding customers' details and profiles and sending them regular mail shots herald the dawn of a relationship. Even a customer who comes back on a regular basis is not necessarily in a relationship of any significance with the organization. You may visit your local supermarket because it is convenient to do so but not want any dialogue or partnership or relationship of any kind with that supermarket. A relationship, in business terms, requires a voluntary patronage of a supplier by a customer over time, when there are other choices available to that customer. In addition, a relationship has to be seen as such by both parties, and a company's perceived relationship with its customers is hollow if the latter do not consider themselves to be loyal to, or in a relationship with, that organization.

Many organizations have also begun to recognize that relationship marketing is not an add-on to their existing strategy and ways of doing business but that it is a philosophy that has to be embraced in its totality and that this – particularly in the case of IT-enabled relationship marketing (that is, CRM) – requires a great deal of financial investment with the cost of software, interactive websites, call centres and other systems proving to be prohibitive for some organizations. Perhaps even more difficult than meeting the costs is the fact that relationship marketing requires a total change in organizational culture where so many practices have to be changed: for example, adoption of a customer orientation by the whole organization, long-term thinking, new remuneration and reward structures. The business world traditionally assesses success on a short-term basis, in terms of monthly, weekly or even daily sales and market share figures. To begin to think in terms of customer share, as required in a relational strategy, instead of market share, to think of share of a customer's wallet rather than the number of customers coming through the door and to reward your sales people for re-selling to existing customers and for looking after them rather than paying commission only for new sales, require a massive cultural shift.

Additionally, despite some misconceptions, it is not recommended that companies engage in relationship marketing with all their customers, nor that relationship marketing is suitable for all companies in all sectors. Companies should contemplate investing in a long-term relationship with those customers whose lifetime value they calculate to be worth the investment. Also, it has to be recognized that different customers have different desire levels and propensity to engage in a long-term relationship with suppliers. According to Gronroos (2000), for example, customers may be segmented into three groups, where those in 'transactional mode' do not seek contact from supplier, those in 'active relational mode' actively

Figure 4.1 The six markets model: a broadened view of marketing
Source: Christopher et al. (2000) *Relationship Marketing: Bringing Quality, Customer Service and Marketing Together*, Oxford: Butterworth-Heinemann, p. 21

look for contact with suppliers and service providers and those in 'passive relational mode' would like to know that they can contact suppliers if they so wished, but seldom do.

While, generally, it is the relationship with customers that is often in focus, the importance of the organization's relationship with other stakeholders should not be forgotten. The success of a relational strategy with customers depends on the quality of an organization's relationship with all those that it is involved with in creating and delivering value. Different authors have referred to a large number of stakeholders. The following is one model depicting markets of concern for the organization in its relationship marketing strategy.

In the above model:

- **Referral markets** – This include customers, intermediaries and any source that may refer customers to the organization.

- **Employee markets** – This refers to the potential employees of an organization, for example recent graduates.

- **Influence markets** – This includes government and regulatory bodies.

- **Internal markets or internal marketing** – This is thought to be of great importance in implementing a relationship marketing strategy, but there is no universal consensus as to what it means. It may be fair though to suggest that most people would agree internal marketing implies the application of the marketing concept internally within the organization. Put simply, this involves promotion of the company mission, objectives and a customer orientation philosophy amongst all staff, so that they all buy in and pull in the same direction. It also involves identifying and satisfying employee needs in terms of self-development, participation and promotion. Communications play a significant role in internal marketing. The use of regular appraisals, briefing meetings with staff, team-building exercises, suggestion boxes, staff development programmes, equal opportunity initiatives and in-house newsletters, Intranet and so on are all tools used in internal marketing.

Finally, relationship marketing is not advocated for all companies and all industries. It is thought that the most suitable sectors for relationship marketing are service industries, where customer anxiety is high during the purchase, where either regular or periodic transactions are required and where there is a good opportunity for customization of products and communication. Also, complexity of service and the need for reassurance and uncertainty (Berry, 1983; Lovelock, 1983) and turbulence in the market environment (Zeithaml, 1981) have been suggested to create fertile grounds for relationship marketing.

What is relationship marketing?

Many definitions of the concept are offered in the literature. For example, Berry's (1983) definition emphasizes 'enhancing customer relationships' in 'multi-service organizations', whereas Gummesson's (1994) definition views relationship marketing as 'relationships, networks and interaction', and Ballantyne's (1994) definition refers to 'exchange relationships' that evolve to provide 'continuous and stable links in the supply chain'. It seems, however, that most textbooks and academics are adopting the definition offered by Gronroos (1994). According to him, in a relational sense:

> *Marketing is to establish, maintain and enhance relationships with customers and other partners, at a profit, so that the objectives of both parties are met. This is achieved by a mutual exchange and fulfillment of promises.*

From the above definition, it is possible to deduce that the following are some of the essential characteristics of relationship marketing.

Long-term orientation

Long-term orientation of the relationship marketing concept as opposed to the short-term orientation of transaction marketing has been stressed by numerous writers (Gronroos, 1990; Gummesson, 1987; Palmer, 1996; Christopher et al., 2000). Comparing transaction marketing with relationship marketing within the service sector, Storbacka et al. (1994) suggest that 'In a relationship perspective the focus is not on service encounters (or transactions) as such' and that 'the encounter is rather seen as an element in an ongoing sequence of episodes between the customer and the service firm'. Relationship marketing aims to close the loop between getting customers and keeping them (Christopher et al., 2000).

Communication and achievement of mutual objectives

The traditional marketing concept views the supplier as active and the buyer as passive, whereas the relationship approach 'clearly views marketing as an interactive process in a social context where relationship building and management are a vital cornerstone' (Gronroos, 1994). Whereas traditional marketing emphasizes competition as the driving force of a market economy, relationship marketing puts collaboration in focus (Gummesson, 1996). The idea of collaboration as an alternative strategy implies that, in return for the loyalty of the customer, the supplier listens to, and co-operates with, the customer to provide individual and customized solutions for problems. This new approach to marketing 'enables marketers to mass-customize products, tailor services and personalize dialogue with consumers' (Peppers and Rogers, 1995).

The relationship marketing concept places heavy emphasis on the importance of communications between the customer and the supplier as well as emphasizing mutual satisfaction of objectives. This essentially requires an ongoing two-way communication between the customer and the supplier, where customers are able to take the initiative in communicating. In consumer markets, where individually tailored products are often not a viable option, because of the large number of customers involved, mass-customized products are modified and offered to micro-segments of the market, supplemented by one-to-one communication that is made possible using modern technology. Today, this is possible not only in face-to-face encounters but also through well-designed websites, call centres and so on, making two-way communication a reality.

It is suggested (Payne et al., 1996) that relationship building should follow an elaborate process whereby suppliers move prospects up on the ladder of loyalty turning them into customers, then clients, followed by supporters and advocates and finally into partners. The advocate stage is where the supplier begins to reap the benefit of word-of-mouth or voluntary promotion by customers, and partnership is relationship marketing at its perfect form. It would be fair to propose that different types of communications and messages will be required for each stage of the process as well as for different individuals or micro-segments of customers.

Fulfilment of promises by all the parties involved

This characteristic can be examined mainly in the context of trust and commitment. Indeed, it may be proposed that the trust and commitment theories of relationship marketing best explain how long-term mutual exchange relationships can be created, maintained and enhanced. If a long-term relationship is to be created and successfully maintained, it would be safe to assume that there has to be trust between the parties involved. Long-term relationships and keeping of promises require investment in time, resources, emotional bonding and forsaking of others. Gronroos (1996) advocates a trusting relationship with customers as opposed to an adversarial one, whereas Grossman (1998) defines trust as 'the degree of confidence one feels in a relationship' and goes on to add that trust has three elements: predictability, dependability and faith. Moorman et al. (1992) define trust as 'a willingness to rely on an exchange partner in whom one has confidence'.

Morgan and Hunt (1994) define commitment as 'an exchange partner believing that an ongoing relationship is so important as to warrant maximum efforts at maintaining it'. Bejou and Palmer (1998) assert 'commitment implies that both parties will be loyal, reliable and show stability in relation to the agreement they have with the other party'. The extent to which the principles of relationship marketing could be imported from the business-to-business (B2B) sector and applied to the consumer markets has been much debated, as have the conditions which are pertinent to the development of customer–supplier relationships, as discussed earlier. There is, however, widespread agreement that a relationship marketing strategy could help with differentiating a company and result in customer loyalty. This in turn would reduce the company's costs of recruiting new customers, enable it to cross-sell more easily to existing customers and also help it to benefit from favourable word-of-mouth advertising.

The concept of relationship marketing is mainly concerned with the customer-supplier interface and is, to a large extent, distinct from branding relationships (e.g. you could be loyal to a particular brand of perfume but not be bothered as to where you buy it from). For a discussion of brand relationships, see Ranchhod (2004).

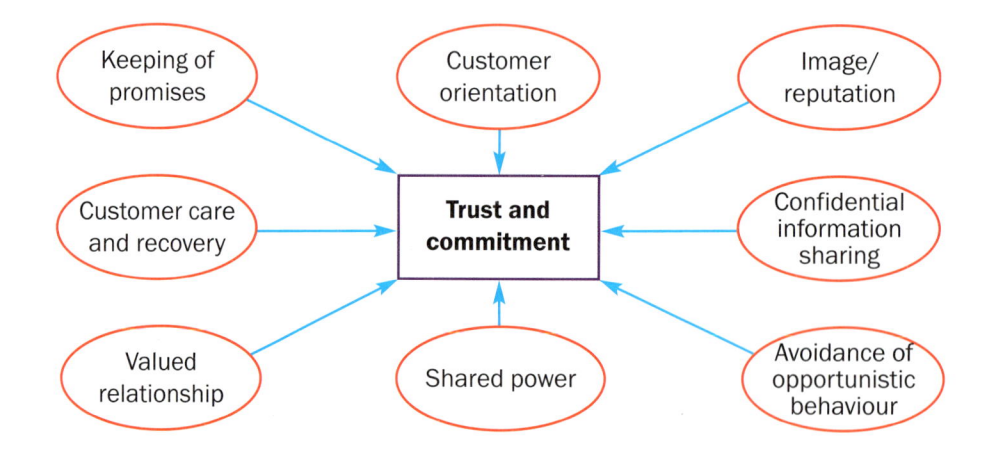

Figure 4.2 Creating trust and commitment
Source: Little and Marandi (2003)

References

Anderson, R. and Srinivasan, S. (2002) E-satisfaction and e-loyalty: A contingency framework, *Psychology and Marketing*, **20**(2): 123-318.

Ballantyne, D. (1994) Marketing at the crossroads, Editorial, *Asia-Australia Marketing Journal*, **2**(1), August.

Bejou, D., Palmer, A. (1998) Service failure and loyalty: An exploratory empirical study of airline customers, *Journal of Services Marketing*, **12**(1).

Berry, L.L. (1983) Relationship Marketing, in L.L. Berry et al. (eds), Emerging perspectives of services marketing, *American Marketing Association*, Chicago, IL.

Christopher, M., Payne, A. and Ballantyne, D. (2000) *Relationship Marketing: Bringing Quality, Customer Service and Marketing Together*, Oxford: Butterworth-Heinemann.

Garvin, D.A. (1998) *Managing Quality*, New York: The Free Press.

Gronroos, C. (1990) Relationship approach to marketing in service contexts: The marketing and organizational behaviour interface, *Journal of Business Research*, **20**.

Gronroos, C. (1994) From marketing mix to relationship marketing: Towards a paradigm shift in marketing, *Management Decision*, **32**(2).

Gronroos, C. (1996) The rise and fall of modern marketing and its rebirth, in S.A. Shaw and N. Hood (eds), *Marketing in Evolution: Essays in Honour of Michael J. Baker*, New York: Macmillan.

Gronroos, C. (2000) *Service Management and Marketing – A Customer Relationship Approach*, 2nd edition, Chichester: John Wiley and Sons.

Grossman, R.P. (1998) Developing and managing effective consumer relationships, *Journal of Product and Brand Management*, **59**, January.

Gummesson, E. (1987) The new marketing – developing long-term interactive relationships, *Long Range Planning*, **59**, January.

Gummesson, E. (1994) Making relationship marketing operational, *International Journal of Service Industries Management*, **5**(5).

Gummesson, E. (1996) Relationship marketing and imaginary organizations: A synthesis (Nordic Perspective on Relationship Marketing), *European Journal of Marketing*, **30**(2).

Little, E., Marandi, E. (2003) *Relationship Marketing Management*, London: Thomson Learning.

Lovelock, C.H. (1983) Classifying services to gain strategic marketing insight, *Journal of Marketing*, **47**, Summer.

Moorman, C., Zaltman, G. and Deshpande, R. (1992) Relationships between providers and users of market research: The dynamics of trust within and between organizations, *Journal of Marketing Research*, **29**, August.

Morgan, R.M. and Hunt, S.D. (1994) The commitment-trust theory of relationship marketing, *Journal of Marketing*, **58**, July.

Palmer, A. (1996) Relationship marketing: A universal paradigm or management fad?, *The Learning Organisation*, **3**(3): 18–25.

Payne, A., Christopher, M. and Peck, H. (1996) *Relationship Marketing for Competitive Advantage-Winning and Keeping Customers*, Butterworth-Heinemann.

Peppers, D., Rogers, M. (1995) A new marketing paradigm: Share of customer, not market share, *Managing Service Quality*, **5**(3).

Ranchhod, A. (2004) *Marketing Strategies: A Twenty-first Century Approach*, Harlow: Prentice Hall.

Storbacka, K. Strandvik, T. and Gronroos, C. (1994) Managing customer relationships for profit: The dynamics of relationship quality, *International Journal of Service Industry Management*, **5**(5).

Zeithaml, V.A. (1981) How consumers' evaluation processes differ between goods and services, in H.H. Donnelly and W.R. George (eds), *Marketing of Services*, Chicago, IL: AMA.

Key account management (KAM)

Source: Little, E. and Marandi, E. (2003) Relationship Marketing Management, London: Thomson Learning. Reproduced with kind permission of Thomson Learning.

Introduction

Key account management (KAM) is a common manifestation of relationship marketing (RM) in B2B markets. With its roots in selling, the theory and practice of KAM is narrower in scope than that of relationship marketing – it can be seen as the application of 'external' RM principles in a B2B context, predominately from a supplier's perspective. Nevertheless, the subject offers valuable insights into the practical considerations of implementing RM and hence can, in turn, inform the development of the broader theory.

This unit begins by defining KAM, its costs and benefits, before looking at the nature of the B2B relationships and the key stages in their development. Decision-making frameworks for identifying key accounts and developing KAM programmes are then considered. After considering the subsidiary topic of global account management (GAM), the section ends with a discussion of the contribution that KAM can make to the wider theory of RM, and whether KAM practices in turn can be informed by more general work on RM.

What is key account management?

KAM defined

KAM is a management practice aimed at optimizing the relationship between a supplying organization and a buying organization. As usual in the marketing literature, there is some debate over the precise meaning of the term 'key account management'. Further confusion is created by the fact that KAM is used interchangeably with national account management (NAM), strategic account management (SAM) and account management (AM), although there appear to be no significant distinctions between the meanings of the four terms. Nevertheless, there is general consensus that KAM consists of three elements. Kempeners and van der Hart (1999: 311) represent these elements well by defining [key] account management as follows:

> *The process of building and maintaining relationships over an extended period, which cuts across multiple levels, functions and operating units in both the selling organization and in carefully selected customers (accounts) that contribute to the company's objectives now or in the future.*

As reflected in this definition, the practice of KAM is characterized by:

◆ **The conscious selection of key accounts** – The starting point of KAM is the identification of customers which will equate to strategic partners. All KAM programmes must, therefore, employ a mechanism for selecting these key accounts, based on the strategic objectives of the organization.

- **The development and maintenance of long-term relationships** – Having identified the key customers, the organization must have strategies and systems in place to build and maintain a business relationship with that customer.

- **The establishment of cross-functional processes for servicing accounts** – This is a common feature of all definitions and examples of KAM. To enable the other two features of the KAM programme, the organizational structure and systems must enable multi-functional processes based around individual accounts.

KAM activities

Homburg et al. (2002) identify KAM by the activities that the suppliers undertake to build and maintain relationships. These include:

- Special pricing
- Customization of products and services
- Development of special products or services
- Joint co-ordination of workflow
- Information sharing
- Taking over the customer's business processes

McDonald (2000) focuses on the communication ties between the two companies, which move from the 'bow-tie' formation shown in Figure 4.3 to a 'diamond' structure (Figure 4.4). Such a shift in structure can be both a response to and a stimulus for relationship development.

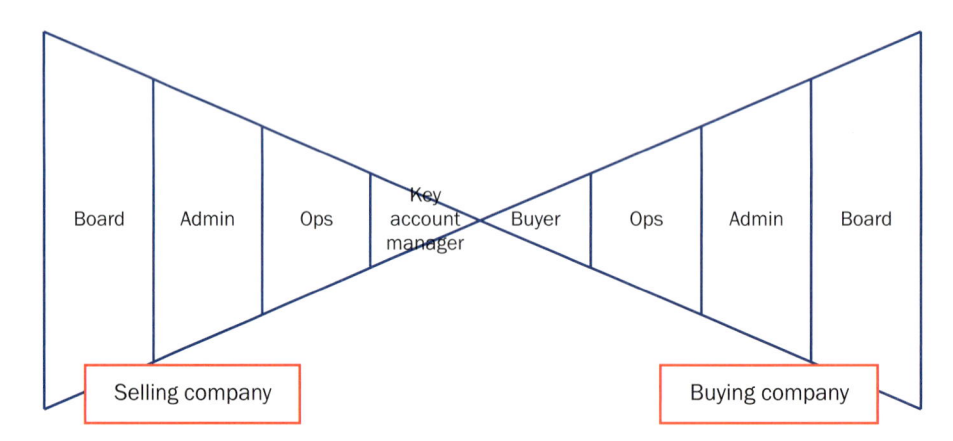

Figure 4.3 The bow-tie structure (evident early in KAM relationships)
Source: McDonald, M. (2000) Key account management – a domain review, *The Marketing Review*, **1**: 15–34. Reprinted with permission of Westburn Publishers Ltd.

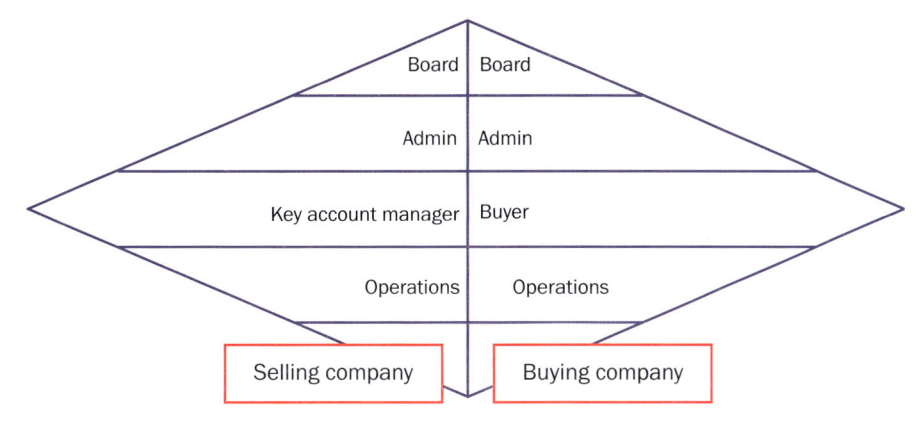

Figure 4.4 The diamond structure
Source: McDonald, M. (2000) Key account Management – a domain review, *The Marketing Review*, **1**: 15–34. Reprinted with permission of Westburn Publishers Ltd.

The rationale for KAM

Before examining the mechanics of KAM and its implementation, it is worth considering the advantages (and penalties) of the practice. These are summarized in Figure 4.5. The supplier benefits from increased turnover, because the proper selection and development of accounts implies, amongst other things, the cultivation of the high-volume, high-value customers. At the same time, costs associated with the winning of new customers, such as marketing research and communications, are reduced. Ellram (1991) further notes that the long-term relationships give the supplier the opportunity to plan its production and logistics with greater certainty, perfecting repetitive operations. Hence, both production and transaction costs may be reduced. The buyer, in turn, benefits from products and services that are specifically tailored to its needs, while receiving some of the benefit of the supplier's cost reductions in the form of price discounts.

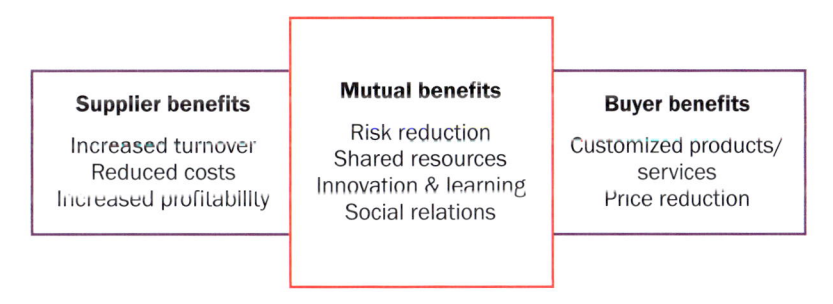

Figure 4.5 Benefits of key account management

It is the mutual benefits, however, that bring the greatest strategic advantages to the parties involved. Both parties enjoy reduced risk, alleviating the threat of both short-term crises in supply and demand and long-term planning uncertainty. By pooling their resources, the two companies not only make efficiency gains but also are able to explore business opportunities that might require a prohibitively high investment were they operating individually. Resources here refer to intangible assets, such as brand image, skills, information and organizational competences as well as to tangible assets. By sharing information, for example, the two parties may be able to develop products, process or strategies that could not have been developed individually. Similarly, one party may be able to capitalize on the brand image of its partner by association to gain access to new markets or buyers. Finally, Ojasalo (2001) notes that the benefits of KAM may occur at the individual as well the organizational level, through the enhanced social interaction arising from the bonds that inevitably form between individuals in the two companies. Given the effect this has an employee satisfaction and motivation, this would have indirect benefits at the organizational level.

It should be stressed, however, that these benefits arise from the successful implementation of KAM and represent the greatest benefits that can accrue. It will be seen that the development of KAM infrastructure involves a significant investment in terms of management time, staffing and training; an investment that will probably not create a return during the early stages of the relationship. The proper selection of key accounts and the proper development and maintenance of these relationships are critical to the long-term profitability of any KAM programme.

The key account development cycle

Stages in the key account development cycle

As with all relationships, key account relationships develop over time and require different treatment at different stages in this development. The literature offers two competing models of key account development, although the differences between them are nominal. The explanation offered below is a synthesis of the two.

Pre- and early-KAM

These stages are described by McDonald et al. (1997) as the 'scanning and attraction stages'. Here, the supplier is concerned with the identification of potential key accounts and gaining information by which the selection decision can be made. The move into early-KAM is characterized by the willingness of the supplier to make adjustments to its standard offering. The types of information needed to select key accounts are discussed in the next section. Given the fact that customers in the pre- or early-KAM stages of development are of relatively low importance to the organization, sales representatives play the central role in this process, with no special infrastructure or resources being devoted to the customer (Millman and Wilson, 1995). The focus of the relationship remains on the product and on a set of relatively discrete (albeit repetitive) transactions.

Mid-KAM

Here, the focus of the relationship begins to shift to process, as trust and commitment develop between the two parties. Hence, the range of value-added services offered by the supplier assume as great an importance in the eyes of the buyer as the product and its price. Both begin to view the relationship as long term, although the buyer will still maintain contact with alternative suppliers. The number of contact points between the two companies will increase, and the management of the account will tend to shift towards more senior levels of the organizations, as it takes on greater strategic importance.

Partnership and synergistic KAM (mature KAM)

At this point in the relationship, the boundaries between the two companies reduce as the structural and social bonds between them strengthen. The sharing of sensitive information and joint problem-solving will be common practice, and both formal and informal contacts will occur regularly at all levels of both the organizations. Synergistic KAM is described by McDonald et al. (1997) as 'quasi-integration' – a state in which the two organizations operate jointly.

Uncoupling KAM

Relationship disintegration may occur at any stage. McDonald et al. find that relationship breakdown is most frequently attributed to a breach of trust. Millman and Wilson stress, however, that relationship dissolution should not necessarily be viewed as a failure, because it may be in the interests of a party to end a relationship. Whether intentional or not the uncoupling stage should be managed carefully to reduce the social and economic impact on the organization.

Implications of the key account development cycle

Clearly the different stages of the cycle bring differing levels of investment and varying returns. The early- and mid-KAM stages are particularly demanding for the supplier, requiring investment in activities such as information gathering, communications and the developing of value-added services in an attempt to gain the confidence of the buyer. The major benefits of KAM, however, occur in the later stages. The supplier must, therefore, ensure that the balance of its relationship portfolio is maintained, so that the superior returns from mature relationships can fund the development of those in the early- or mid-KAM stages.

Identifying key accounts

The need for selection criteria

Given the cost/benefit implications of the key account development cycle, the need for the careful selection of potential key accounts is critical. Millman and Wilson (1995) describe the example of a business relationship between two multinational companies agreeing to develop jointly an advanced pigmentation system. Although the selling company saw the project as the start of a long-term strategic relationship, the buyer viewed it as a one-off project. The buyer terminated the arrangement after two years, leaving the seller shocked and bitter, with no resulting sales gain to soften the blow. If a selling company is to profit from KAM, it must minimize the likelihood of such strategic failures. Although research in the field of KAM is limited, it has been found that companies that explicitly define and identify key accounts are more successful in targeting resources and show a more sophisticated understanding of their customers (Millman and Wilson, 1999). The remainder of this section reviews various criteria for the selection of key accounts suggested by research into KAM.

Relationship history

Obviously, this criterion presumes that KAM is being implemented against a background of established accounts and cannot be easily applied to new prospects. The literature commonly points to longevity as an indicator of the strategic importance of an account, constituting evidence of commitment and trust, both of which are important ingredients of strategic relationships (McDonald, 2000). Ojasalo (2001) points out, however, that longevity is no guarantee of profitability.

Volume

Theorists are virtually unanimous in identifying sales volume as a key determinant in the selection of key accounts (Krapfel et al., 1991; McDonald et al., 1997; Campbell and Cunningham, 1983). Research suggests that practitioners also find this criterion simple to apply, because it is easily quantified and readily accepted by key players within the organization. When 'selling' the importance of the account internally, key account managers found that sales turnover was well recognized throughout the business (McDonald et al., 1997). It should be stressed that potential sales volume is as important as current – the same research found that achieving links with fast growing companies or companies in developing markets was also a prime strategic consideration.

Profitability

Ojasalo (2001) points out that high sales volume does not always lead to profitability, and to be of value, the total revenue from an account must exceed its servicing costs within a given timeframe. The quantification of profitability, however, is not straightforward. The majority of costs associated with the servicing of key accounts involve services, management time and the resolution of day-to-day problems. These intangible activities are difficult to cost, particularly in organizations where a single team or manager handles more than one account. Similarly, the benefits accruing from a relationship may be equally nebulous and difficult to quantify – gains in areas such as innovation, learning and reputation are hard to assess in anything but qualitative terms. Hence, Millman and Wilson (1999) found that the assessments of the net value of business relationships tended to rely on the subjective judgment of those involved in their operationalization.

Status

Ojasalo (2001) identifies the fact that organizations often derive benefit from association with a reputable partner. McDonald et al. (1997), in his research, found that some selling companies actively targeted national or multinational or 'blue-chip' companies, because the prestige associated with these organizations facilitated the winning of further customers. It was also noted that companies with a good reputation were more likely to focus on long-term value-creating activities rather than short-term cost issues and hence were more receptive to KAM initiatives.

Ease of replacement

This criterion is relevant to the decision to develop rather than to initiate a key account relationship, because it applies to existing customers only. Krapfel et al. (1991) recommend that by calculating the cost of replacing an existing customer or supplier, an organization can obtain a useful quantitative measure of the relationship's value.

Resources synergies

Campbell and Cunningham (1983) identify this as a separate criterion, whereas Millman and Wilson (1999) subsume it within broader considerations of 'strategic fit'. The selling organization will be able to service the account more effectively if it is able to leverage any resources or competences that distinguish it from its competitors. Hence, it should look for partners among organizations that would benefit particularly from its unique strengths. Similarly, it should ensure that these partners command resources that may in turn benefit the selling organization.

Strategic compatibility

Millman and Wilson's (1999) notion of strategic fit also encompass the alignment of organizational goals, *modus operandi*, culture and relational norms. Similarly, McDonald et al. (1997) note that not all organizations seem willing or able to maintain long-term relationships; so, receptivity to a KAM programme is an important consideration. More practical considerations such as compatibility between present and intended product and market arenas and even such mundane issues as the physical location should not be ignored.

Criteria for selecting a key supplier

The literature tends to view KAM from the perspective of the supplier, and most of the criteria outlined above have been formulated with the supplier in mind. Many apply equally well to the buying company that is considering the development of strategic relationships with its supplier – the volume criterion, for example, becomes a question of whether the supplier can reliably fulfil current and future orders in the volume needed by the buyer. Similarly, issues of strategic compatibility or resource fit are mutual concerns. In addition, the research of McDonald et al. (1999: 748) identified that the buying company is likely to weigh the following factors in its choice of strategic partner:

- **Product quality** – Whether goods or service, the quality of the product and the relevance of value-added service will be of prime importance to the buying organization.

- **Ease of doing business** – Aggravation and problem-solving are significant costs to the buying organization, and purchasing officers look very favourably on those suppliers that minimize these costs.

- **People quality** – Purchasing officers took account of the personality and skills of key contacts in the selling company, valuing such qualities as honesty, integrity and, above all, 'a spirit of understanding'.

By understanding the criteria that the customer will apply in selecting suppliers, the supplier will be in a better position to design a KAM system that suits their needs.

Serving key accounts: KAM activities

Adding value for key accounts

Having identified the key accounts, the next stage in the KAM process is to identify the means by which the relationship can be developed (Cann, 1998). This can in part be addressed by the installation of special resources dedicated to the servicing of the account, as discussed in the next section. However, before investing in such resources, the organization must have a clear idea of the activities to which they will be applied. There is a clear, although tacit, consensus in the literature that such activities involve adding value rather than cutting prices. Homburg et al. (2002) refer in passing to 'special pricing', and Ojasalo (2001) implies the use of discounting by listing cost savings as one of the benefits to buyers of key account relationships. Otherwise, the KAM literature is silent regarding the potential of pricing as a tactic in relationship development, focusing instead on the means by which added value can be generated – McDonald et al. (1997) even found that suppliers actively targeted non-price-sensitive accounts, so that the investment made in the account could be recouped through premium pricing.

Figure 4.6 summarizes the key activities or tactics that may be employed. These are arranged as a hierarchy of measures. Although the position of each element in the hierarchy is not definitive, it serves as a rough indicator of those elements that are basic prerequisites of any strategic relationship and those that characterize highly developed partnerships.

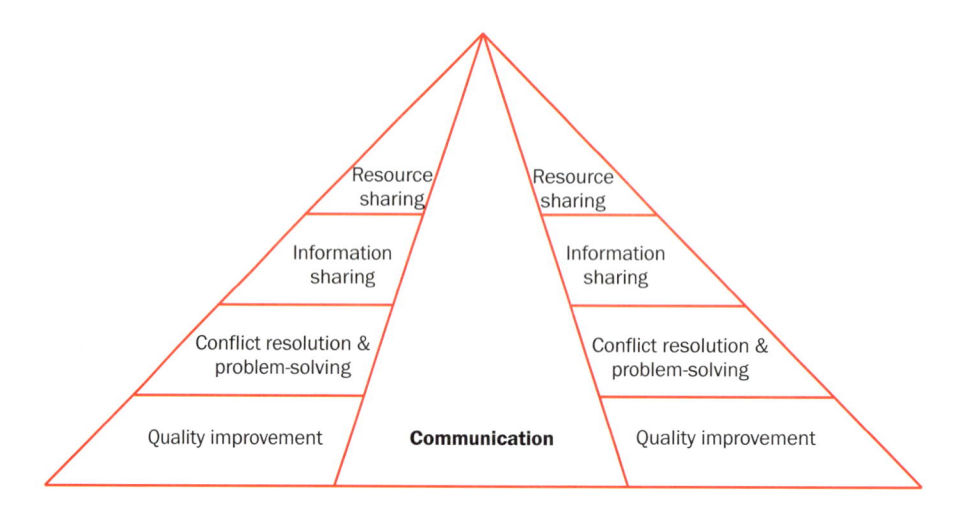

Figure 4.6 Adding value to key accounts

Quality improvement

This is perhaps the fundamental element of KAM and the pre-requisite of a strategic relationship most commonly cited by buyers (McDonald et al., 1997; Millman and Wilson, 1995). In the words of Millman and Wilson (1999: 332), 'The desire to serve key customers better must be matched by the capability to do so.' Given the long-term focus of strategic relationships, product excellence at any one moment is less important than the capability to continuously develop product offerings in response to market conditions, buyer requirements and competitor activity. As, in all but the earliest stages of the relationship, the supplier's total offering is likely to involve a significant service element, even suppliers of manufactured goods must be able to reassure buyers of the quality of their processes and people, as well as its manufacturing capability (McDonald et al., 1997). Hence, the focus from the outset is on internal process quality rather than product quality.

Customization

Again, this can be seen as a pre-requisite of any relationship. To initiate any degree of exclusivity in the relationship, the supplier must be able to offer the buyer something that its competitors cannot. Customization may derive from the physical modification of tangible goods or from the development of tailored services or transaction routines.

Conflict resolution and problem-solving

Selnes (1998) found that the flexibility of the supplier in accepting responsibility for resolving the buyer's problems was a key determinant of a buyer's trust in their supplier, which in turn was a key antecedent of motivation to enhance the relationship. Responsiveness is often considered to be a dimension of service quality, because the ability of the supplier to resolve differences with or the difficulties of the buyer will determine the latter's satisfaction with repeated transactions over time (Parasuraman, Zeithaml and Berry, 1988). It is listed separately here because it represents an important step away from a focus on specific, product-related transactions and towards the development of a total offering based on joint processes.

Information sharing

Millman and Wilson (1995) found that mature relationships are characterized by the free exchange of commercially sensitive information between the two parties. Selnes (1998) states that the sharing of information can stimulate relationship enhancement in two ways. First, information is a valuable resource that can greatly enhance the operations planning of the buyer. Second, willingness to yield potentially sensitive information is taken by the buyer as an expression of trust – an important antecedent of relationship development.

Resource sharing

Perhaps the pinnacle of key account relationship building is the ability of the two parties to share resources for mutual advantage. Whether through temporary joint ventures, or the development of permanent systems or structures, the sharing of resources is both a result of and a stimulus for very close bonds between organizations.

Communication

Communication occupies a special place in the servicing of key accounts, because it underpins all of the other tactics and is universally cited as being of central importance to the initiation, development and maintenance of key accounts. The two major models of KAM development identify the various stages by the nature and extent of the communication channels existing between the two companies (McDonald, 2000). A key tactic for relationship development is therefore the development of communication channels between buyer and supplier.

Schultz and Evans (2002) in their research suggest that the nature of communication is important:

- ◆ **Informality** – Customers are heavily concerned with interaction efficiency and find informal methods less cumbersome than formal channels. Perhaps more important, informal communication is strongly linked to trust, suggesting that it is perceived to be more open and frank than carefully managed interaction.

- ◆ **Bi-directionality** – To add value to the relationship, communication must be two way, with suppliers both listening to and acting on feedback from the customer, and keeping them informed.

- ◆ **Frequency** – In keeping with customers' preference for informal modes of communication, frequent, short episodes of interaction make customers feel they are being 'kept in touch with'.

- ◆ **Strategic content** – The content of communication is just as important as the mode and frequency. Customers respond better to communication which they feel to be of strategic importance, reacting badly to being bombarded with trivial detail.

Servicing key accounts: developing a KAM infrastructure

Identifying the type of KAM system

Having identified the key accounts, the next stage in the development of KAM is the design of the system through which they will be serviced. Shapiro and Moriarty (1984) describe five major types of key account 'programme':

1. **No programme** – No formal system or infrastructure is developed.
2. **Part-time programme** – People with other roles take on the additional responsibility of managing the account.
3. **Full-time programme (unit level)** – The system is operated by fully dedicated staff but decentralized at business unit or division level.
4. **Corporate-level programme** – The system is run centrally by dedicated staff.
5. **National account division** – A separate operating unit is dedicated to the account.

From a study of some 400 German and US suppliers, Homburg et al. (2002) identified eight distinct types of KAM system:

1. **Top-management KAM** – Involves highly formalized KAM programmes. As the label suggests, such programmes exhibit the highest degree of top-management involvement and are usually located at the organization's headquarters. Most have dedicated sales managers responsible for key accounts and make extensive use of key account teams. Collaborative activities such as the co-ordination of the manufacturing schedules are of high intensity, and the supplier is proactive in developing such activities. Despite this positive picture, access to functional resources is low.

2   **Middle-management KAM** – Is also highly formalized but attracts less involvement from senior management. The intensity of collaborative activities and the proactivity of the supplier are only of medium level. Key account managers tend to be locally based, and enjoy less prominent positions in the corporate hierarchy than their counterparts in top-management KAM systems. Access to functional resources is low.

3   **Operating-level KAM** – Is also relatively formalized, involving standardized procedures and contributing significant value to the key accounts. Senior management involvement, however, is lower still, and a still greater proportion of account managers are based at local level. Access to functional resources is low.

4   **Cross-functional, dominant KAM** – Offers the most positive picture against all criteria. Access to resources is high, and senior management involvement is significant. Processes and structures are well developed, and key account managers enjoy a prominent role. Proactivity and intensity of collaboration are both high. Of all the organizations surveyed, those employing this form of KAM system key account managers spend the greatest proportion of their time on external activities.

5   **Unstructured KAM** – Systems are characterized by a lack of formality and standardization and a reactive stance to collaborative activity. With little top-management involvement, account managers in this group spend the lowest proportion of their time on external activities.

6   **Isolated KAM** – Is a system in which KAM activities are instigated by local sales effort, but lacks support from the central business units. Although the involvement of senior management is medium, access to functional resources is limited, and selling centre *esprit de corp* is low.

7   **Country-club KAM** – Systems exhibit a high degree of involvement from top management, but little else. Structures and processes are poorly developed, and teams are hardly ever formed. Special activities are neither intense nor proactive. The authors suggest that this form of KAM amounts to little more than representation by senior managers.

8   **No KAM** – Operators may pay lip-service to a KAM system, often by awarding sales or general managers the title 'account co-ordinator' or similar. However, no special activities of any significance are undertaken for their key customers.

Homburg et al. took a number of measures of the success of the various companies, both at the account level (i.e. how well the particular relationships were performing) and at the organizational level (i.e. how well the business as a whole was performing). Perhaps predictably, the no KAM and isolated KAM approaches performed the worst, whereas cross-functional, dominant KAM companies performed particularly well against organization-level outcomes. Top-management KAM systems were found to be associated with the most profitable companies, suggesting that greater gains from other approaches are offset by higher costs.

This research offers valuable insights into the range of KAM systems that may be applied. It is also possible that the various systems, rather than being alternatives, are stages in the development of KAM systems. The key conclusion arising from the research is the desirability that senior management be actively involved in the design and implementation of KAM systems, rather than delegating the task to local sales managers.

The role of the account manager

The role of the key account manager will vary considerably depending on the nature of the organization, its environment and the KAM system in force. Millman and Wilson (1995), however, tentatively suggest a list of functions that are commonly associated with such posts:

- Maintaining the sales/profitability of key accounts
- Customizing the seller's total offering to key accounts
- Facilitating inter-level or inter-functional processes that add value to the total offering
- Promoting the KAM concept within the organization
- Promoting the interests of the account within the organization

On the basis of the research by Homburg et al. described above and work by other authors (e.g. Millman and Wilson, 1996; McDonald et al., 1997; Schultz and Evans, 2002), it is clear that the key account manager plays a crucial role in the implementation of KAM. Decisions on the responsibility, authority and resources allocated to key account managers will be critical in determining the effectiveness of the programme. Kempeners and van der Hart (1999) suggest the following checklist:

- **Full- or part-time system** – Should account managers be dedicated full time to the servicing of key accounts or should they also have other responsibilities?
- **The position of account managers in the system** – Should they be integrated into the sales department or should a new organizational layer be created? Should they be physically located at head office or locally? Should different levels of KAM be created?
- **Allocation of responsibility** – How many accounts should each manger control?
- **Allocation of authority** – What resources should the account manager control? Should these be held centrally or dedicated entirely to the account manager?

These questions have significant implications for the organization's structure, because the KAM framework will have to be integrated with existing structures and processes. Research by Homburg et al. (2002) indicates that, if medium-term profitability is the chief focus, a centralized, highly developed key account executive function is not always the optimum solution, because of the cost of installing and maintaining such a system. It is possible, however, that the superior returns of such a system pay dividends in the longer term.

Skills of the key account manager

Given the importance of the key account manager, a significant amount of research has been conducted into the skills necessary to perform this function. According to Millman and Wilson (1995: 17), the demands of the role require:

> High calibre people who are not only sufficiently 'rounded' to be able to diagnose/ analyse complex commercial and technical situations; but also equipped to cope with highly politicized interaction, together with personal tensions and ambiguities inherent in the boundary-spanning role.

Shultz and Evans (2002) also single out communication skills as the key competence required of key account representatives, particularly the ability to share information of a strategic nature rather than communicating predominantly on tactical issues. Research by McDonald et al. (1997) adds the following requirements:

- Integrity
- Product service knowledge
- Understanding the buying company's business and business environment
- Selling/negotiating skills

Possession of these skills and competences is understandably rare, and organizations seeking to implement KAM must be prepared to invest heavily in the selection, retention and development of suitable candidates.

The key account team

The use of key account teams to support the manager varies considerably between different examples of KAM systems, with account managers in some companies having no support from teams (Kempener and van der Hart, 1999; Homburg et al., 2002). Homburg et al. (2002) found that the companies that performed best at the operational or account level made extensive use of teams. Shultz and Evans (2002) recommend the use of key account teams. Not only do they enable frequent contact with the customer, but they also help the flow of information in the selling organization, so that relevant information about the customer and the account is transferred to all points of customer contact.

According to Kempener and van der Hart, key account team decisions relate to the constitution and control of teams:

- **Constitution of account teams** – The role of the account team is to support cross-functional activities. To be of value, therefore, the teams should comprise members from all functions that have a hand in servicing the account. Team members may be full- or part-time, and certain members (or indeed entire teams) may be involved only on an ad hoc basis, to solve a particular problem.

- **Control of account teams** – The most formalized control structure involves the key account manager with line-management responsibility for a dedicated, full-time team. Where part-time or ad hoc members are involved, however, line-management responsibility may be shared, or rest wholly with a manager in a functional department.

Clearly, there are significant trade-offs here between efficiency and effectiveness, as demonstrated in the finding of Homburg et al. that the most formalized and 'successful' systems were not necessarily the most profitable. Moreover, the development of a permanent structure would be inappropriate in the early stages of a relationship – it is implicit in the notion of the account development cycle that supplier investments increase as trust develops between the two parties, and the chance of exit reduces (McDonald, 2000; Millman and Wilson, 1995). As with the various options for designing the role of the key account manager, so the different account team structures might be used by the same organization at different stages of the account's development.

The relevance of KAM to relationship marketing

A specific application of RM

Theories of KAM have been developed in high-value, low-volume, B2B markets, usually as an extension of theories of personal selling. This naturally sets limits on the applicability of KAM to RM practices in other types of market, particular to mass markets. Nevertheless, the KAM literature illustrates some important general principles of RM.

The need for senior management support

Both the empirical research and theoretical work provide strong evidence to suggest that KAM strategies will not work without the active support of senior management. This reinforces the general principle that RM requires a fundamental change in the values, goals and resource priorities of the organization and will not be successful if viewed as a tactical issue. In the early stages at least, RM initiatives must be championed by influential members of the organization's management if they are to succeed.

The need for cross-functional co-ordination

KAM programmes appear to work better when they are supported by teams arranged around customers rather than functional areas. The development of KAM relationships involves a move away from the focus on rigid structures producing standardized offerings and towards a more flexible network structure that can adapt to changing customer requirements, calling on new members and resources as circumstances require. This mirrors the consensus in the more general literature that RM is best supported by a network structure based on process rather than functional areas (see Chapters 5 and 6).

The importance of communication

Finally, the KAM literature underlines the central role of communication in building and maintaining the trust on which relationships depend. Whether dealing with customers, employees, channel members or referral markets, the management of relationships hinges on the development of open dialogue between the parties involved. This is as true for mass, consumer markets as for B2B sectors.

References

Campbell, M., Cunningham, M. (1983) Customer analysis for strategic developments in industrial markets, *Strategic Management Journal*, **4**(4): 369–481.

Cann, C. (1998) Eight steps to building a business-to-business relationship, *Journal of Business and Industrial Marketing*, **13**(4/5): 395–405.

Ellram, L.E. (1991) Supply chain management, *International Journal of Physical Distribution and Logistics Management*, **21**(1): 13–22.

Homburg, C., Workman, Jr. J., Jensen, O. (2002) A configurational perspective on key account management, *Journal of Marketing*, **66**(2): 38.

Kempeners, M., van der Hart, H. (1999) 'Designing account management organizations', *Journal of Business and Industrial Marketing*, **14**(4), 310–355.

Krapfel, Jr., Salmond, D. and Spekman, R. (1991) A strategic approach to managing buyer-seller relationships, *European Journal of Marketing*, **25**(9): 22–48.

McDonald, M. (2000) Key account management – a domain review, *The Marketing Review*, **1**: 15–34.

McDonald, M., Millman, T. and Rogers, G. (1997) Key account management: Theory, practice and challenges, *Journal of Marketing Management*, **13**: 737–757.

Millman, T., Wilson, K. (1995) From key account selling to key account management, *Journal of Marketing Practice: Applied Marketing Science*, **1**(1): 9–21.

Millman, T., Wilson, K. (1996) Processual issues in key account management, *Journal of Business and Industrial Marketing*, **14**(4): 328–337.

Millman, T., Wilson, K. (1999) Processual issues in key account management: Underpinning the customer-facing organization, *Journal of Business and Industrial Marketing*, **14**(4): 328–337.

Ojasalo, J. (2001) Key account management at company and individual levels in business-to-business relationships, *Journal of Business and Industrial Marketing*, **16**(3): 199–218.

Parasuraman, A., Zeithaml, V. and Berry, L. (1988) SERVQUAL: A multiple item scale for measuring consumer perceptions of service quality, *Journal of Retailing*, **64**(1): 12–40.

Schulz, R., Evans, K. (2002) Strategic collaborative communication by key account representatives, *Journal of Personal Selling and Sales Management*, **22**(1): 23–32.

Selnes, F. (1998) Antecedents and consequences of trust and satisfaction in buyer-seller relationships, *European Journal of Marketing*, **32**(3): 305–322.

Shapiro, B.P., Moriarty, R.T. (1984) Organising the National Account Force, *Working paper*, Marketing Science Institute, MA.

Using the KAM contemporary issue within case studies

KAM has become increasingly important for many organizations as they attempt to develop effective strategies for dealing with the various segments that they operate in. For instance, in B2B marketing, KAM is highly relevant. In past cases such as WCI and Enzymes Ltd, growth was possible and sustainable through KAM. In business to consumer markets, each account is an important account, especially in a case such as Reiss. In this instance, some of the more tangible aspects of relationship marketing such as acquisition, retention and adaptation come into play. So a better understanding of KAM for the B2B markets can also help with trying to understand wider issues surrounding relationship marketing.

Unit 4: Contemporary issues in marketing

Sustainability and strategy

Source: We are grateful to Pearson Education for granting us the permission to use Chapter 4 from *Marketing Strategies: A Contemporary Approach* by Ashok Ranchhod and Calin Gurau.

Introduction

As the world's population grows and some 90 million more individuals are added to the planet each year, many marketers are questioning some of the basic tenets of marketing. Is it right to expect continued growth? Should we be marketing goods that are likely to harm the planet? Should instead marketing concentrate on products that are 'green'? These and many other questions are being asked not just by marketers but by the general consumers themselves. In recent surveys, it has been shown that consumers are concerned about the products that they purchase; however, cost may be a factor in choosing products as well.

Nonetheless, in Germany, 88% of consumers are ready to switch brands to greener products, while the corresponding figures in Italy and Spain were 84% and 82% respectively (Wasik, 1996). In the US, the green market is estimated to include 52 million households (Ottman, 1993). In 1996, MORI categorised 36% of its British poll respondents as 'green consumers', on the basis of their claim to have 'selected one product over another because of its environmentally friendly packaging, formulation or advertising' (Worcester, 1997). This compares favourably with only 19% of consumers in 1988 (although it continued the steady decline from a peak of 50% in 1990). This makes it important for marketers to actually understand and respond to customer needs. Although marketers may attempt to do this, recent studies seem to indicate that there is a big difference between customer intent

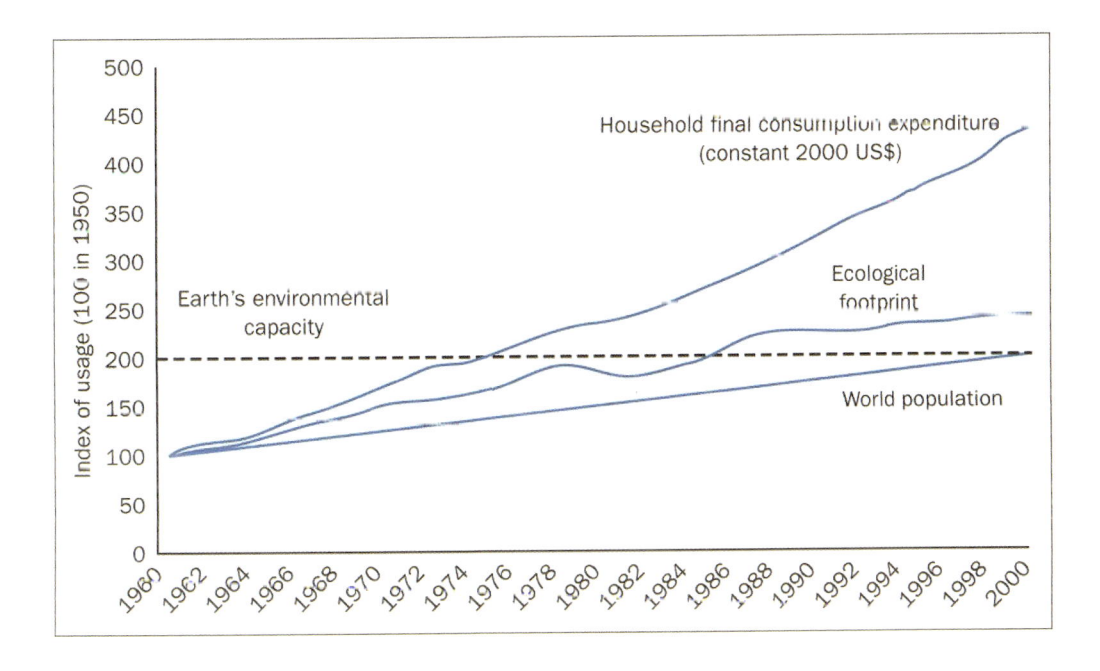

Figure 4.7 Household consumption expenditure

and execution in the market-place. Figure 4.7 Illustrates how human consumption patterns are now beyond the earth's ability to sustain itself. It appears that consumers do not really wish to slow down consumption and even if they have good intentions, most of them do not seem to be particularly inclined to purchase green products.

Evolution of population, household consumption and ecological footprint: The World (1960-2000)

This trend is regarded as the 4:40 effect. Most green products struggle to get to a 1-4 per cent market share, because although around 40 per cent of adults believe in the purchase of green products, only around four percent actually translate this into reality. Promoting sustainable consumption within the general populace is a real challenge to marketers. In their recent report, UNEP (Talk the Walk, 2005) argue that marketing may actually hold the key to changing consumer attitudes by incorporating sustainability into the marketing mix.

> *Sustainable production, sustainable service and product design, sustainable procurement, green marketing ... these programs are all good for the environment, but they are also good for the economy (saving costs, developing domestic markets, seizing export opportunities) and they are also good for social progress (helping to spread good labor conditions, helping to create decent jobs).*
>
> Monique Barbut, Director, UNEP DTIE

This area is discussed in detail towards the end of the unit.

A further question to ask is: are the provisions of certain products and services sustainable? Sustainability is about understanding the interactions of various stakeholders in an organization. Maximizing profits and looking for short-term gains in market share may, in the long run, be so harmful to certain groups of stakeholders that the company itself may suffer bad publicity. These stakeholders are the employees, the local community and government agencies. The main stakeholder is probably the planet itself, and increasingly the public feels that business firms should take responsibility for environmental damage inflicted on parts of the earth in the pursuit of profit. An example of this is the cost paid by General Electric Company in the USA for removing two million cubic metres of contaminated sludge from the Hudson River (New Scientist, 2001). For 35 years, the company poured some 500,000 kilogrammes of polychlorinated biphenyls (PCBs) into the river, before they were banned in 1977. Residents living near the river bank claim to have suffered from a variety of PCB-related illnesses, ranging from cancer to physical deformities. As a result of this, the US Environmental Protection Agency has decided to remove the sludge and have asked GEC to foot the $500 million bill.

In a situation like this, when the factors are however complex, the fact remains that the consumers actually bought electrical equipment that was manufactured by GEC during all this period, being generally unaware of the pollution problems. The onus, therefore, remains on companies to ensure that their products and services are environmentally friendly or not and whether their practices are environmentally sustainable or not. This information also needs to filter through to the consumer.

In this chapter, we will explore various notions of sustainability, ranging from 'green' products to sustainable and ethical production. The aim of this chapter is to understand the implications of being environmentally friendly and how by taking such a stance, a company could create a sustainable competitive advantage in marketing. The consumer paradox and short-termism promoted through stock markets, sometimes does not help companies that are trying to be ethical in their approach. For example, consider Gap Inc. as discussed by Vogel (2006):

> *A few years ago the company, like many other apparel retailers, Gap Inc., found itself criticized for the labor practices of its suppliers. It has responded in an exemplary fashion and arguably now has one of the most responsible and effective programs to help ensure that the workers who produce its products are treated fairly. These policies made business sense in that they prevented its brand from being tarnished by continued activist pressures, and assured its current and prospective employees that the firm had strong social commitments. More recently, the Gap has experienced financial difficulties. These difficulties are completely unrelated to its social performance. Rather they are entirely due to the fact that its fickle consumers now regard its products as less attractive or appealing than those of other brands. Not surprisingly, many financial analysts have become less sanguine about its future earnings and its share price has become depressed. In short, whatever the business implications of the Gap's responsible outsourcing policies, investors are either unaware or uninterested in them. All that matters to them are Gap's future sales.*
>
> *This does not mean that the Gap should not have adopted responsible procurement policies or that it should now abandon them. Nor does it mean that other highly visible companies should avoid similar policies in order to protect their reputations. What it does imply is that we should not expect the financial markets to appreciate or reward these efforts. Instead of bemoaning the unwillingness of the financial markets and the media to reward CSR policies, perhaps we should be grateful that they do not penalize them.*

Understanding environmental marketing

For many consumers, the term 'green' may evoke a range of different emotions and understanding. For some, it may mean products that do not harm the environment, for others it may mean products that have been made without harming the environment. Many may include ethical and moral considerations such as fair trade with the developing nations. For some it could be charitable ventures such as Oxfam. From these examples, it can be seen that the term 'environmentally-friendly' encompasses a myriad of meanings for individuals, depending on their range of experiences and perspectives. The main issue here is the merging of the social concerns with ecological concerns. Many marketing specialists would argue that these are now inseparable (Peattie, 1995). Others people consider that simply being green is not enough and that ethical issues also need to be taken into account. This is backed up by research into the notion of 'environmental justice' within the USA (Oyewole, 2001). The main contention is that many companies site chemical plants and dump toxic waste near poor or deprived communities. This is also part of a global concern where some products are cheaply made by communities who are too poor to complain about environmental issues, needing jobs and money to sustain themselves. Sometimes pollution is exported from the rich countries to the poor countries, as noted by UNEP (2005):

> *Every year, 20 to 50 million tonnes of electrical and electronic equipment waste ('e-waste') are generated world-wide, which could bring serious risks to human health and the environment. While 4 million PCs are discarded per year in China alone. (http://www.greenpeace.org/raw/content/international/press/reports/recycling-of-electronic-waste.pdf)*

The key pollutants presently used are amongst many: lead, tin, antimony, cadmium, mercury, polychlorinated biphenyls (PCBs), polybrominated diphenyl ethers (PBDEs), polychlorinated napthalenes (PCNs), nonyl phenols (NP) and triphenyl phosphate (TPP). Each of these substances is toxic and creates problems for humans, interfering with their metabolic systems in harmful ways, and creating cancers, bone diseases, internal organ damage and weakening of the immune system. At the same time, pollutants released into the soil and water systems contaminate the ecosystem with devastating effect on plant and animal life, affecting the whole food chain. The key countries accepting e-waste are India and China. As their economies grow, they in turn will be producing significant amounts of e-waste themselves as mentioned in the quote. Hand in hand with this, crisis-ridden governments such as Indonesia, the Philippines, South Korea and Thailand cut back on environmental spending (French, 2000). For instance, in Russia, the budget for protected areas was cut by 40 per cent. The globalization of commerce is intensifying the environmental agenda, with many countries being increasingly concerned about the effect of global consumption trends on the environment. This is shown in the diagrams below (Worldwatch Institute, 2000). The quotes are provided by the Institute.

Energy and climate

> *As our growing population intensified the burning of coal and oil to produce power, the carbon locked in millions of years worth of ancient plant growth was released into the air, laying a heat-retaining blanket of carbon dioxide over the planet. As a result, earth's temperature increased significantly. Climate scientists had predicted that this increase would disrupt weather. Indeed, annual damages from weather disasters have increased over 40-fold.*

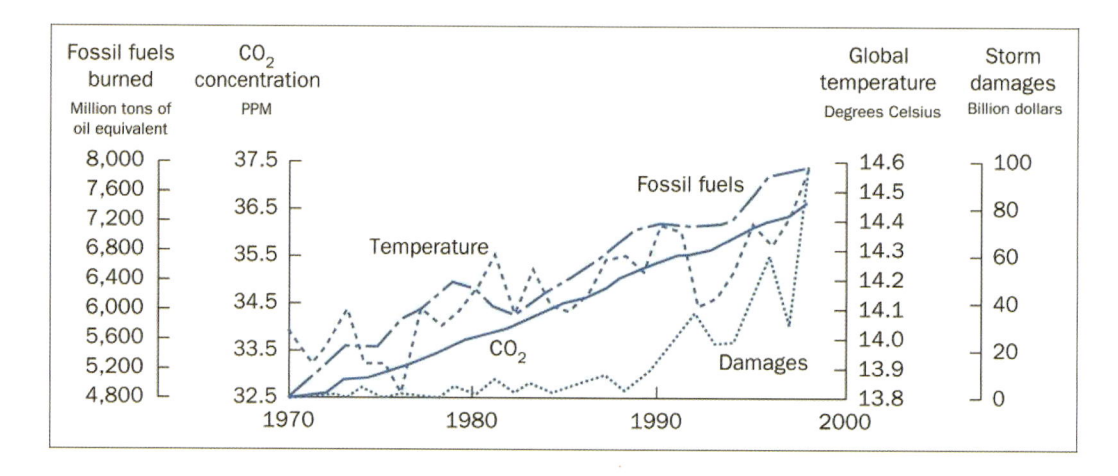

Figure 4.8 Energy and the climate

Unit 4: Contemporary issues in marketing

Chemicals and the biological boomerang

Our consumption of chemicals has exploded, with about three new synthetic chemicals introduced each day. Almost nothing is known about the long-term health and environmental effects of new synthetics, so we have been ambushed again and again by belated discoveries. One of the most ominous signs of this is the evolution of pesticide-resistant pests, as the use of pesticides increases.

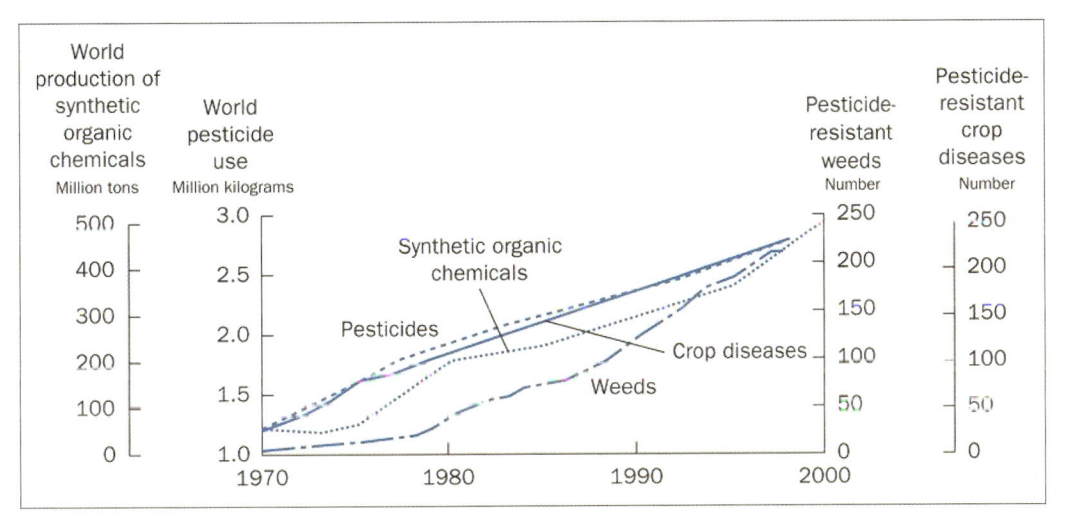

Figure 4.9 Chemicals and the biological boomerang

Commerce and the oceans

The global economy has more than doubled in the past 30 years, putting pressure on most countries to increase export income. Many have tried to increase revenues by selling more ocean fish – for which there is growing demand, since the increase in crop yields no longer keeps pace with population growth. Result: over-fishing is decimating one stock after another, and the catch is getting thinner and thinner.

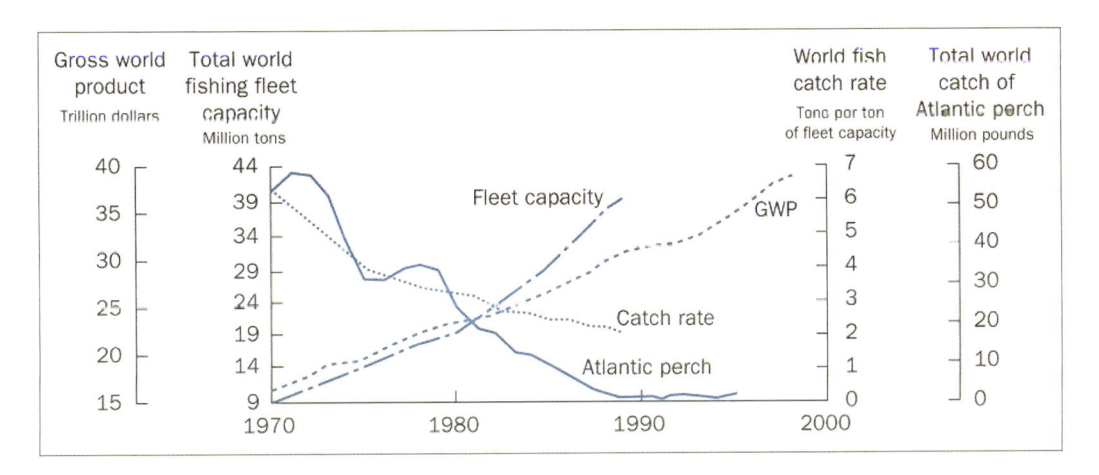

Figure 4.10 Commerce and the oceans

95

Unit 4: Contemporary issues in marketing

As the world's population expands, placing ever increasing pressures on the environment, many major institutions are researching the impact of how certain scenarios are likely to affect the planet. Recently, the United Nations Environmental Programme (UNEP) produced an excellent and very detailed report named GEO-3 (2002), which outlines the various ways in which the Earth would evolve under differing policy initiatives. They acknowledge the fact that, currently, all these initiatives are probably in progress, but in sustainability terms the most important initiatives must attempt to save the planet. The key scenarios are:

- **Markets First** – Most of the world adopts the values and expectations prevailing in today's industrialized countries. The wealth of nations and the optimal play of market forces dominate social and political agendas. Trust is placed in further globalization and liberalization to enhance corporate wealth, create new enterprises and livelihoods, and so help people and communities to afford to insure against — or pay to fix — social and environmental problems. Ethical investors, together with citizen and consumer groups, try to exercise growing corrective influence but are undermined by economic imperatives. The powers of state officials, planners and lawmakers to regulate society, economy and the environment continue to be overwhelmed by expanding demands.

    Much of the current marketing literature focuses on this type of scenario. Much emphasis is placed on increasing consumption and expanding markets. Strategies proposed rarely take into account human, social and environmental costs.

- **Policy First** – Decisive initiatives are taken by governments in an attempt to reach specific social and environmental goals. A co-ordinated pro-environment and anti-poverty drive balances the momentum for economic development at any cost. Environmental and social costs and gains are factored into policy measures, regulatory frameworks and planning processes. All these are reinforced by fiscal levers or incentives such as carbon taxes and tax breaks. International 'soft law' treaties and binding instruments affecting environment and development are integrated into unified blueprints and their status in law is upgraded, though fresh provision is made for open consultation processes to allow for regional and local variants.

    There are attempts being made in this direction by governments. Such a major initiative is the Kyoto Protocol, limiting the emission of greenhouse gases, primarily Carbon Dioxide. The protocol, which became legally binding at midnight New York time (0500 GMT) on 16 February, demands a 5.2 per cent cut in greenhouse gas emissions from the industrialized world as a whole, by 2012. However, it is clear that not all nations are wiling to sign this agreement, the USA, India and China being some very important examples. The USA government feels that the arguments are flawed, though an increasing number of states are following their own agenda on limiting CO_2 and greenhouse gas emissions. However, some 41 countries, accounting for 55 per cent of greenhouse gas emissions, have ratified the treaty, pledging to cut these emissions by 5.2 per cent by 2012.

- **Security First** – This scenario assumes a world of striking disparities where inequality and conflict prevail. Socio-economic and environmental stresses give rise to waves of protest and counteraction. As such troubles become increasingly prevalent, the more powerful and wealthy groups focus on self-protection, creating enclaves akin to the present-day 'gated communities'. Such islands of advantage provide a degree of enhanced security and economic benefits for dependent communities in their immediate surroundings, but they exclude the disadvantaged mass of outsiders. Welfare and regulatory services fall into disuse but market forces continue to operate outside the walls.

Security First can occur in regions within countries and between countries. Within countries we have rich and poor localities, with people generally living in differing economic environments. Increasingly, some areas are 'gated' and privileged. Some countries also have very strict border controls to prevent labour movement from the poor to the rich regions. One could argue that the failure of the recent Doha round of trade talks still favours the rich nations, maintaining such 'gated communities' around a sea of poorer nations.

◆ Sustainability First – A new environment and development paradigm emerges in response to the challenge of sustainability, supported by new, more equitable values and institutions. A more visionary state of affairs prevails, where radical shifts in the way people interact with one another and with the world around them, stimulate and support sustainable policy measures and accountable corporate behaviour. There is much fuller collaboration between governments, citizens and other stakeholder

Markets first	Policy first
Most of the world adopts the values and expectations prevailing in today's industrialised countries. The wealth of nations and the optimal play of market forces dominate social and political agendas. Trust is placed in further globalisation and liberisation, which will enhance corporate wealth, create new enterprises and livelihoods and so help people and communities to afford to insure against – or pay to fix – social and environmental problems. Ethical investors, together with citizens' and consumer groups, try to exercise growing corrective influence, but are undermined by economic imperatives. The powers of state officials, planners and lawmakers to regulate society, economy and the environment continue to be overwhelmed by expanding demands.	Decisive initiatives are taken by governments in an attempt to reach specific social and environmental goals. A coordinated pro-environment and anti-poverty drive balances the momentum for economic development at any cost. Environmental and social costs and gains are factored into policy measures, regulatory frameworks and planning processes. All these are reinforced by fiscal levers or incentives, such as carbon taxes and tax breaks. International 'soft law' treaties and binding instruments affecting environment and development are integrated into unified blueprints and their status in law is upgraded, though fresh provision is made for open consultation processes to allow for regional and local variants.
Security first	**Sustainability first**
This scenario assumes a world of striking disparities where inequality and conflict prevail. Socio-economic and environmental stresses give rise to waves of protest and counteraction. As such troubles become increasingly prevalent, the more powerful and wealthy groups focus self-protection, creating enclaves akin to the present-day 'gated communities'. Such islands of advantage provide a degree of enhanced security and economic benefits for dependent communities in their immediate surroundings, but they exclude the disadvantaged mass of outsiders. Welfare and regulatory services fall into disuse, but market forces continue to operate outside the walls.	A new environment and development paradigm emerges in response to the challenge of sustainability, supported by new, more equitable values and institutions. A more visionary state of affairs prevails, where radical shifts in the way people interact with one another and with the world around them stimulate and support sustainable policy measures and accountable corporate behaviour. There is much fuller collaboration between governments, citizens and other stakeholder groups in decision-making on issues of close common concern. A consensus is reached on what needs to be done to satisfy basic needs and realise personal goals without beggaring others or spoiling the outlook for posterity.

Figure 4.11 Different world economic scenarios, 2002–2032

Unit 4: Contemporary issues in marketing

groups in decision-making on issues of close common concern. A consensus is reached on what needs to be done to satisfy basic needs and realize personal goals, without beggaring others or spoiling the outlook for posterity.

This is happening in patches around the world. However, much of the world is poor and sustainability often gives way to making money first as an option. However, environmental groups, charity organizations and certain governments are going for Sustainability First as an option. Countries such as Austria and Germany are leading the way. Regional pockets in other countries are also pursuing this option; however, in general, consumer awareness about environmental issues is poor in both the rich and poor countries.

What is interesting is that they have followed this up with scientific analysis of how each scenario will affect the way in which the planet will evolve in terms of pollution, poverty eradication and land degradation. The scenarios depict what would happen between 2002 and 2032. A synopsis is provided in Figure 4.11 (above).

At the same time some calculations have been made on global CO_2 generation. The graphic representations are provided in Figures 4.12, 4.13 and 4.14.

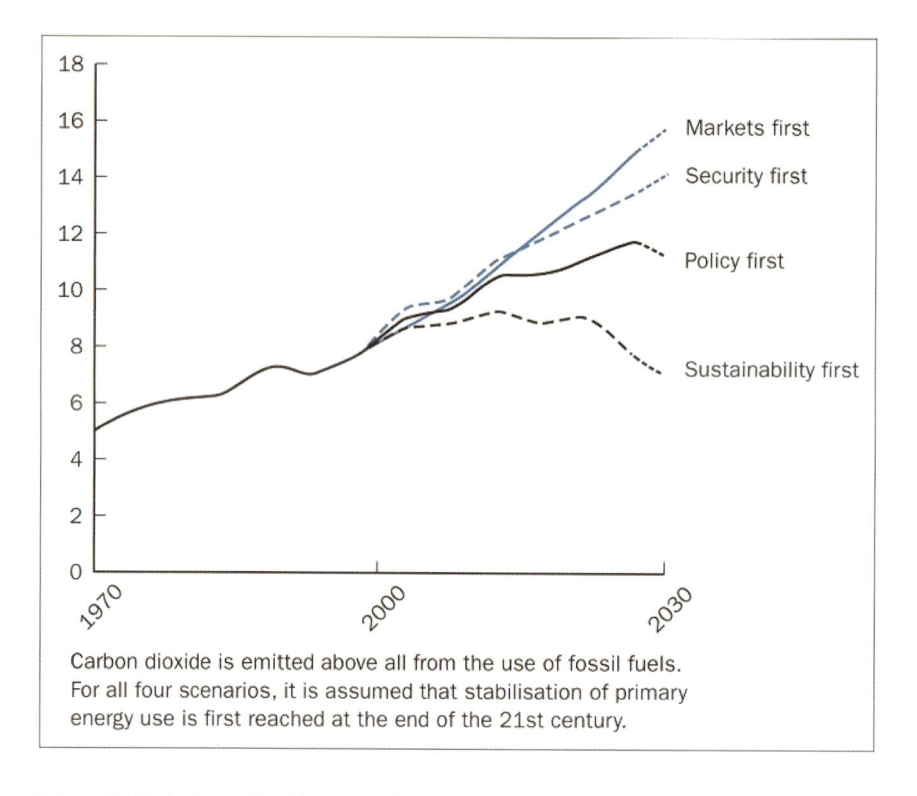

Carbon dioxide is emitted above all from the use of fossil fuels. For all four scenarios, it is assumed that stabilisation of primary energy use is first reached at the end of the 21st century.

Figure 4.12 Carbon dioxide emissions from all sources

Unit 4: Contemporary issues in marketing

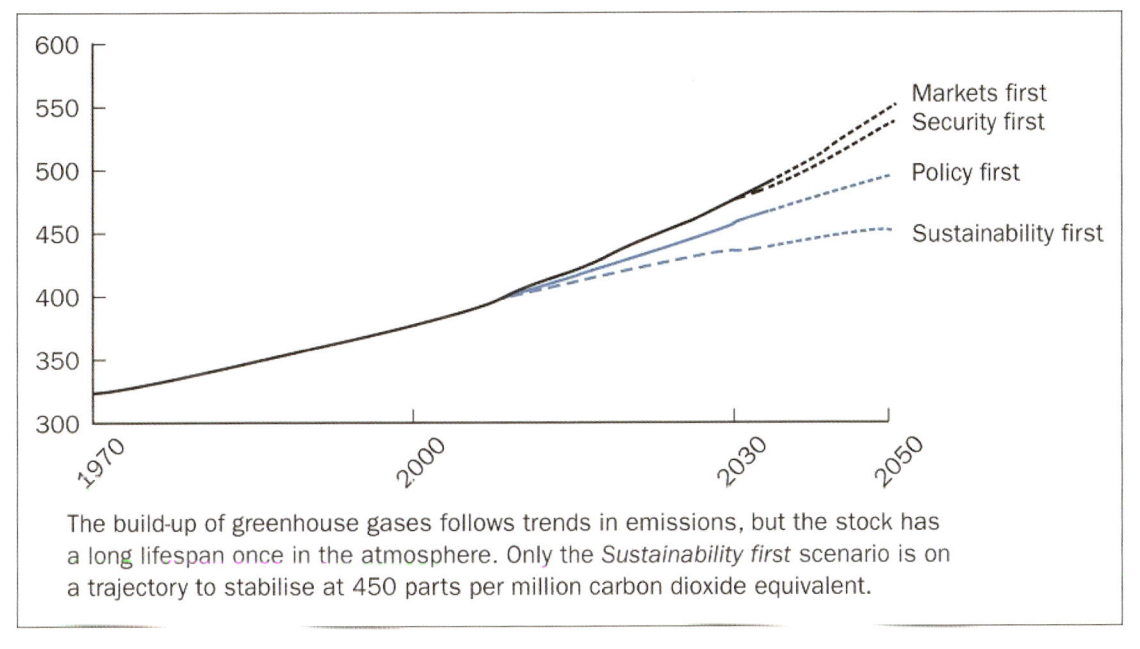

The build-up of greenhouse gases follows trends in emissions, but the stock has a long lifespan once in the atmosphere. Only the *Sustainability first* scenario is on a trajectory to stabilise at 450 parts per million carbon dioxide equivalent.

Figure 4.13 Atmospheric concentrations of carbon dioxide

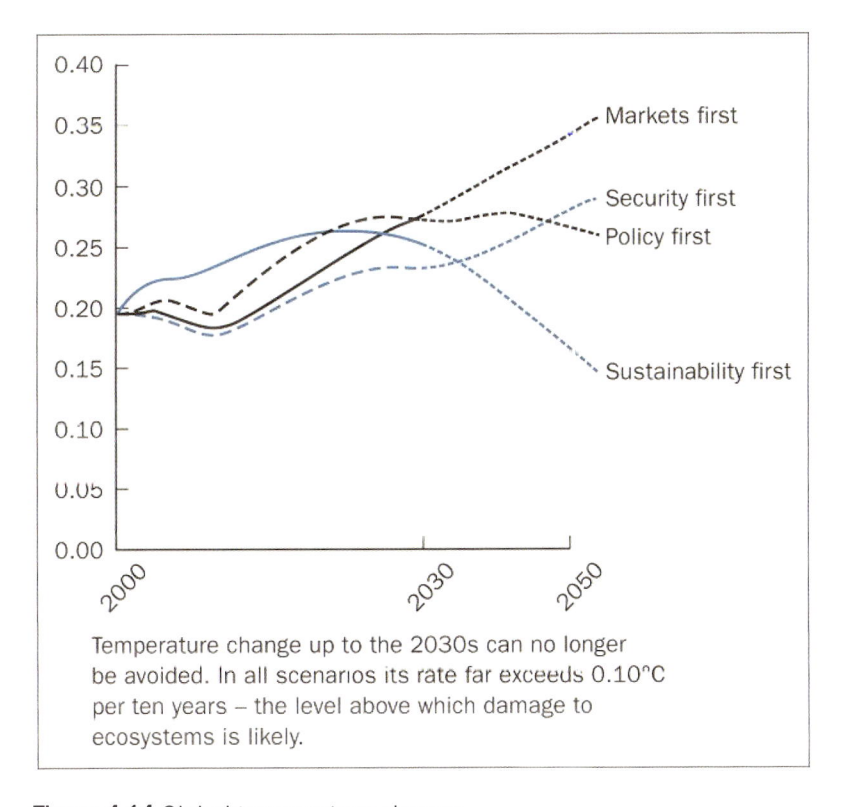

Temperature change up to the 2030s can no longer be avoided. In all scenarios its rate far exceeds 0.10°C per ten years – the level above which damage to ecosystems is likely.

Figure 4.14 Global temperature change

Unit 4: Contemporary issues in marketing

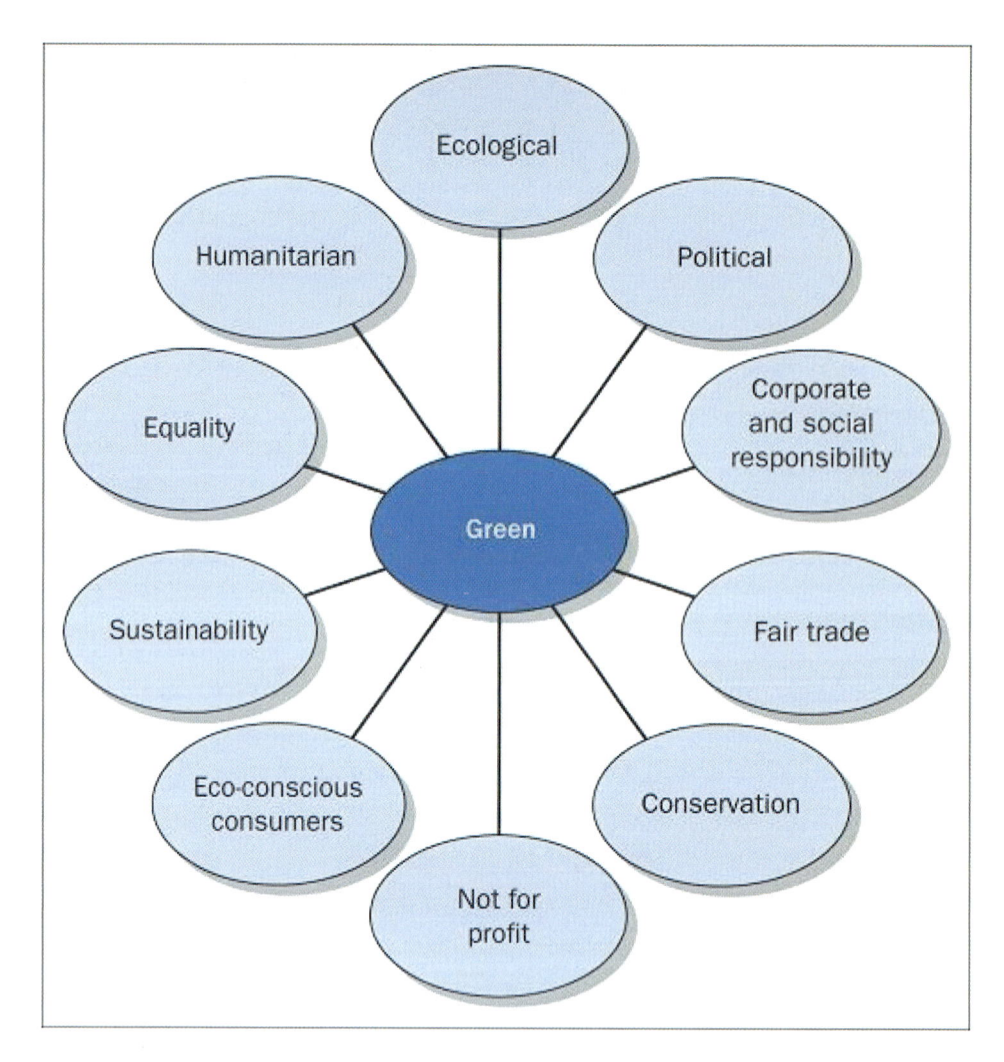

Figure 4.15 Green marketing

Diagram showing "Green" at the centre connected to: Ecological, Political, Corporate and social responsibility, Fair trade, Conservation, Not for profit, Eco-conscious consumers, Sustainability, Equality, Humanitarian.

These scenarios show how fragile the whole eco system has become. Further pressures on the environment will seriously affect the life of every single individual on the planet. Even communities that feel that they live in gated secure areas are not immune from land degradation and pollution. Therefore, as production, marketing and consumption become increasingly global, environmental issues affect every one of us. For marketers, who are often concerned with single products or brands, it is often difficult to disentangle the various interconnecting strands affecting the manufacturing of a single product. A complex piece of machinery, such as a car, may well have certain components that have not been either ethically or environmentally produced. Some marketers would even say that the production and use of a car itself is environmentally unfriendly, as each car in use adds to the local and global pollution. Given this range of views, we need to understand the different ways in which green marketing is perceived. Marketers may also have a significant role to play in enlightening consumers and bringing about positive change.

In many ways, to be totally green means that the human population must eschew any luxuries beyond self-sufficiency. As the history of marketing shows, consumption has always played a large part in human existence. For this reason, many marketers feel that being totally green is unattainable, therefore the term 'greener' should be used (Charter and Polonsky, 1999). Figure 4.16 also shows that many products are now global and the way in which consumption at the local level also has global implications.

GREEN MARKETING LAYERS

- Local production
- International trading
- International marketing
- Local branding
- Consumer/consumption

Local pollution

Local ethical issues

Planetary impact of pollution

Local environmental degradation

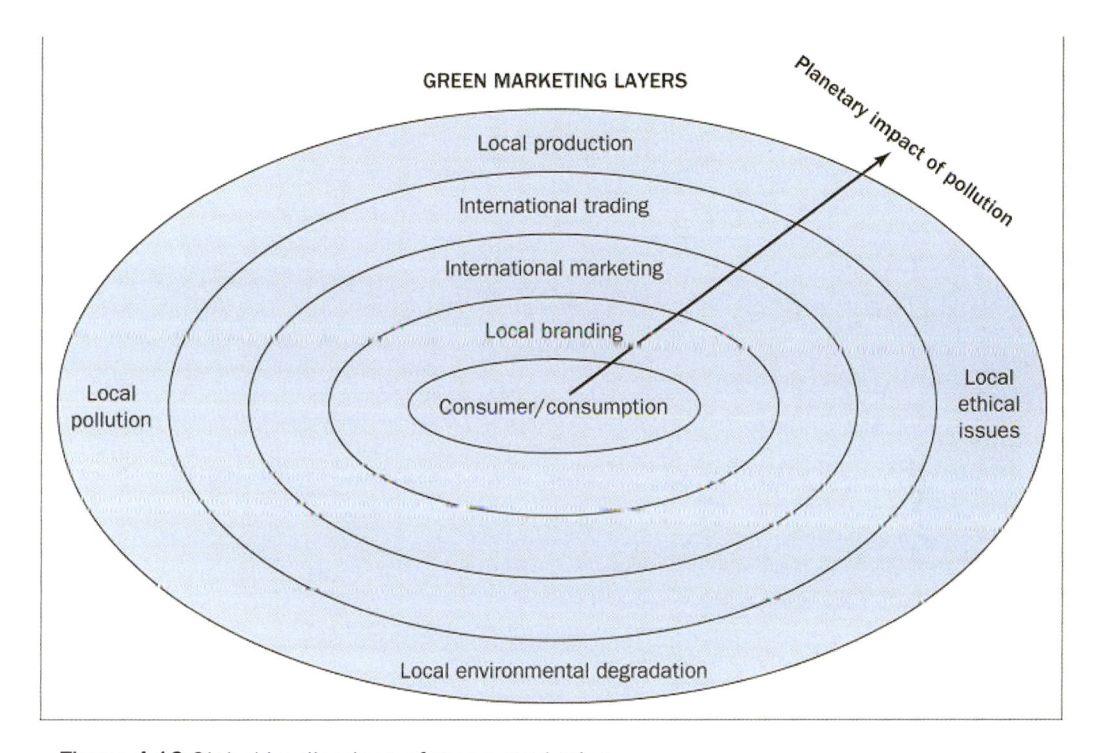

Figure 4.16 Global implications of green marketing

In order to understand how products can be defined as being green, many complicated analytical systems have evolved over the years. As a result, at present many multinationals are taking the green issues more seriously. McDonald's, for instance, has spent a great deal of money on improving its ability to recycle its materials, but has been quiet on discussing the impact the company has on the environment as a result of the mass production of beef. It has instituted a number of programmes in order to combat energy wastage (Wasik, 1996):

- **McRecycle USA Programme** The company claims to purchase over $100 million of recycled packaging. Switching from white to brown bags has saved bleaching costs and prevented a greater degree of chemical pollution.

- **Recycled Materials in Construction** – The company sets aside 25% of its construction budget for recycled materials for construction.

- **Energy Efficiency** – In partnering with the US Environmental Protection Agency, the company instituted a 'Green Lights' Programme. Eco-efficient lighting was used in stores. The stores themselves were made more energy efficient. The energy saved has resulted in preventing over 30 tons of carbon dioxide being released into the air.

- **Waste Reduction Action Plan (WRAP)** – The focus of this programme was to cut the amount of waste materials going to landfill sites by using recycled materials and paper.

Interestingly, the biggest failure amongst these various programmes was in the recycling within the shop environment. Consumers were generally oblivious to this issue! So the final question is, is McDonald's offering a green product? This a difficult question to answer because the company has obviously tried hard to improve its products and services through various ecological efficiency programmes. On the other hand, the morality of mass-producing beef remains unresolved. Some would argue that even this brings necessary employment in poorer areas, while others could consider that such farming is harmful to the environment. Recently, an unlikely alliance was formed between Greenpeace and McDonald's when Greenpeace highlighted the fact that many of the chickens sold at McDonald's were fed on soya imported from newly deforested areas in the Amazon. Not only did McDonald's produce a two-year moratorium on the use of such feed but it also formed an alliance with other high street retailers to stop using soya produced in the Amazon area. Greenpeace is demanding that the moratorium stays until proper procedures for legality and governance are in place, asking the creation of an agreement with the Brazilian Government and key stakeholders on the long-term protection of the Amazon rainforest (John Sauven, 2006, *The Guardian*).

In the light of these fundamental questions, we can only argue for greener marketing.

Greener marketing may well colour different companies in different shades of green (see Figure 4.17). Again, it is important to note that both social and ecological issues are inextricably intertwined and a truly green company should address both issues simultaneously. This approach is the correct route to creating sustainable businesses and environments. The Nike case illustrates the particular problems faced by an organization caught exploiting workers and then, as a result of public pressure, attempting to set things right.

Products and services with a modicum of respect for the environment. Socially and ethically not concerned or ignorant.

Understands ecological efficiency and incorporates this into products. Some social issues addressed, but shareholder returns take precedence.

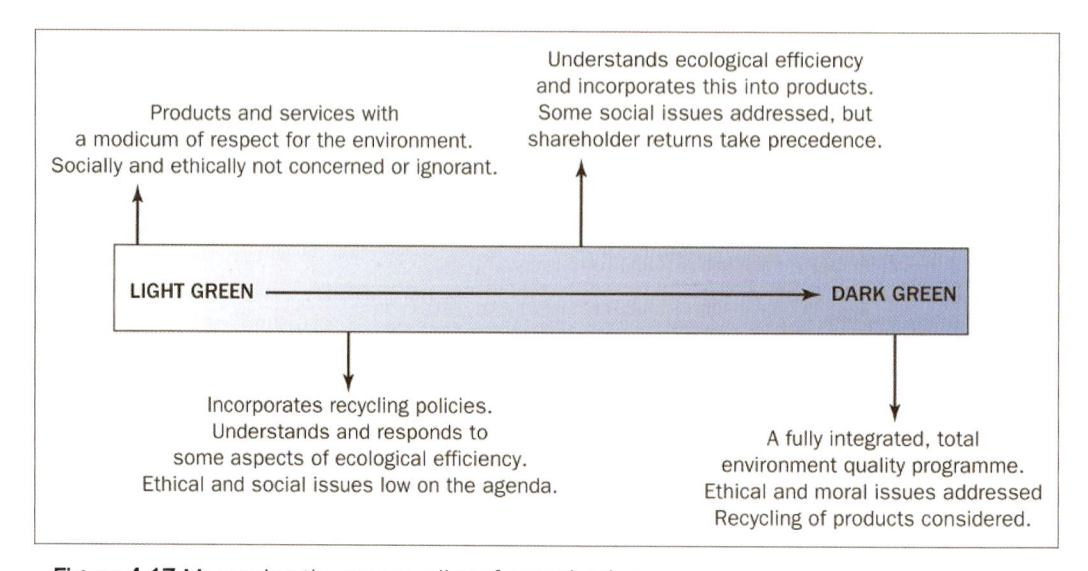

LIGHT GREEN ⟶ DARK GREEN

Incorporates recycling policies. Understands and responds to some aspects of ecological efficiency. Ethical and social issues low on the agenda.

A fully integrated, total environment quality programme. Ethical and moral issues addressed. Recycling of products considered.

Figure 4.17 Measuring the green policy of organizations

Case study: Nike Corporation

Consider Nike, the $8 billion footwear and apparel company, which has become a lightning rod for activists, consumers, the media and others, who have taken aim at the company's workplace, environmental and human rights practices. According to its critics, Nike has engaged in a variety of practices that have exploited Third World workers and the communities where they live. The images proffered by Nike's critics are vivid: women and young children toiling for long hours for low pay in squalid conditions, breathing fumes of toxic chemicals, unable to protest for fear of losing their jobs, manufacturing goods whose price tags exceed their monthly pay.

Nike acknowledges that in the past it was less than vigilant in monitoring the practices of its factories -- although nearly all of them are contracted to independent manufacturers. It has now launched an aggressive and ambitious effort not only to correct such situations but also to set a shining example for its industry. The company has begun using sustainability as a design criterion to reduce the use of toxic materials and generation of waste in its manufacturing process. Nike cut the use of solvents in its adhesives by 800,000 gallons in one year and has a goal of reducing its use of volatile organic compounds per unit of production by 90 per cent by 2001. The company also supports organic cotton farming by providing incentives for farmers to switch to organic production.

None of this seems to have stemmed the tide of criticism. In recent years, Nike has been named among the ten 'worst' international corporations by Multinational Monitor magazine. It had an Indonesian factory looted and burned by protesters and suffered criticisms by US women's groups, who pilloried the company for commercials that call for empowering women while poorly paying its predominantly female overseas workers. Its home town, Portland, Oregon, adopted a resolution urging its troubled school district to 'respectfully decline' a $500,000 cash donation because of the company's alleged human rights abuses.

The experiences of Nike and other companies that have come under intense public scrutiny because of perceived wrongdoings suggest that consumers' expectations of brands are changing. It is no longer enough that a company delivers good-quality products. In the search for differentiation, the battleground shifts from the tangible -- pounds of chemicals and other wastes released into the environment -- to the intangible -- ethics, values and corporate culture.

The above case illustrates the part ethics play in understanding sustainable marketing strategies. Another way of considering sustainability lies in taking a different view on the commonly quoted product life cycle.

Unit 4: Contemporary issues in marketing

The Life Cycle Analysis (LCA) concept – life cycle thinking

One way of considering the creation and utilization of environmentally-friendly products and services is the LCA concept. The LCA is recognized both as a concept and as an analytical environmental management tool (SPOLD, 1995). This concept, sometimes termed 'life cycle thinking', helps everyone (consumers and producers alike) to understand the overall environmental implications of the services required by society. The analysis based on this concept promotes the consideration of the cradle-to-grave implications of any actions taken, forcing the managers to move beyond the supply chain and sector-based considerations of the environment, and to consider the wider implications of economic activities.

Recently, Greenpeace has advocated the use of a similar dial to the one adopted in this book, for consumer electronics.

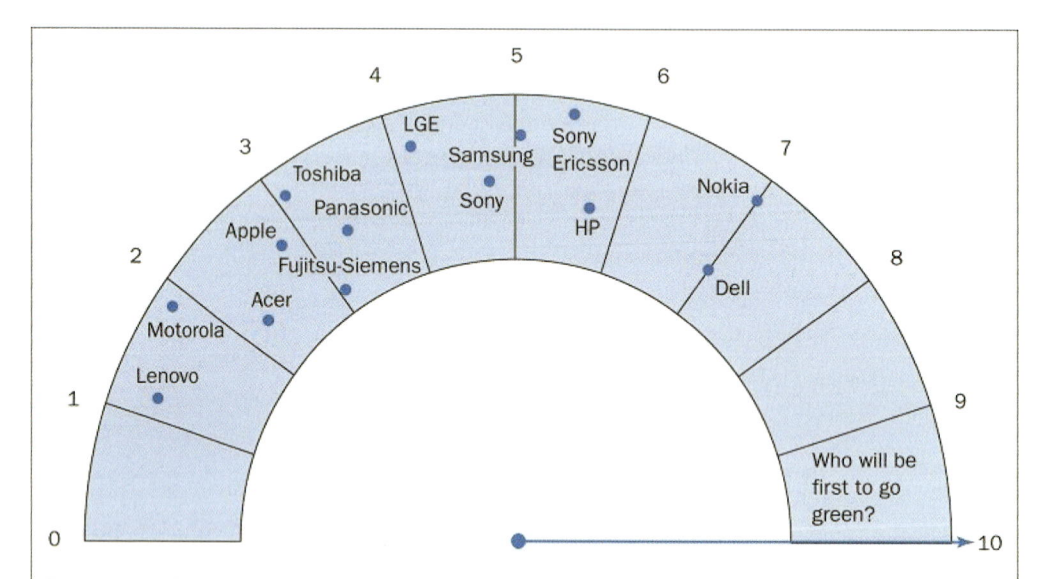

The criteria reflect the demands of the Toxic Tech campaign to the electronic companies. Our two demands are that companies should:
- clean up their products by eliminating hazardous substances
- take back and recycle their products once they become obsolete.

The two issues are connected. The use of harmful chemicals in electronics prevents them from being recycled safely when products are discarded. Each company was given a score out of 30 which was then divided by 3 to give a mark out of 10 for simplicity.

Figure 4.18 Greenpeace guide to greener electronics

Greenpeace scores the companies on the electronics scorecard as follows:

Chemicals policy and practice (5 criteria)

1. A chemicals policy based on the Precautionary Principle
2. Chemicals management: supply-chain management of chemicals via, for example, banned/restricted substance lists or a policy to identify problematic substances for future elimination/substitution

3   Timeline for phasing out all use of vinyl plastic (PVC)

4   Timeline for phasing out all use of brominated flame retardants (not just those banned by EU's RoHS Directive)

5   PVC- and BFR-free models of electronic products on the market

Policy and practice on producer responsibility for taking back their discarded products and recycling (4 criteria)

1   Support for individual (financial) producer responsibility – producers should finance the end-of-life management of their products by taking back and reusing/recycling their own-brand discarded products.

2   Provides voluntary take-back and recycling in every country where it sells its products, even in the absence of national laws requiring producer responsibility for electronic waste.

3   Provides clear information for individual customers on take-back policies and recycling services in all countries where there are sales of its products.

4   Reports on amount of waste electrical and electronic equipment (WEEE) collected and recycled.

Nokia leads the way on eliminating toxic chemicals. Since the end of 2005 all new models of mobiles are free of polyvinyl chloride (PVC) and all new models are free of brominated flame retardents (BFRs) from the start of 2007. Nokia loses points for failing to provide an adequate definition of what precautionary principle means in practice. On the other hand, Nokia scores well on producer responsibility for its electronic waste. The company actively

Nokia = 7/10	Bad (0)	Partially bad (1+)	Partially good (2+)	Good (2+)
Precautionary principle		■		
Chemicals management				■
Timeline for PVC phaseout				■
Timeline for BFR phaseout				■
PVC-free and/or BFR-free models (Companies score double for this)			■	
Individual producer responsibility			■	
Voluntary take-back				■
Information to individual customers			■	
Amounts recycled		■		

Figure 4.19 Nokia's electronic scorecard

supports and lobbies for individual producer responsibility, which means that each company should take care of the electronic waste from its own-brand products. However, Nokia loses points for not providing data on the amounts of actual mobiles recycled. Further detailed analysis for each company is provided by Greenpeace on their website (http://www.green-peace.org/international/news/green-electronics-guide-ewaste250806).

This type of classification is important as these companies produce huge amounts of e-waste globally, some of which goes for recycling in places such as India and China, where they contribute to environmental degradation and endanger human health. Any positive inputs into the way products are made, commercialized and consumed are important for both the consumer and the recycler.

Case study: APRIL takes a leaf out of the green book

By Anna Jenkinson

Asia is not renowned for being the most advanced region as far as environmental awareness goes. Just think of the car-clogged, highly-polluted streets of many of Asia's big cities, the lack of paper recycling systems throughout much of the region or even the poor quality of drinking water in some places further off the beaten track.

But a mixed track record is no excuse for Asian industries today and many of the region's major pulp and paper manufacturers are facing up to the 'green challenge'. One such company is Indonesia's Riau Andalan Pulp and Paper (RAPP), part of the Asia Pacific Resources International (APRIL) group. On the environmental front, RAPP was arguably helped along by its co-operation, albeit short lived, with Finland's UPM-Kymmene. 'The presence of a European company helped raise environmental awareness and performance', according to Canesio P Munoz, the company's environmental manager. But since the the alliance broke down and RAPP was left standing on its own two feet, there has been no let-up in the company's momentum for greener and cleaner operations.

At present, RAPP is constructing a second pulp line at its Kerinci mill in the Riau province on the Indonesian island of Sumatra. As the company starts to expand toward a two million ton/yr pulp capacity target, the mill is becoming increasingly aware of the need to meet stringent environmental targets to satisfy both local and international demands. The company is targeting a first quarter 2001 start-up date for the new line at the Riau mill.

As part of its environmental commitment, APRIL is working on its first annual environmental report. But it is not just a moral sense of concern for the mill's surroundings that is driving APRIL -- pressure is coming from many quarters. Local people have lodged complaints about skin-related diseases and fish depletion in the nearby Kampar river. As a result of these allegations, non-governmental organizations (NGOs) have leveled criticisms at the pulp and paper mill. There have also been some critical voices from overseas, for example in Europe.

In an attempt to put these fears and accusations to rest, APRIL has appointed independent bodies to carry out research and help prove that the Indonesian mill operates in line with international standards and, in some cases, beats these targets (Table 4.1).

Table 4.1 RAPP effluent load as compared to international standards (kg/ton)

Parameter cluster rules		Indonesia		Canada		Sweden
		RAPP (Early 2000)		(BC)		Existing mills
New mills		(Oct 1999)				
BOD5	8.5	4.5	8.7	8.05	5.5	2.93
COD	29.75	No spec	31	No spec	No spec	11.22
TSS	8.5	7.0	4.0	16.4	9.5	4.41
pH	6-9	5-9	5-9	5-9	5-9	7.1 8.2
AOX	No spec	1.5	0.23	0.623	0.272	0.12

No spec – No specification

Outside approval

One independent body that RAPP selected was the Finnish Environmental Research Group which carried out an environmental impact assessment at the mill. The report was published last September and concluded that RAPP's industrial complex contained low levels of pollutants and that the external treatment seemed to work efficiently, although improvements of nutrient dosage could be carried out. The Finnish group also came to the conclusion that the risk for humans coming into contact with the Kampar river water was "negligible or non-existent". As for the river's fish life, investigations suggested that the level of pulp mill effluent contaminants was low enough not to have any serious effect on the animals:

Soon after the Finnish report, RAPP launched a one-year program with local NGOs to carry out further studies into the effects of the pulp and paper operations on the quality of the local river. The gist of these investigations is to sample biodata from the Kampar river every three months and compare examples taken from upstream, downstream and at the point of effluent discharge from the pulp mill.

The research is a three-pronged effort, with local NGO Riau Mandiri assessing the water quality, the Fisheries department of the University of Riau in charge of the river biology/ecology and the University of Singapore investigating health-related matters.

The preliminary results are good news for RAPP, with no strong condemnations being thrown in its direction. The water quality is described as 'generally good', although Riau Mandiri is looking further into the COD (chemical oxygen demand) and BOD (biological oxygen demand) readings, which have recently started to rise. The University of Riau has not noticed any significant difference to the natural river life either. In fact, fish stocks actually increased due to higher nitrogen and phosphorous levels in the effluent treatment. The university team continues to assess the quality of the fish stocks as it seems that sulphur levels are slightly higher than normal, though.

On top of that, the reports from local people about skin irritations are not being blamed on RAPP and it is thought that plants may be the problem. The findings of one Riau University study suggest that it is 'unlikely' that river water is a cause of inflammatory skin problems among villagers. Monitoring will continue, though, until a more conclusive verdict is reached.

It is certainly in RAPP's interests to co-operate with the NGOs and prove the mill's case wherever possible, as the NGOs can act as a powerful lobbyist. As Riau Mandiri spokesperson, Anny Hardiyanti, says, 'After a year's monitoring, if we find negative results, we will urge the company to address the problem. And if the problem is not addressed, we will launch a campaign against the company responsible.' Added to that, the NGO is not afraid of carrying out threats of action. It has already launched several campaigns against other companies, which were found to be polluting another nearby river in the region.

Forest sustenance

A key tenet of APRIL's environmental policy is striving toward fully sustainable forest management. The Indonesian mill's long-term goal is to achieve sustainable forest management certification. But as an interim step, the mill is focusing on an ISO 14001 certificate for its forestry operations, which it hopes to receive by the end of this year. If the company sticks to the timetable, certification would come just a few months after RAPP was awarded ISO 9002 for its pulp and paper operations.

ISO 14001 is an environmental management system, which provides criteria for assessing a company's use of air, water, soil and resources. The drive toward this certification comes from RAPP's customers around the globe, and particularly from European consumers.

Part of the company's efforts toward full sustainability is the development of its acacia plantations. Planting started back in 1993 and some of the plantations are already mature, but the company is waiting until next year before harvesting the area for strategic reasons. RAPP aims to make a full switch from mixed tropical hardwood to acacia plantations by 2008.

The company has also carried out extensive tests on the plantations and is extremely pleased with the yield and quality results. The plantations are expected to yield 210 m^3/ha at harvest and achieve a wood to pulp conversion rate of 4.5 m^3/ton/ib. As a result, RAPP hopes to gain the double advantage of higher yields and limiting any adverse effects on the environment.

By RAPP's calculations, the mill will need 127,500 ha of plantations to supply pulp line #1 which has an 850,000 ton/yr capacity (Table 4.2). Pulp line #2A is due to come on line by the first quarter of 2001, bringing total capacity up to 1.3 million tons/yr. RAPP calculates that it will need 195,000 ha/yr of acacia plantations to meet this pulp capacity, and it is no surprise perhaps that the company happens to have exactly this amount available. Originally the government allocated 280,000 ha of land to RAPP for conversion into plantations. The area chosen by the government was so-called

Table 4.2 Plantation supplies at RAPP

		Line 1	Line 1+2A	Line 1+2A+2B
Pulp mill capacity		850,000	1,300,000	2,000,000
Acacia growth rate				
Mean annual increment	M³/ha/a	30	30	30
Rotation	Yr	7	7	7
Yield at harvest	M³/ha	210	210	210
Wood to pulp conversion				
Acacia species	M³/t/ib	4.5	4.5	4.5
Wood and HTI requirement				
Annual acacia input	M³/yr	3,825,000	5,850,000	9,000,000
Total net HTI area required	Ha	127,500	195,000	300,000
Land resources for tree				
Plantation development				
RAPP HTI concessions area	Ha	195,000	195,000	195,000
Associated companies/jvs	Ha	0	0	85,000
Tree farms	Ha	0	0	20,000
TOTAL AREA	ha	195,000	195,000	300,000

HTI = Hutan Tanaman Industri

'non-productive land' -- in other words the land had already been logged over and exploited. Some of this area must be maintained as a greenbelt area to protect wildlife and ensure biodiversity in the area, leaving the company with the magic number of 195,000 ha/yr for converting into plantations.

Indonesia's social scene

On paper, the land transfer sounds like a relatively simple procedure -- the government allocates land and the company decides to convert the area into plantations. In practice, though, there are many more hurdles to be cleared. For example, some of the allocated land is next to local settlements and the communities claim that the ground is theirs in accordance with 'community rights'. Companies such as RAPP are only able to operate effectively by avoiding conflicts with these local communities. This involves talking with the people, suggesting alternative sources of income and convincing them that they will

Unit 4: Contemporary issues in marketing

not lose out. As environmental manager, Munoz, says, 'We don't drive people out. Resolutions are always reached by consensus.'

Of the total area allocated to RAPP, some 60,000 ha of land were termed so-called 'problem areas'. So far, the company has resolved approximately half of the issues. RAPP is all too aware of the need to work with the local people to avoid potentially serious problems. For example, last December the Kerinci mill was brought to a standstill as demonstrators took to the streets in protest over a labour dispute. And in the new era of 'reformation' which is flourishing in Indonesia, local communities are becoming increasingly aware of their rights and companies such as RAPP clearly want to avoid conflicts wherever possible.

To date, RAPP has employed a host of community development (CD) projects to try and keep the peace with the locals. The CD programmes have existed since 1993, although the initiative was significantly expanded in 1998. Last year alone, the company implemented programmes in six local villages. RAPP has carried out initiatives such as building a mosque, providing drinking water, building bridges to overcome transportation difficulties and training the villagers to cultivate unused land for productive and profitable uses.

RAPP's budget for CD programmes in 2000 is $2 million and the company's management believes that it is money well spent. Not only does it benefit the local people but it also promotes good relations with neighbouring communities and improves the skills of potential employees for the pulp and paper mill.

One village called Gunung Sahilan chose to develop oil palm plantations with the company's CD program funds. As a result, APRIL teamed up with an associated company, Asian Agri, which is active in the oil palm industry. The alliance has worked well and the villagers seem extremely pleased with the project's success. But when asked if he was satisfied, the village chief replied, 'We don't need more, but we want more.' A note of warning to RAPP, perhaps, that it cannot sit back and relax. The company must constantly remain attentive to the demands of the local people just as much as, if not more than, those of the international community.

The case illustrates the various factors involved in a company striving to be green. The chain to the final consumer however, can be quite long.

Paper/Pulp production → Packaging / Printing (newspapers/books) / Paper products → Consumer → Disposal/ Recycling

Consider the Life Cycle of the products taking into account the various stages of responsibilities.

According to SPOLD, life cycle thinking reflects the acceptance that key company stakeholders cannot strictly limit their responsibilities only to those phases of the product life cycle, process or activity in which they are actively involved. This approach expands the scope of their responsibility to include environmental implications along the entire life cycle of the product, process or activity. The direct effect of this type of thinking is that all processors, manufacturers, distributors, retailers, users and waste managers involved in the product life cycle share responsibility towards the environment.

The individual share of responsibility for each of these actors will be greatest in the parts of the life cycle under their direct control and least in the other stages of the cycle. Life cycle thinking has been applied to much of the legislation emanating from the European Commission, especially with regards to product and waste policy. The concept of producer responsibility is at the heart of waste strategy, and it follows life cycle thinking. An example of this is given in Figure 4.20.

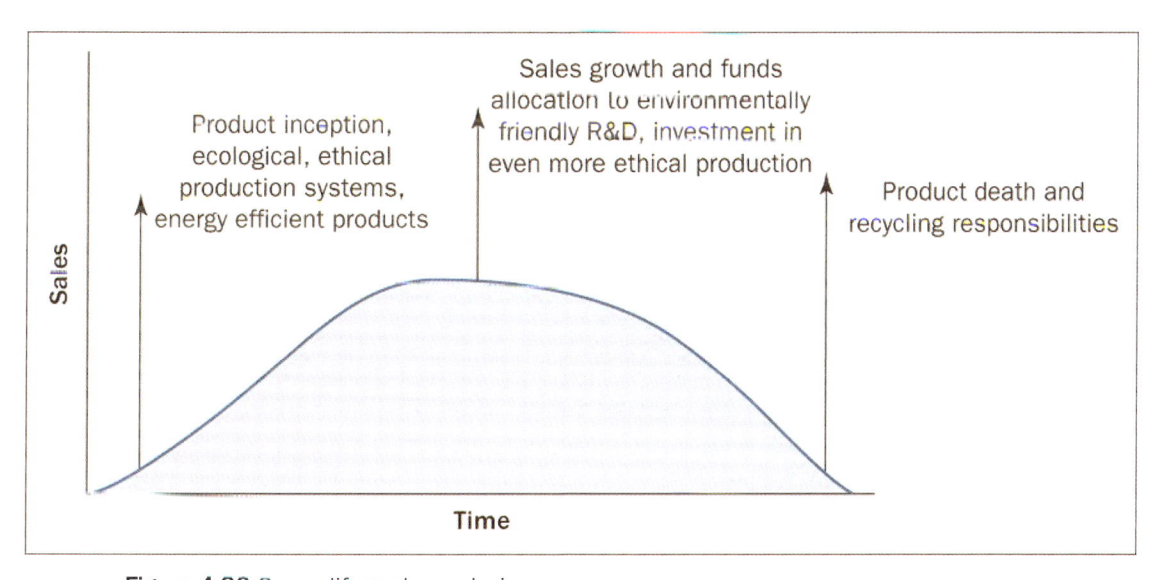

Figure 4.20 Green life cycle analysis

Currently, there are various concepts that are related to developing ecologically sound products. Some of these are as follows:

◆ **Design for the environment** – There are many initiatives for reducing the negative environmental impacts that a product may unleash. These effects could be concentrated at the production, usage or disposal stage. In designing for the environment, technologists are concerned with reducing energy consumption (both in the production of an item, as well as when it is in use) and generally conserving resources. The main trends are:

1   The incorporation of information from LCA into design
2   The definition of environmental objectives

3. A focus on the relationship between the product and the consumer and how the design can encourage environmentally responsible behaviour in the consumer

According to the US EPA (1992), life cycle design is *'A systems-oriented approach for designing more ecologically and economically sustainable product systems, which integrates environmental requirements into the earliest stages of design. In LCD, environmental performance, cost, cultural and legal requirements are balanced.'*

- **Clean technology** – Clean technology is the means of providing a human benefit which, overall, uses less resources and causes less environmental damage than alternative means with which it is in direct economic competition (Clift, 1995).

- **Industrial ecology** – This is generally concerned with the evolution of technology and economic systems in such a way that human activities mimic mature biological systems with regards to being self-contained in their material and resource use (Allenby, 1994). Governments and non-governmental organizations often use this idea when they assess the sustainability of industrial processes.

- **Total quality environment management** – This concept synthesises environmental management and total quality management (TQM) (GEMI, 1993). TQEM relies on the following basic parts:

    1. **Identify customers** – The definition of quality dependent on what the customers want (a broader definition of customers is taken and they include consumers, legislators, environmental groups and society at large).

    2. **Continuous improvement** – A systematic approach directed towards continuously improving organizational processes and activities.

    3. **Do the job right the first time** – In terms of the environment, eliminate problems at the outset. Quality failures may be detrimental to the environment and also incur financial costs, without providing benefits to the consumer.

    4. **Take a systems approach** – Each part of environmental management is considered to be a 'system'. This includes people, equipment and processes. Weak links in the system should be addressed.

In general, the plan-do-check-act (PDCA) cycle is followed in parallel with typical TQM programmes.

All these concepts are inter-linked and there is now a concerted approach to take a more holistic view by incorporating them into a general framework for sustainable development (SETAC, 1998).

Implications for organizations

For organizations it is becoming increasingly important to incorporate green thinking into their processes and products. Organizations need to consider very carefully how much their activities impact on the planet. Any improvement creates a net benefit for both the consumer and the environment. There are many charges against companies stating that they embrace a green attitude at a superficial level and are generally engaged in 'greenwashing' the public through clever advertising and public relations activities. In fact, even companies like Body Shop have been criticized for exaggerating their claims with regards to promoting sustainable development and the purity of their ingredients (Stauber and Rampton, 1995). In many cases, companies even pursuing a modicum of green policies are not rewarded in the market-place (Wong et al., 1996). Such criticisms could be levelled at almost every corporation. Nonetheless, it is important to realize that corporations can have a major impact on the environment, even by implementing some of the concepts discussed above. For instance:

- Anheuser-Busch has developed an aluminium can that is 33 per cent lighter. This reduced use of aluminium, combined with an overall recycling plan, saves the company $200 million a year.

- Ford Motor Company used more than 60 million two-litre plastic soda bottles in the manufacturing of grille reinforcements, window frames, engine covers and trunk carpets. In 1999, this effort accounted for 7.5 million pounds of plastic.

- Kellogg's plant in Bremen, Germany, employs a wastewater recycling operation that reduces water consumption and wastewater effluent. In India, a Kellogg vapour-absorption system is used to provide plant air conditioning, eliminating the use of ozone-depleting substances. Fluorescent bulbs discarded from Kellogg's plant in New Jersey are sent for recycling, removing potentially hazardous materials from landfills (Rand Corporation, 2000).

In spite of cynical views, these efforts not only save the companies concerned millions, but also save resources. These types of savings are not easily obtainable through the behaviour of individual customers. It is important that companies pursue such strategies. This is evident when you consider that of the 100 largest economies in the world, 51 are global corporations and only 49 are countries (Anderson and Cavanagh, 1996). Mitsubishi was larger than the fourth most populous nation on Earth, Indonesia. General Motors was bigger than Denmark, and Toyota bigger than Norway. Often, large chunks of world trade are actually transactions between different parts of organizations. Companies, therefore, have to be proactive in pursuing ecologically-friendly processes and in introducing 'green' products. In addition to their moral obligation, they are also under pressure from consumers and non-governmental organizations (NGOs such as Greenpeace). In the last 20 years, companies have become much more sensitive to such pressures because of (Bennet and James, 1999):

- The growing economic value of a good corporate reputation and a strong positively regarded brand. These can be put at risk by adverse criticism of environmental and social performance (Fomburn, 1996).

- The growing number of customers who are becoming more 'green conscious', taking social and environmental criteria into account when purchasing goods or services.

- The tremendous flow of information, exchanged at unprecedented levels, through satellite TV stations such as CNN and the Internet. In the future, it is likely that

Unit 4: Contemporary issues in marketing

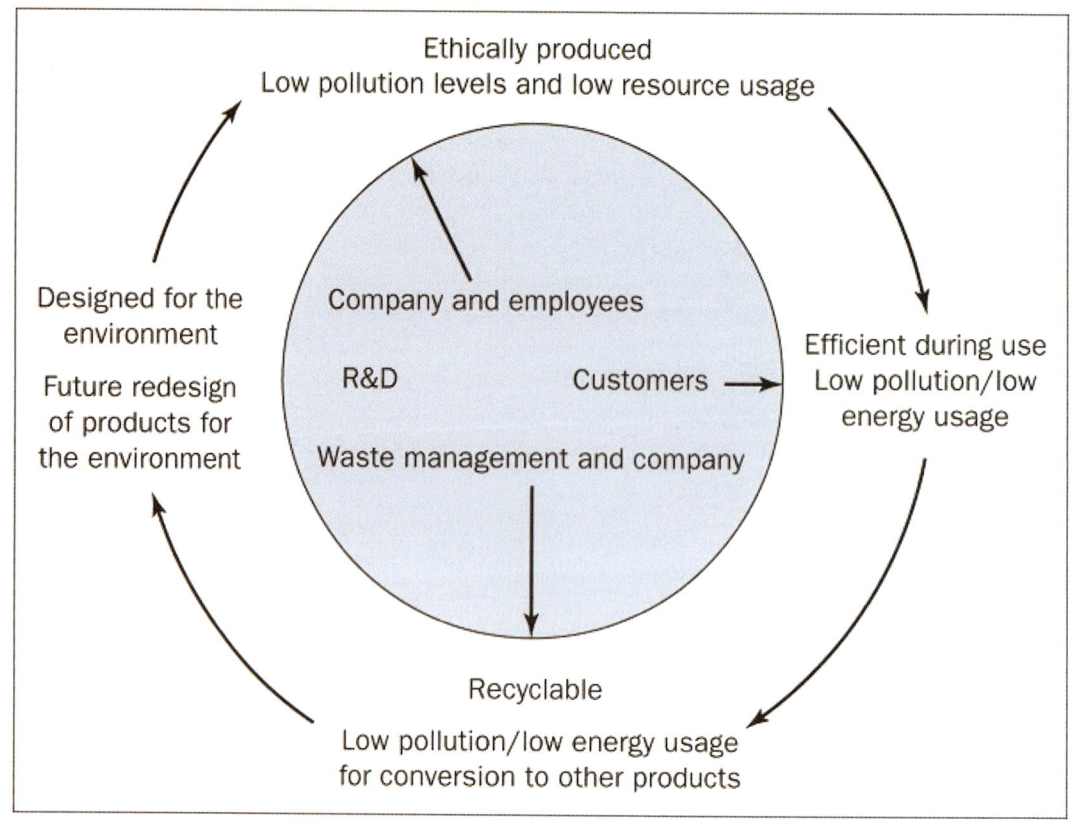

Figure 4.21 Assessing green credentials

Diagram showing a central circle containing: Company and employees, R&D, Customers, Waste management and company. Surrounding labels:
- Ethically produced — Low pollution levels and low resource usage
- Efficient during use — Low pollution/low energy usage
- Recyclable — Low pollution/low energy usage for conversion to other products
- Designed for the environment; Future redesign of products for the environment

Sustainability and ethical matrix

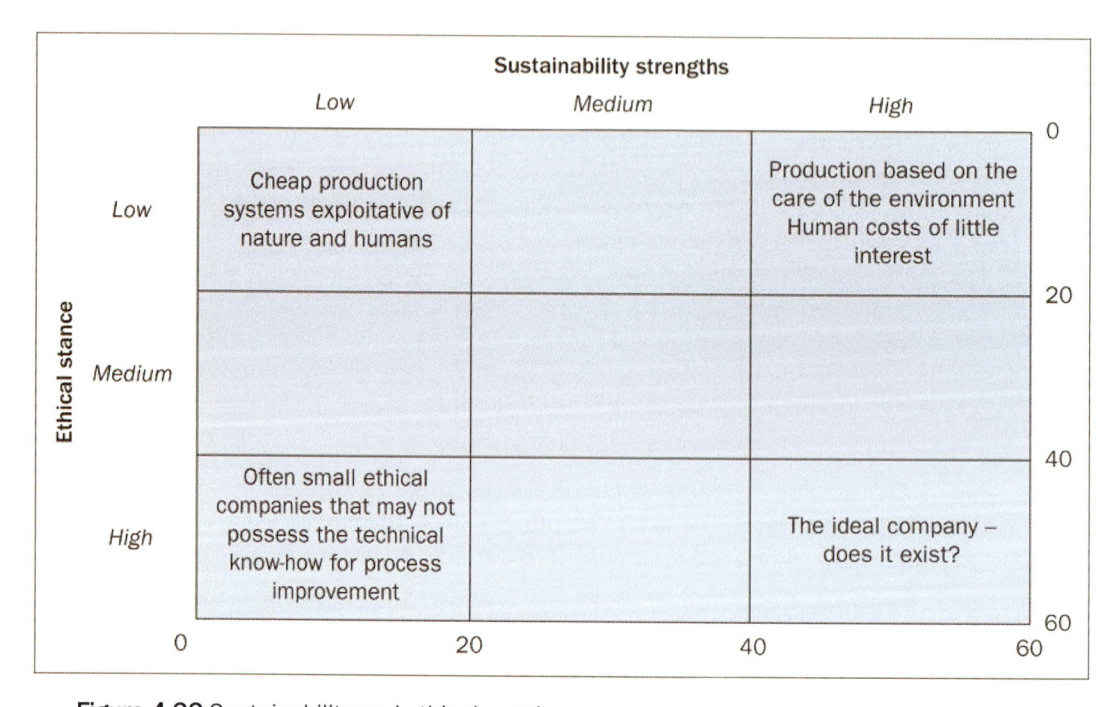

Sustainability strengths across top: Low, Medium, High
Ethical stance down side: Low, Medium, High

	Low	Medium	High
Low	Cheap production systems exploitative of nature and humans		Production based on the care of the environment. Human costs of little interest
Medium			
High	Often small ethical companies that may not possess the technical know-how for process improvement		The ideal company – does it exist?

Axis values: 0, 20, 40, 60 (both axes)

Figure 4.22 Sustainability and ethical matrix

information will also be transferred 'on the move' through mobile communication devices such as Internet-interfacing mobiles and personal digital assistants (PDAs). This flow of information increases the visibility of any enterprise.

- Companies are also dependent on a workforce who is highly educated and often more environmentally literate than their older counterparts.

Interestingly, a recent survey of ethical funds shows that they have performed strongly over the past three years. Many funds have shown growth ranging from 73 per cent to 50 per cent (Bien, 2001). These are early days, but the current results bode well for ethical and green investments. What, then, should companies strive to achieve? Some of the key questions that companies should be addressing are given at the end of the chapter. In many ways, companies should attempt to get into a virtual circle and constantly look forward to the future of their R&D (Figure 4.21).

Considering this type of virtual way in which companies could operate, the competitive advantages that could be gained are considerable. Various authors have tried different types of categorizations. For instance, Hart (2000) has developed a sustainability model, which can be used by companies to rate themselves on the following scale for each quadrant: 1 – nonexistant, 2 – emerging, 3 – established or 4 – institutionalized. Based on this assessment, each individual organization can look for environmental policy gaps, analyse them to understand their sustainability credentials, and begin to plan both internal and external strategies for the future.

Another way of assessing the total commitment of a company to sustainability and ethical consideration is to utilize the matrix shown in Figure 4.22 above.

The following questions were formulated by understanding the various cases of greener organizations (Peattie and Charter, 1997; Piasecki et al., 1999; Crosbie and Knight, 1995). Look at the questions set. Companies scoring 12 points in both sets of questions fall into the top left-hand quadrant. Companies scoring 60 in both sets of questions fall into the bottom right-hand quadrant. The set of questions is designed to show the quadrant in which a company falls, and also points the way for future improvement and the opportunities that may be available.

Unit 4: Contemporary issues in marketing

```
                    Green management questions

                         Very    Poor   Adequate  Good   Very
                         poor                            good

                          1       2       3        4      5

   1.  Design for the environment
   2.  Energy efficiency in manufacturing
   3.  Waste in manufacturing
   4.  Pollution during manufacturing
   5.  Recyclability of packaging
   6.  Lifespan of product
   7.  Energy efficiency during use
   8.  Recyclability of product
   9.  Total quality environmental management
   10. Search for new green product opportunities
   11. Use of pollution control equipment
   12. Compliance consulting


                        Ethical considerations

                          1       2       3        4      5

   1.  Working conditions
   2.  Staff welfare and health care
   3.  Limitation of exposure to pollutants
   4.  Sustainability of operations within
       local ecology
   5.  Involvement of stakeholders in
       environmental issues
   6.  Continuous pollution monitoring
   7.  Management of the end of the
       life cycle without affecting others
       (prevention of dumping in poor areas)
   8.  Respect for fauna and flora
   9.  Adequate compensation to local
       suppliers
   10. Honesty in advertising
   11. Discussions with NGOs
   12. Environment restoration post
       production
```

Figure 4.23 Green management questions

Companies scoring in the medium/medium range (middle of the matrix) can be prone to resorting to strong advertising campaigns and PR in order to 'greenwash' the public. Consumers often have to rely on specialist journals or articles in newspapers for a true indication of a company's policy. There is a great danger for companies to pay lip service to green strategies and not necessarily address the key issues involved. These issues are explored in detail in the hard-hitting book by Stauber and Rampton (1995). As discussed before, a company that is truly following sustainable principles has to be both ethically and environmentally sound. Customers too are realizing that we do not live in a world with infinite resources. In fact the new-world paradigm reflects the fact that we are *a part* of nature and not *apart* from it (Wasik, 1996). The post-modern consumer is more concerned about nature and is likely to look at issues holistically. Table 4.3 illustrates this approach.

Table 4.3 Old versus new paradigms

Old world view	New world view
Continuous unbridled growth	Sustainable, green economics
Conquer nature, reap resources	Biophilia (affinity for nature)
Environmental compliance	Eco-auditing
Marketing to fill needs	Marketing to sustain life
Materialism	Personalism
Industrial production	Industrial ecology
Design for obsolescence, disposal	Design for environment
Cost accounting (profit/loss statements)	Full cost accounting
Departmentalism, reductionism	Holism

Green consumer behaviour

According to a survey carried out by the Wirthlin Group (Wirthlin Worldwide, 2000), two thirds of American consumers agreed that 'environmental standards cannot be too high and continuing improvements must be made regardless of the costs.' In 1999, a Gallup poll survey found that 68 per cent of Americans worried a great deal about the pollution of drinking water and 53 per cent about the contamination of soil and water by toxic waste. Understanding the complexity of the human/ecological interface requires a degree of scientific understanding. Yet surveys conducted by the National Science Foundation suggest that, even using lenient standards, only about 11 per cent of citizens understand enough of the vocabulary and concepts of science in general, in order to be considered scientifically literate (National Science Foundation, 1998).

This is an especially important issue when companies are advertising the green benefits of their products. How many consumers will actually understand the claims made? Are they likely to understand the scientific reasoning behind particular policies or are they likely to be emotively manipulated by the press in a simplistic manner? Quite often, people are very likely to understand only simple cause-and-effect relationships. According to Coyle the NEETF president (NEETF/Roper, 2000):

> ...[P]eople understand that cars pollute, or that species become extinct when habitat is destroyed. But when there are two or more steps involved ... such as energy production from fossil-fuelled power stations contributing to climate change, thereby

warming ocean waters sufficiently to inhibit the production of plankton for fish, thus impairing the survival of marine life ... public understanding drops precipitously. Each year, the National Environmental Education & Training Foundation (NEETF) issues a 10-question survey on environmental awareness; in a typical year, Americans averaged fewer than 25 per cent correct answers to basic environmental literacy questions. Furthermore, myths and misconceptions persist. Surveys indicate that many Americans still believe that trash bags can be made to biodegrade in landfills (virtually nothing degrades in landfills). Many people still believe aerosol cans contain ozone-destroying ingredients (chlorofluorocarbons were banned from aerosols in 1978) and that landfills are brimming with plastic (plastic accounts for just 9 per cent of municipal solid waste, paper and cardboard are four times as much).

This can be illustrated by an energy and environmental profile analysis of children's single-use and reusable cloth diapers carried out by Franklin Associates in 1992, and explained in Fuller (1999). For many consumers, the intuitive understanding is that plastic/paper diapers are vastly energy consuming and polluting. The comparative scientific analysis however shows that the environmental answers are not clear cut. The results show that:

- Home cloth diapers consume 33 per cent more energy than single use diapers and 12 per cent more energy than commercial cloth diapers.
- Single-use diapers produce about twice the total solid waste by volume in comparison with home or commercial cloth diapers.
- Home cloth diapers produce nearly twice the total atmospheric emissions in comparison with single-use diapers or commercial cloth diapers.
- Home or commercial diapers produce about seven times the total water-borne waste of single-use diapers.
- The manufacturing of home or commercial cloth diapers consume more than twice the water volume used for single-use diapers.

Many criticisms can be levelled at such an analysis and, indeed, some authors argue that single-use diapers also contribute to air pollution, via incineration. They may also be the cause of allergic skin reactions. Nonetheless, the case illustrates the complexity of issues involved when undertaking some sort of life cycle analysis for products. In these circumstances consumers should also to be able to follow complex arguments in order to make valid judgements.

Roper Starch (Rand Corporation, 2000), who produce the Green Gauge Report on the environment and environmentally-conscious purchase decisions, showed how consumer attitudes broke down in the 2000 survey:

- **11% True-Blue Greens** – The recyclers, composters, letter-writers and volunteers of the world, the ones most likely to go out of their way to buy organic foods, recycled paper products, rechargeable batteries, less toxic paints and other goods with environmentally preferable attributes.
- **5% Greenback Greens** – Those who will contribute to environmental organizations or spend more for green products, but not consider changes in lifestyles or housekeeping due to environmental concerns.
- **33% Sprouts** – Those who care about the environment, but who will only spend slightly more for environmentally sensitive products.

- **18% Grousers** – These are people who care about the environment but view it as someone else's problem; Grousers don't seek environmentally-sensitive goods or consider green-minded lifestyle changes.

- **33% Basic Brown** – People who are essentially unconcerned about the environment.

There is another way of slicing the consumers and that is the traditional method of classifying consumers as:

1. **Traditionalists** – Those who believe in the nostalgic image of small towns and conservative churches.

2. **Moderns** – These are individuals who are more materialistic and consumer oriented. They are generally individuals who see life through the same filters as Time magazine.

3. **The cultural creatives** – This is a new category, discussed by Dr. Paul Ray (Rand Corporation, 2000) as a result of market research studies in consumer behaviour. The cultural creatives (CCs) have often been involved in, or care about, three to six social movements. These are:

    - Very strong environmentalism
    - The condition of the whole planet
    - Civil rights
    - Peace
    - Social justice
    - New spiritualities
    - Organic food
    - Holistic health

Many follow personal paths and spiritual goals. These individuals account for a high proportion of people using alternative healthcare products and other lifestyle of health and sustainability (LOHAS) products and service. These individuals are very good at putting their own big picture together from a diverse range of sources of information. They compare and contrast, attempting to understand the real issues. They are the least likely to be 'green-washed' by aggressive advertising. In addition to this, to fully appreciate the sustainable lifestyle, the Natural Business Communications and the Natural Marketing Institute believe that the greater paradigm of such existence is LOHAS. The LOHAS market comprises five core market segments — sustainable economy, healthy lifestyles, personal development, alternative healthcare and ecological lifestyles. The five segments combined represented a $226.8 billion US market and an estimated $546 billion global market in 2000. Within each of these five segments there are many specific categories of products and services across a vast array of businesses and industries. The chart below shows the total size for the five key LOHAS segments and the associated industry categories.

The ecological lifestyles and sustainable economy segments represent nearly 75 per cent of the global market, if the US breakdown is emulated around the world. Considering the complexity of the green consumer profile, several interrelated factors have to be taken into account, as shown in Table 4.4. However, the examples and the discussions presented above show that a new breed of consumer is indeed emerging. This new consumer is characterized by a need to protect the environment and to lead an ethically correct lifestyle. The market trends show that these consumers are growing in numbers. Companies wishing to understand this new segment's potential customers need to address their marketing offer in a sensible and honest manner. They also need to consider the way in which markets may move in the future.

Table 4.4 Key LOHAS segments and industries (Rand Corporatio, 2000)

LOHAS market segment	Total in $ million
Sustainable economy	$76,470
Healthy lifestyles	$27,811
Alternative healthcare	$30,698
Personal development (mind, body, spirit)	$10,628
Ecological lifestyles	$81,178
TOTAL US LOHAS MARKET	**$226.8 billion**

Green marketing strategies

In many cases, companies take reactive stances to green issues. The lack of proactive initiatives often damage the credibility of a company and the profitability of products that are sold. It is therefore important for companies that are seriously concerned about green issues to be more proactive and pursue a market orientation that is green in its design. In order to gain competitive advantage, companies have to exhibit the following characteristics:

- Offering products that address the ethical, moral and sustainability issues described above.
- Producing goods which are not only commercially viable but which also meet consumer needs.
- Using some of the profits for environmental and social improvement at the source of production.
- Segmenting the markets effectively, so that the complexity of the niche markets and the 'new' consumers are understood and targeted accordingly.
- Communicating honest and credible messages to the customers. These messages should be transparent and should be understood by internal and external stakeholders, as well as by consumers.
- The transportation and logistics systems should mirror the company's aims and objectives of lessening pollution, being environmentally friendly etc.

- Developing a marketing perspective that takes a cradle-to-grave ecological approach for products.
- In cases where products are complex, offering certain levels of educational marketing literature.
- Presenting advertising in a clear and concise manner.
- Understanding the future needs of customers and stakeholders.

The cases illustrated below are examples of how companies are dealing with green issues and face consumer reluctance to purchase green goods in spite of good intentions. They are taken from Makower (2006).

Case study: Electrolux: Efficiency = Green

The Swedish appliance giant doesn't go out of its way to market its products as environmental, says Karl Edsjö, Project Manager, Electrolux Sustainability Department in Stockholm. The company promotes products' energy-saving advantages on labels, but that is required in both Europe and the US. However, the company does play up its products' efficiency. 'It's worked very well to educate people about energy,' says Edsjö. 'If they choose the most efficient product, that's the most important thing for us.'

Promoting 'efficiency' has unwittingly translated into 'green' for Electrolux, leading consumers to 'assume our products are environmentally friendly,' Edsjö told me. That reputation also reduces pressure on Electrolux when new environmental concerns arise. For example, there is growing concern in some European countries over the health and environmental impacts of some flame retardants. 'It's a small concern at the moment, but we're pretty sure this will be a bigger issue in the future,' says Edsjö. He believes that Electrolux's reputation for environmental proactivity will make the company immune from consumer activism on this issue. 'They know that as soon as there is a solution, we will apply it to all our products.'

'To inform consumers is tricky,' says Edjsö. 'We'd like them to be more environmentally aware. We have a principle of both delivering the best technology, but also marketing it well to promote it well.'

But despite its green image and its holistic thinking, even Electrolux can get frustrated by consumers' less than willingness to embrace some company efforts aimed at aligning environmental sustainability with business success. For example, it piloted an initiative in Sweden in which consumers were given a washing machine (for a small installation fee), then charged on a per-use basis of 10 Swedish kronor (about US $1). One objective was that the consumer didn't have to worry about the appliance, relying on Electrolux to keep the most efficient machines in operation, thereby minimizing their energy and water needs.

The program was met with a decisive yawn by consumers, who apparently didn't want to change the way they paid for doing the wash at home. Edsjö believes the experiment may have been doomed by flawed methodology and hopes it will be revived some day. As he puts it: 'It's resting -- but there's still some big interest.'

Case study: Philips – durability trumps green

Netherlands-based Philips' flagship environmental consumer products are compact fluorescent light bulbs (CFLs), which it has marketed since 1978. For years, energy-saving and longer-lasting CFLs languished in the US market, despite their success in Europe, which experiences much higher energy costs. (The penetration rate for CFLs in Holland, where Philips is based, is around 50 per cent, compared with less than 10 per cent in the US.) Among other things, US consumers didn't care for the quality of CFLs' light output, and the fact that they didn't fit many existing lighting fixtures.

Things changed as the bulbs got cheaper, the quality of their light better, and their adaptability into various fixtures increased. Equally important was a key name change that reflected some green-marketing realities; Philips stopped calling the bulb 'Earth Light' and changed the name to 'Marathon'.

'After sales flattened, we went out and did primary research to find out why and whether we were reaching the hearts and minds of the audience with the name Earth Light,' explains Steve Goldmacher, Director, Corporate Communications for Philips Lighting in the US.

In its research, Philips found a great deal of sympathy (50 per cent positive, 25 per cent neutral) for green issues, combined with outright fear (60 per cent positive, 10 per cent neutral). And almost half (45 per cent) appear to be quite sympathetic to green-marketing efforts, requiring additional information about the environmental benefits of the products they buy. *Nevertheless, a much lower percentage are willing to change their lifestyles (20 per cent) or pay more (25 per cent).*

'It turned out the environment wasn't their primary need,' says Goldmacher. 'Environmental responsibility was the number four or five purchase criterion. Number one is that they wanted the bulb to last longer. The longer a light bulb lasted was the most important criterion. Being green is wonderful, but no one wants to pay the extra nickel.'

Case study: Toyota – green without compromise

Toyota's Prius may be the first major consumer product that fits nearly all of the criteria for success in the green-consumer market-place. It comes from a trusted company and can be bought wherever the company's products are sold; it looks and feels like a 'conventional' product and doesn't require consumers to change their habits to use; it is (almost) comparably priced to purchase and can save consumers money to operate; and it has added benefits -- it both saves money and is stylishly cool.

But when the Prius was launched in the US market in 2000, Toyota didn't play up its environmental attributes, according to Ed La Roque, National Advanced Technology Vehicle Manager. The emphasis was on saving gas and money. Those early marketing efforts were aimed at early adapters -- the technology buffs that wanted the latest, coolest thing -- today's iPod crowd. Environmentalists were a relatively small subset of that population. The product's original tagline was 'Prius/genius,' showing 'not only the intelligence of the new technology but also the creative Web-based marketing approach.' The first 2,000 or so vehicles were sold online – a key medium for early adopters.

Before rolling out the Prius, Toyota embarked on a two-year effort to develop a dialogue with consumers. That resulted in a pool of more than 40,000 interested consumers – or 'handraisers,' in industry-speak. These prospects were given early access to a Prius Web site and its special order feature. 'Our focus groups and studies confirmed that people want an environmentally friendly product at a fair price, but that they didn't want any compromises,' says La Roque.

Of course, Toyota turned to an increasingly green message, says La Roque. 'We are really talking about gallons saved and the positive impact on the environment. I think a lot of it has to do with Middle East situation and global warming. The whole environmental focus has come more to the forefront.'

One key ally are celebrities. 'The Hollywood community really embraced Prius,' says La Roque. 'There are a number of celebrity owners. It's their way of making a statement. And it's been a great benefit for us to have that unsolicited testimonial.' Example: Cameron Diaz appeared on the 'Tonight Show' the day she picked up her Prius and made it part of the interview.

Toyota has since transitioned to the current phase – what it calls the 'early majority buyer – sort of in between early adopter and mainstream,' explains La Roque. The strategy's success is shown in the form of months-long waiting lists for the Prius, and the rush to market by Toyota's competitors with other hybrid models.

In the end, however, the Prius' success was all about quality. 'It's very important that companies interested in promoting environmental products deliver,' says La Roque. 'We think we've delivered a great product for the market. We like to think we set a good example for other companies selling hybrids. There's no doubt that we get a good halo effect on the overall Toyota brand.'

Source: http://www.worldchanging.com/archives/003502.html

A recent UNEP report (Talk the Walk, 2005) discusses how marketing could help to change social attitudes towards consumption. In essence, as discussed above, consumer behaviour results from a range of interactions among factors such as public policy, cultural identity, media coverage of sustainability issues and corporate marketing, not to mention cultural imprints, as well as societal and family influences. This complexity increases the difficulty of assessing the impact of marketing efforts on consumer behaviour, as the range of variables can be extremely high. The variables can range from product features, service augmentation, pricing, promotion, retail strategy, distribution, or credit offers, to name just a few. Within this context it is instructive to look at these interactions through the diagram proposed below.

Companies sometimes feel that they are blamed for unsustainable consumption even though they make efforts to inform consumers, and this is encapsulated in the following quote:

Unit 4: Contemporary issues in marketing

Despite contributions to sustainable development, advertising's role and effects have been questioned. Advertising has been blamed for spreading Western lifestyles around the world and for promoting excessive consumption in developed countries.
(Procter & Gamble 2003 sustainability report)

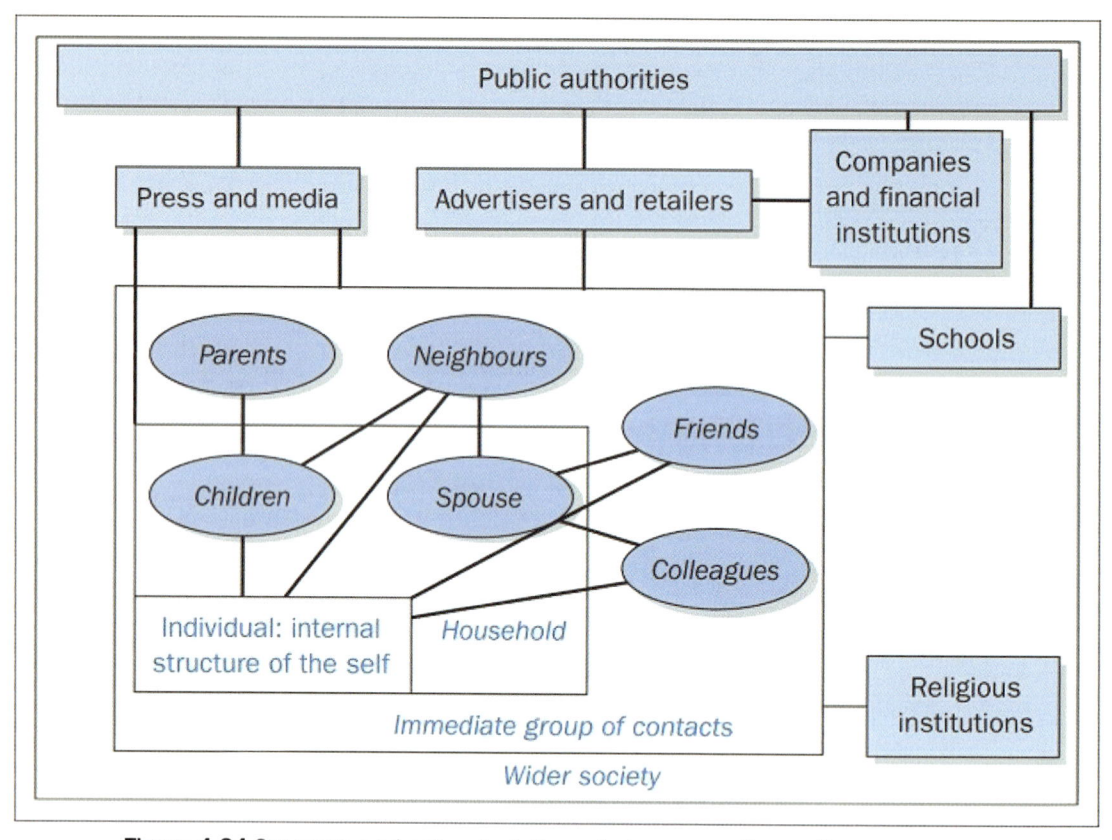

Figure 4.24 Structure and networks influencing consumption patterns

This is an interesting proposition as the model in Figure 4.24 shows multiple influences on consumption patterns. According to MORI (2003), 74 per cent of the UK public that was surveyed would purchase from companies that promulgated am ethical and green policy if they had the information available to them. This offers a golden opportunity to companies to market and advertise their products and services accordingly. One of the key arguments put forward by the UNDEP report is a model that incorporates three different areas of marketing to encourage sustainable lifestyles marketing. As explained before, according to the LOHAS segmentation criteria, large segments of the population are interested in sustainable lifestyles encompassing a range of different products and services. This model incorporates:

◆ Responsible marketing – Some companies are beginning to embrace policies and strategies to promote sustainable behaviour to consumers, especially with regards to over-consumption of food or alcohol that results in health damage, either in the form of alcohol-related diseases or in obesity. For example, according to a report prepared by Business in the Community (http://www.bitc.org.uk/about_bitc/index.html).

Coca-Cola Great Britain is responding to the challenge through a total business approach led by a cross-functional senior management team. Four key areas of strategic focus are actively being addressed:

1. Providing and raising awareness of a widening choice of products, particularly making diet and low sugar choices more attractive through continuing taste enhancement.

2. Helping consumers make a more informed choice. Their consumer research showed that around 43 per cent of consumers did not know that diet Coke is sugar-free and it suggested that a sugar-free message is more motivating to consumers than the actual number of calories listed. The sugar-free message now features on all diet Coke packs.

3. Ensuring responsible sales and marketing, by reinforcing their 50-year policy of not targeting under-12s in any media, upholding their Schools Code of Practice including its commitment to not place vending machines in primary schools and give secondary schools the opportunity to provide a wide choice of products from water, 100 per cent juice, a variety of diet, low sugar as well as regular carbonated drinks, and as well as offering unbranded machines.

4. Encouraging physical activity amongst young people and thereby challenging the rise in sedentary lifestyles.

- Green marketing – This area of marketing is largely concerned with environmental value-added propositions related to the product that is being sold to the consumer. Such value addition could consist of many of the points previously discussed, such as packaging, environmentally-safe production techniques, recyclability, reusability, environmentally-friendly sourcing etc. Good examples of this have been provided within the e-goods dial produced by Greenpeace (Figure 4.18).

- Social marketing – This area of marketing is regarded by many authors as related to advertising and public relations. Its main application is linked to programmes aimed at raising awareness and promoting sustainable behaviour (McKenzie-Mohr and Smith, 1999). Often, these programmes are promoted by local councils or government information offices and attempt to increase the adoption of positive social behaviour, such as: recycling, sensible eating, low energy usage or low car usage, amongst many other initiatives. For instance a 'buy-recycled' campaign was launched by the King County Commission staff in 1993, in Washington State. The programme was essentially a partnership with retailers to boost sales of recycled products. Every element of the campaign strategy was designed to do one of three things: show consumers the importance of buying recycled, tell them where they could buy recycled-content products and show them existing product choices. In the end, the campaign produced good results with sales of recycled paper towels, napkins and toilet tissue increasing by 74 per cent (http://www.toolsofchange.com/English/firstsplit.asp).

As marketing evolves in the future, these areas of importance will need to overlap regularly when companies develop and execute their strategies. Understanding green consumer behaviour is a difficult and complex matter, because of the factors influencing decision-making and consumption. In order to embrace all the complexity of this process, the model represented in Figure 4.25 has to be cross-related with the key points highlighted in Figure 4.26.

Unit 4: Contemporary issues in marketing

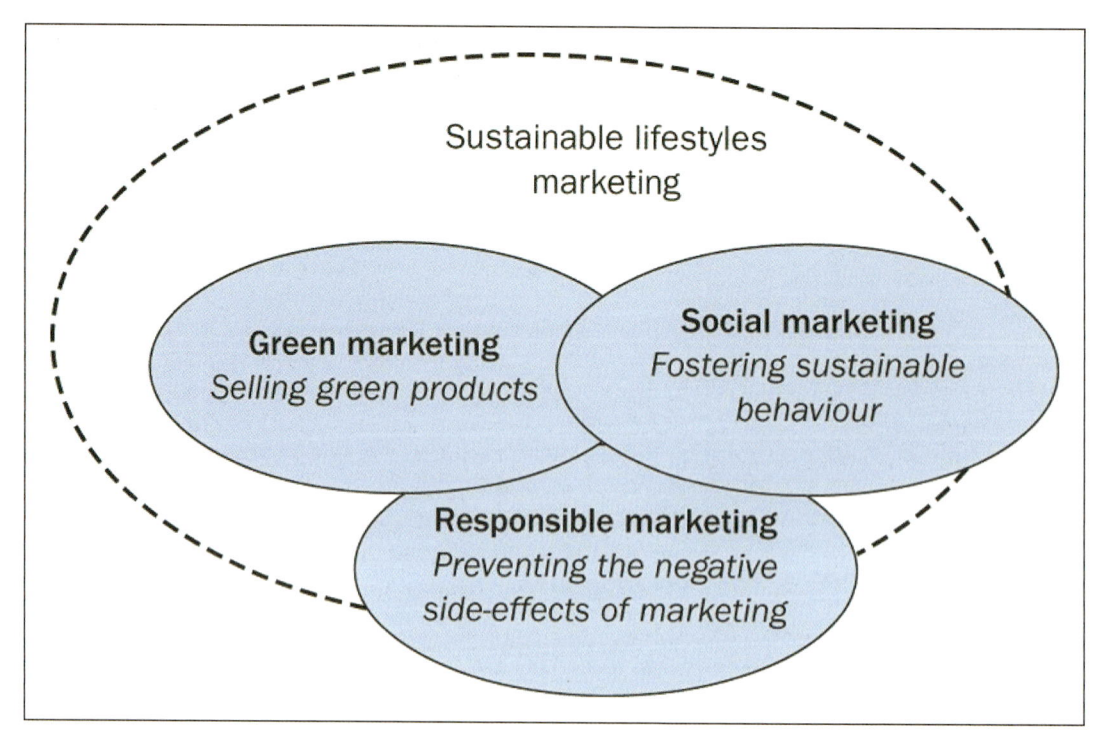

Figure 4.25 A sustainable lifestyles marketing model

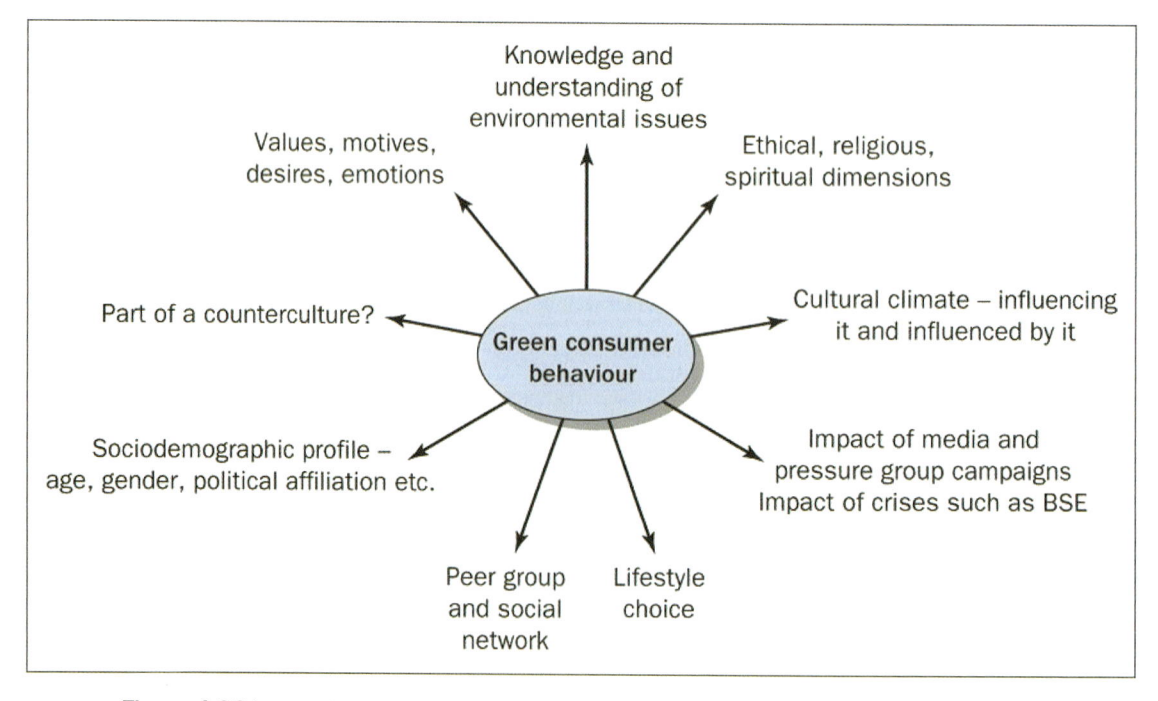

Figure 4.26 Inter-related green consumer factors
Source: Wagner, S. A. (2001) *Understanding green consumer behaviour*, London and New York: Routledge.

126

Unit 4: Contemporary issues in marketing

As the environment takes a pivotal point in the survival of the human race, marketers have a duty not only to anticipate consumer needs but to form them, so that better consumption decisions are made. Companies are beginning to take cognisance of this but unfortunately the majority of consumers are lagging behind. Future technological and biotechnological advances could spell either triumphs or disasters for the environment. Already there is considerable disquiet over the introduction of GM foods. The way in which foods are produced, distributed, commercialized and perceived has been radically changed in the last 20 years by the advent of new technologies such as genetic engineering.

The creation of genetically modified foods and organisms has increased the general public awareness of the elements and the quality of foods. The main concern over GM foods centres on the fact that they have not been tested conclusively in people's diets using rigorous standards (Cottrill, 1998). The negative perceptions surrounding GM foods lie deep in the myths and fears of the modern civilization (the expression 'Frankenstein foods' is a good example) (MacMillan, 2000). Given these negative and in many cases serious concerns about the possible consequences of the environmental spread of 'rogue' genes via cross-pollination, the public are concerned about clarity of messages and product labelling. As a reaction against GM foods and continuing health scares, organic food sales have grown rapidly. The growing and consumption of organic foods, by many, is seen as ecologically friendly and sustainable. Therefore developing marketing strategies that entice, educate and excite consumers in favour of products and services that are sustainable is crucial. Table 4.5 illustrates the possible strategies that companies should adopt when attempting to expand sustainable consumption.

	Limited role	Reactive Role	Proactive Role
Inspiration	Copy pioneers	Acquire pioneers	Be pioneer
Target	Opinion leaders	Niche market	Mass market
Attribute to Brands	None	Differentiating	Entrystake
Claims backed by	No evidence	Green labels	Green labels + Product reprting
Connection with Lobbying	Supports defensive lobbying	Disconnected	Supported by positive lobbying
Other marketing practices	Opposed/Disconnected	Compliance driven	Aligned with sustainability goals

Source: Utopies2008 www.utopies.com

Table 4.5 The evolving role of green products and sustainable lifestyles marketing in mainstream companies' strategy

According to Datamonitor, organic sales in the United States reached $5.4 billion in 1998 and were estimated at $6.4 billion in 1999. Datamonitor (1999) projects sales will continue to grow at approximately 20 per cent per year, reaching $7.76 billion in the year 2000, $9.35 billion in 2001, slightly more than $11 billion in 2002, and slightly more than $13 billion in 2003. Sales during the 1990s grew by 20-24 per cent per year. Organic produce still remains the leading category, although such categories as organic frozen foods, organic dairy, organic bakery items/cereals, organic baby food and organic ready meals are growing at a faster rate. Another aspect of future consumer trends may be the need for convenience, access to product use and a desire to be free from material possessions.

It is quite possible that in the future companies may have to design products that can be shared amongst different individuals. For instance, cars could be pooled within cities and individuals could subscribe to leasing and using cars as and when necessary, picking them up and droping them at their destination. Many other items including recreation products such as surfboards could be leased in such a manner. This type of consumption points the way towards a shared existence, away from the individualistic pursuit of gathering material goods.

Summary

This chapter outlines the major environmental threats to the planet through the consumption patterns of organizations and consumers. It also shows the way in which companies can look at what being green means and how they can translate this into effective action and competitive advantage. It is clear that consumption patterns and consumer actions are going to change as we move further into the 21st Century. Marketing has a key role to play in the greening of companies and the environment and in developing consumer tastes that protect the natural environment more. At the same time it offers a chance to improve the social status of poorer and less well-endowed sections of the developing world. Sustainability issues and ethics go hand in hand and the opportunities that exist are immense for companies that can think and act holistically in meeting the growing demand for greener products. At the same time there is a great onus and opportunity for marketers to begin to change consumer behaviour to create a sustainable future for the world.

Questions for discussion

1. How difficult is it for companies to embrace green marketing strategies?
2. How is consumer behaviour likely to change in the future?
3. How can companies develop strategies for implementing green consumer behaviour?

References

Allenby, B. (1994) Industrial ecology gets down to earth, *IEEE Circuits and Devices*, **10**(1): 20-24.

Anderson, S. and Cavanagh, J. (1996) Top 200: *The Rise of Global Corporate Power*, Institute for Policy Studies, Washington DC.

Anonymous (2000) The State of the World, Worldwatch Institute.

Anonymous (2001) Clean me a river, *New Scientist*, **171** (2303): 17.

Bennet, M. and James, P. (1999) *Sustainable Measures: Evaluating and Reporting of Environment and Social Performance*, Sheffield, UK: Greenleaf Publishing.

Bien, M. (2001) Ethical Investing, Even a Blue Chip Share Can be Green, *The Independent*, February 25 (Foreign Edition). UK.

Charter, M. and Polonsky, M.J. (1999) *Greener Marketing: A Global Perspective on Greening Marketing Practice*, Sheffield, UK: Greenleaf Publishing.

Clift, R. (1995. Clean Technology: an Introduction, *Journal of Chemical Technology and Biotechnology*, **62**: 321-26.

Cottrill, K. (1998) Out of the Lab and Onto the Table, *Journal of Business Strategy*, **19**(2): 38-39.

Crosbie, L. and Knight, K. (1995) *Strategy for Sustainable Business: environmental opportunity and strategic choice*, Maidenhead, UK: McGraw-Hill Book Company Europe.

Datamonitor (1999) *Organic Trade Association and Datamonitor* (Datamonitor's 1999 US Organics Report), Datamonitor.

EPA (1992) *Life Cycle Design Guidance Manual*, Environmental Protection Agency (EPA), EPA 600 1R-92/226, Cincinnati, USA. http://www.epa.gov.

Fornburn, C. (1996) *Reputation, Realising Value from the Corporate Image*. Casmbridge, MA: Harvard Business School Press.

French, H. (2000) Coping with Ecological Globalization, in *The State of the World*. World Institute, New York and London: W.W. Norfton and Company, 184-211.

Fuller, D.A. (1999) *Sustainable Marketing: Managerial-Ecological Issues*, Industrial Examples Sage, Publications Ltd.

GEMI – Global Environmental Management Initiative (1993) *Total Quality Environmental Management*, GEMI, Washington.

GEO-3 (2002) Global Environment Outlook http://www.unep.org/geo/geo3.

Hart, S. L. (2000) *Beyond Greening: Strategies for a Sustainable World*, Business and the Environment, Boston, MA: Harvard Business School Publishing.

Jenkinson, A. (2001) APRIL takes a leaf out of the green book, *Pulp and Paper International*, **42**(8): 19-21.

MacMillan, A. (2000) *Genetically Modified Foods: the British Debate*, http://cbc.ca/news/viewpoint/correspondents/mamillan_gmf.html.

Makower, J. (1994) Beyond the bottom line: putting social responsibility to work for your business and the world, Simon Schuster.

Makower, J. (2006) Green Marketing: Lessons from the Leaders, http://www.worldchanging.com/archives/003502.html.

McKenzie-Mohr, D. and Smith, W. (1999) Fostering Sustainable Behavior, An Introduction to Community-Based Social Marketing, Gabriola Island, British Columbia, Canada: New Society Publishers.

MORI (2003) 'Green Choice' is still a middle class affair, http://www.ipsos-mori.com/polls/2003/ncc.shtml.

National Science Foundation (1998) Science and Engineering Indicators -- 1998, http://www.nsf.gov/sbe/srs/seind98/frames.htm.

NEETF/Roper (2000) *The Ninth Annual National Report Card on Environmental Attitudes, Knowledge and Behaviours*, NEETF/Roper.

Ottman, J. (1993) *Green Marketing: Challenges & Opportunities for the New Marketing Age*, Lincolnwood, IL: NTC Books.

Oyewole, P. (2001) Social Costs of Environmental Justice Associated with the Practice of Green Marketing, *Journal of Business Ethics*, **29**: 239-251.

Peattie, K. (1995) *Environmental Marketing Management*, London: Pitman.

Peattie, K. and Charter, M. (1997) Green Marketing. In McDonagh, P. and Prothero. A. (eds), *Green Management: A Reader*, London: Dryden Press, 388-412.

Piasecki, W. B., Fletcher, K.A. and Mendelson, F.J. (1999) *Environmental Management and Business Management: Leadership Skills for the 21st Century*, John Wiley and Sons.

Procter & Gamble (2003) Sustainability report: Linking Opportunity with Responsibility, http://www.pg.com/content/pdf/01_about_pg/corporate_citizenship/sustainability/reports/sustainability_report_2003.pdf.

Rand Corporation (2000) *Consumer Power and Green Consumption*. http://www.rand.org/scitech/stpi/ourfuture/Consumer/Section6.html.

Sauven, J. (2006) The Odd Couple, *The Guardian,* August 2.

SETAC (1998) *Evolution and development of the conceptual framework and methodology of life-cycle impact assessment*, http://setac.org/files/addendum.pdf.

SPOLD (1995) Synthesis Report on the Social Value of LCA Workshop, SPOLD/IMSA (obtainable from Proctor and Gamble Services Company, Temsalaan 100, 1853 Strombeek-Bever, Belgium; Fax +32 2 568 4812. *Spold terminated its activities at the end of 2001. Its history may be obtained on* http://www.spold.org/whatis.html.

Stauber, J and Rampton, S. (1995) *Toxic Sludge is good for you: Lies, Damn Lies and the Public Relations Industry*, Monore, ME: Common Courage Press.

Talk the Walk (2005) Advancing Sustainable Lifestyles through Marketing Communications, http://www.Uneptie.org/pc/sustain/reports/advertising/Talk_the_Walk.pdf.

UNEP (2005) UNEP Annual Report, http://www.unep.org/Documents.multilingual/Default.asp?DocumentID=67&ArticleID=5125&l=en.

Vogel, D. (2006) The Market for Virtue: The Potential and Limits of Corporate Social Responsibility, The Brookings Institution, Washington USA.

Wasik, J.F. (1996) *Green Marketing and Management: a Global Perspective*, Cambridge, MA: Blackwell.

Wirthlin Institute (2000) Environmental Update, **10**(8), http://209.204.197.52/publicns/Twr1100.pdf.

Wong, V., Turner, W. and Stoneman, P. (1996) Marketing Strategies and Market Prospects for Environmentally-Friendly Consumer Products, *British Journal of Management*, **7**(3): 263-81.

Worcester, R. (1997) Public Opinion and the Environment. in Jacobs, Michael (ed): *Greening the Millennium? The New Politics of the Environment*. Oxford: Blackwell.

http://www.bitc.org.uk/about_bitc/index.html

http://www.toolsofchange.com/English/firstsplit.asp

http://www.greenpeace.org/international/news/green-electronics-guide-ewaste250806.

http://www.greenpeace.org/raw/content/international/press/reports/recycling-of-electronic-waste.pdf.

Corporate identity

Attempting to improve public image and create a public identity is an ancient practice witnessed not least of all in flags and other symbols used to rally the masses and unite them. In recent times, businesses have adopted the practice of nations by adopting a consistent name, logo and tagline. The practice of corporate identity began to assume significant importance in the 1970s, but still confusion exists over the meaning of corporate identity, image and personality. The concept also overlaps with branding but is nevertheless a separate subject area. This section will attempt to provide some understanding of the subject though definitive conclusions can not yet be reached.

The concept of corporate identity is important for the same reason as for branding and relationship marketing – the increasing competition in the marketplace and the need to differentiate. It is also related to the increasing recognition of the importance of integrated marketing communication and associating the organization with certain values that would be appealing to the target audience. This is thought to be helpful in building long-term relationships with customers and other stakeholders. Organizational identity and values are, perhaps, particularly relevant with more politically/ideologically motivated consumers who are interested in social and political issues and encourage some organizations, at least, to consider corporate social responsibility and cause-related marketing. Corporate identity strategy is a systematic attempt at using effective integrated communications to build relationships between an organization and its stakeholders. Corporate identity is the manifestation of an organization's mission statement, values and corporate objectives plus a plethora of visual and behavioural elements that help the organization to project its personality.

Corporate identity – a graphic design approach

Examining the concept in more detail reveals that the original notion of corporate identity was more closely linked to visual identity: logos, organizational nomenclature, buildings, design, stationery and so on. This was basically a graphic design approach and was hugely influential in bringing to the fore the basic elements of importance in designing corporate identity.

One of the influential writers on corporate identity, Olins (1978, 1995) proposed that visual identity can reflect an organization's personality, strategy, branding and communication policies. Olins stresses that in the recent graphic design literature, symbolism has become the focal point and moved from promoting corporate visibility to communicating corporate personality. The graphic design paradigm defines corporate identity as 'an assembly of visual clues -- physical and behavioural -- by which an audience can recognize a company and distinguish it from others and which can be used to represent or symbolize the company' (Abratt, cited in Stuart, 1999).

Corporate identity – integrated communication approach

The integrated communication approach to corporate identity embraces the concept from a PR viewpoint. This approach believes that corporate identity is a tool for the organization to communicate effectively with all of its stakeholders (e.g. Schultz et al., 1994). Emphasis is placed on those processes that are used to strategically create, change and manage an organization's corporate identity and improve its public image. Such processes may begin with the mission statement and positioning of the organization.

Unit 4: Contemporary issues in marketing

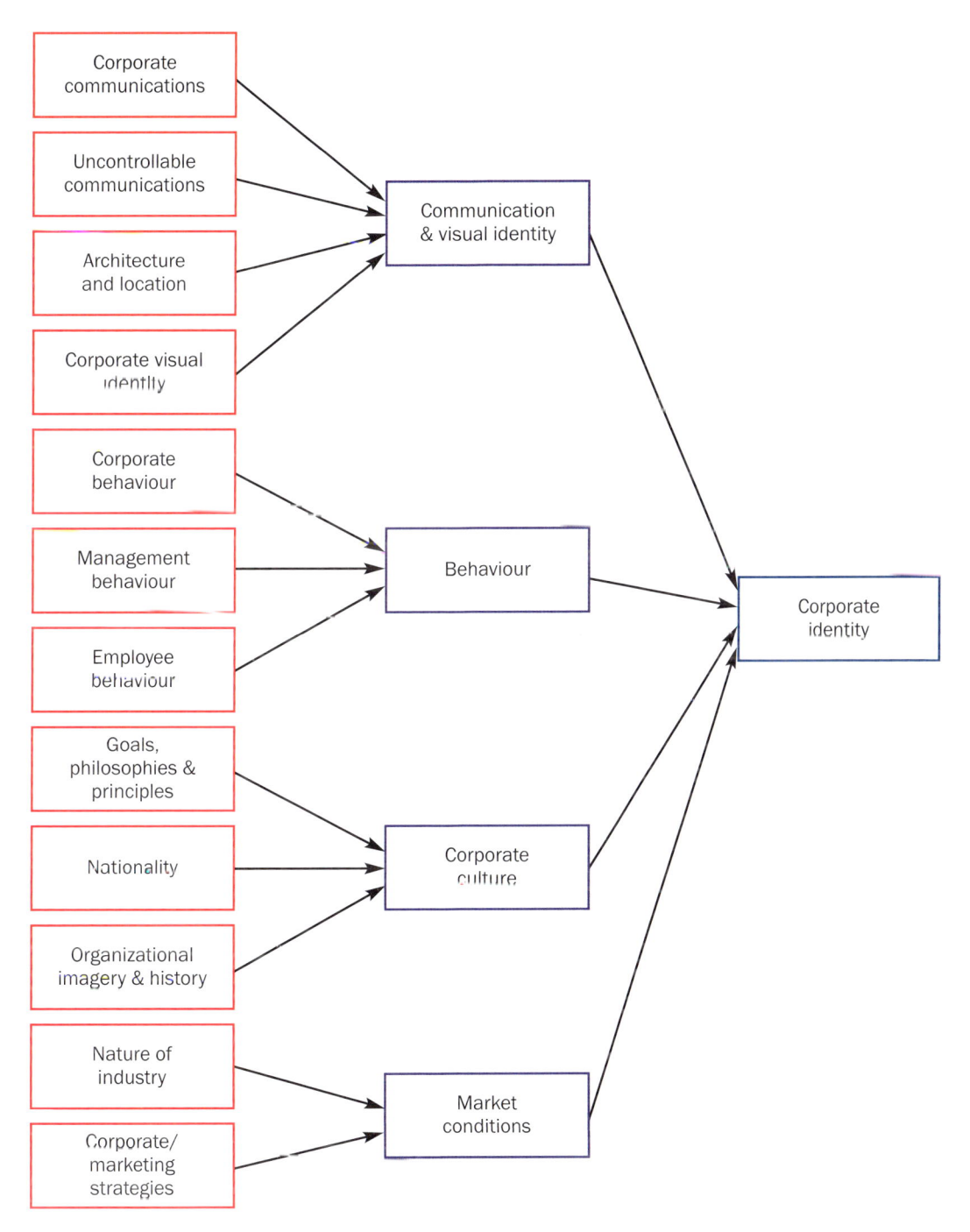

Figure 4.27 Corporate identity and its sub-constructs

Source: Melwar, T.C. and Jenkins, E. (2002) Defining the Corporate Identity Construct, *Corporate Reputation Review*, **5**(1), 76–90.

Synthesis approach

This approach assumes that corporate identity is created through both behavioural and communication strategies, as well as through symbolic elements and visual manifestations. The viewpoint stipulates that image is an expression of corporate personality and as such an externalization of an organization's unique traits, capacities and competencies on a mental, physical and emotional level (Olins, 1995). This approach is a holistic one and regards the organization as an evolving entity.

Defining corporate identity

From the above discussion, it may be discerned that there is not a universal definition of corporate identity. The definition adopted here will be that by Olins (1978) who proposes that corporate identity is 'the tangible manifestation of a corporate personality' and involves the management of all the means that a company uses to present itself through experiences and perceptions to its various publics (Olins, 1995).

Corporate personality

It is suggested that corporate personality is the soul, the spirit of the organization and is unique for every organization (Olins, 1995). It should be pointed out that some authors (Albert and Whetton, 1985) have referred to an organization's character instead of personality.

Corporate/public image

Identity may be suggested to refer to content, whereas image refers to form. When an identity is projected, an image is formed in the individual's mind, and this is how a corporate image is formed (Moffit, 1994).

The role of communications

It is essential that the senior level management effectively communicate the desired corporate identity to all employees and monitor employee behaviour towards customers and other stakeholders. Company's behaviour through its products, services and processes need to be monitored too. Additionally, intentional external communications including advertising, PR, promotions and visual identity elements need to be carefully thought out. Although the communications discussed so far are within the control of the company, other types of communications -- for example, competitor claims, media interpretation, rumours and word of mouth -- are outside the company's direct control but will need to be dealt with effectively by the company. Here, the role of PR becomes apparent.

Integrated communications and consistency are the cornerstones of success in creating and maintaining the desired corporate identity and reputation. Synthesis must exit not just between messages conveyed by different communications tools, used on different occasions, but also between corporate identity and corporate strategy.

References

Albert, S., Whetton, D. (1985) Organisational identity, *Research in Organisational Behaviour*, **7**: 263–295.

Moffit, M.A. (1994) Collapsing and integrating concepts of 'public' and 'image' into a new theory, *Public Relations Review*, **20**(2): 259–2170.

Olins, W. (1978) *The Corporate Personality: An Inquiry into the Nature of Corporate Identity*, London: Design Council.

Olins, W. (1995) *The New Guide to Identity*, London: Gower Publishing.

Schultz, D., Tannenbaum, S.J. and Lauterborn, R.F. (1994) *Integrated Marketing Communications: Pulling It Together and Making it Work*, Chicago: NTC Business Books.

Stuart, H. (1999) Exploring the corporate identity/corporate image interface: An empirical study of accounting firms, *Journal of Communication Management*, **2**(4): 357–371.

Branding

Brands are the major enduring assets of a company, outlasting the company's specific products and facilities (Kotler et al., 2005). A typical definition of branding would be that branding is the process used by a company to distinguish its products from those of its competitors through assigning a name, term, sign, symbol, packaging and design. In reality, though, simply allocating a name to a product and printing a symbol on the package does not really turn a product into a brand, not successfully anyway. Marketing research has to be carried out to determine the physical and emotional needs of target customers, as brands are essentially about emotions, and satisfying of psychological needs. The driver looking proudly at the Mercedes badge on the bonnet of his car is looking at more than a means of transportation, he/she is looking at the vehicle through which the desire to be 'successful' has reached its point of satisfaction. Hence, brands are much more than just names and symbols. They are about feelings, emotions and perceptions and lifestyle statements. To build a successful brand, marketing research should help to make the right decisions about the following:

- **Product benefits** – What are the physical and emotional benefits of buying a brand? In what tangible ways is brand A better than brand B? In what ways and which psychological needs of the target market will brand A satisfy better than brand B?

- **Core values** – Successful brands are built on clear core values, important to the target market, and consistently reinforced through integrated marketing communications. Relevance of such values may be widely different depending on the product category and the target markets and can be revealed through marketing research. Examples of core values are Volvo: safety; BMW: performance, technology, innovation; Pretty Polly: sexy, middle class, young female; Levi: young, sexy, American, original denim jeans; Asda: value for money.

- **Brand associations** – All that is directly or indirectly linked to the brand in the customer's perception. These could include locations, sounds, colours, faces, story lines, attributes and so on. Creating the right associations in the customer's mind is a key aspect of successful branding. Cadbury, the British chocolate manufacturer, keen to promote its 200-year heritage, and its emphasis on quality and tradition uses colour purple in its packaging (royal), as well as a picture of one-and-a-half-pints of milk (quality) and sponsors the longest running TV soap in the UK -- *Coronation Street* (tradition, way of life).

- **Brand image and brand identity** – Brand identity refers to the message sent by the brand owner about the brand. Brand image, on the contrary, is how the target audience perceives the brand. Successful branding implies a great degree of closeness between the two. 'Images surrounding brands enable consumers to form a mental vision of what and who brands stand for. Specific brands are selected when images they convey match the needs, values and lifestyles of consumers' (de Chernatony and McDonald, 1988).

- **Brand personality** – This is the 'character of the brand described in terms of other entities such as people, animals or objects' (Jobber, 2001). For example, a Volvo could possibly be described as a white, middle age, middle-class accountant, whereas a Renault Clio may be described as a young, modern, upwardly mobile woman.

- **Brand names** – Brand names ought to be selected carefully. Ideally a brand name should be short, distinctive, memorable and easy to pronounce. Additionally, a brand name should say something about the product and its benefits and also not have negative meanings in other languages.

- **Branding types (also referred to as branding strategies and branding policies by different authors)** – Companies may choose one or more of the following options:

    1. **Individual branding** – This is when a company uses different brand names for different products (or different versions of the same product), enabling it to position each brand differently in the market, for example up market and down market (Seiko and Pulsar). Here, the failure or success of each brand is of no consequence to other brands of the company, but promotional costs might be high.

    2. **Corporate branding** – This allows a new brand to benefit from the corporate reputation, but a new brand failure can damage that reputation. Also, this approach does not leave much flexibility regarding the positioning of the brand.

    3. **Multi-branding** – Individual differentiation of brands is made possible in this approach and allows for different positioning of the company's different brands with the failure of one not necessarily affecting others. However, promotional costs are normally higher than in corporate branding.

    4. **Range branding** – All the products in a range carry the same brand name, and promotional costs are spread through the range. All the brands within the range may enjoy the same strength while successful, but a failure may affect all the brands in the range. Again, positioning and marketing mix decisions for individual brands are limited as there has to be consistency throughout the range.

5 Private branding/own label brands – In this case, the manufacturer produces under the supplier's own brand name passing all the responsibility for promotion to the supplier. This approach reduces promotional costs but also creates a barrier between the company and the customer.

6 Generic branding – Refers to a brand that does not carry a company name or other distinguishing terms but merely indicates the product category. This option reduces promotional and packaging costs and hence the final price to the customer. This approach means competition is mainly on price and customer service, and psychological elements play a smaller role in differentiation.

7 Brand licensing – This refers to when a company grants permission to another company to use its brand name, in return for a payment or percentage of turnover. This is a good way of earning royalties/fees and expanding the brand quickly. However, problems could arise with regard to such issues as quality control and damage to the brand.

Brand development strategies

- **Brand extension/stretching** – This involves using an existing successful brand to launch new or modified products in a different product category, for example a hi-fi/electronics manufacturer stretching its brand to mobile phones, as in the case of Sony. This is a risky option if consumers find it hard to associate the brand with the new product category. On the contrary, it has the advantage of giving the new product instant recognition through the brand name.

- **Line extension** – This is when new items are added to the product line under the same brand name. This works best if the extension competes with other brands rather than taking the market from the existing items in the line.

- **New brand development** – New brands may be developed for existing or new markets. Ideally, a new brand ought to be capable of real differentiation rather than more or less a copy of existing brands in the market.

Brand revitalization

Every brand has its life cycle, and at some stage, revitalization and re-positioning of the brand may be necessary. Revitalization may be in four shapes (Doyle, 1998):

1 Develop new markets – Saturation of existing markets may be compensated by finding new markets for the brand in geographic areas where the brand may be able to enjoy growth.

2 Enter new segments – This involves attempting to promote the brand to new consumer markets (e.g. different age groups or industry sectors).

3 Find new applications – Finding new uses for existing brands can help revitalize them, for example baking soda used as deodorizer in refrigerators.

4 Increase brand usage rate – There are many ways that a company can attempt to increase the usage of its brands, for example by making it easier to use a brand, by providing incentives to use (loyalty rewards etc.)

Brand positioning

When deciding on the positioning of a brand, various factors need to be taken into consideration. These include the target market in terms of consumers and the competition; the culture and history of the brand (how it has developed over the years); brand assets and attributes in terms of what makes the brand different from competitors; brand values, images and personality; and finally physical and psychological benefits to consumers.

Brand re-positioning

As successful brands take a long time and a large investment to establish themselves, it is not possible to re-position a brand overnight and to change consumers' perceptions. Given adequate marketing research and sustained and integrated marketing communications, however, it is possible to successfully re-position a brand. There are many different types of re-positioning. The two main types are:

1. **Real re-positioning** – This is achieved as a result of product modification and updating.
2. **Psychological re-positioning** – This is about changing consumer beliefs about a brand through advertising and other forms of communications. A recent example of this is Skoda's positioning in the car market, which has over a decade moved from being a very poorly regarded car to a relatively respectable one.

Additional points:

- **Brand equity** – The value of a brand, based on the extent to which it has high brand loyalty, name awareness, perceived quality, strong brand associations and other assets such as patents, trademarks and channel relationships. A brand with strong brand equity is a valuable asset (Kotler et al., 2005). The value of a brand may be shown on a company's balance sheet, although in practice it is very difficult to measure.

- **Global brands** – These are brands that are marketed across national boundaries with the same strategy, the same positioning with little or no change in the marketing mix, for example Coca-Cola. Successful global branding is much more difficult than domestic branding, not least of all because of cultural differences that still exist despite globalization gradually eroding such differences. Branding is essentially built around the concept of core values, and values are the most fundamental components of culture. Cultural differences basically refer to differences, first and foremost, in values and also in attitudes, beliefs and customs. Values are enduring beliefs about right or wrong, good or bad, which we hold as members of society as well as consumers, and which shape our behaviour. Culture will therefore affect whether consumers desire a brand in the first place, how strongly they desire it, to what use they will put it and how often they will use it. Culture will also heavily influence the promotion of brands. As brands are built through associations and images, careful thought will have to be applied to such matters as nudity, gender roles, respect for elders, religious symbols and so on. For example, recently Harrods had to withdraw bikinis depicting the image of Buddha after there was uproar among the Buddhist community.

References

de Chernatony, L., McDonald, M. (1998) *Creating Powerful Brands in Consumer, Service and Industrial Markets*, Oxford: Butterworth-Heinemann.

Doyle, P. (1998) *Marketing Management and Strategy*, 2nd edition, London: Prentice Hall.

Jobber, D. (2001) *Principles and Practice of Marketing*, 3rd edition, Maidenhead: McGraw-Hill.

Kotler, P., Wong, V., Saunders, J. and Armstrong, G. (2005) *Principles of Marketing*, 4th European edition, Harlow: Prentice Hall.

Case history: Re-branding of Skoda

Q: What do you call a Skoda with two exhaust pipes?

A: A wheel barrow!

Skoda began manufacturing cars in Communist Czechoslovakia and has been in business for more than 100 years (www.archives.tcm) and prior to 1989 used old technology and produced basic models. In the Communist state most people could not afford cars and any model had to have economy as the main value attached to a car. After the 1989 revolution a commercial partner was sought, to help the company shed the 'clunky industrial design' image of its cars (www.archives.tcm), and in 1991 Volkswagon (VW) of Germany, a manufacturer associated with advanced car technology, purchased a 30 per cent stake in Skoda. In 2001, VW took total control of the business and attempted to move away from a 'cheap' brand to a 'value-for-money brand' (www.tutor2u.net). The first VW backed model, the Octavia, did not sell well despite unanimously good reviews in the press, and 60 per cent of people questioned still said 'they would never buy a Skoda' (www.tutor2u.net). So it was time to think seriously about re-branding the car and the communications strategy of the brand.

The UK had enjoyed an unprecedented period of sustained economic growth, low unemployment, abundance of credit and consumer spending. The car market was buoyant and sales increased over the past decade. While most people predicted that the economy will slow down somewhat and that competition in most markets will intensify, no one believed there was a recession on the horizon.

An SWOT analysis of the brand showed:

- **Weakness** – Prior to re-branding in the 1990s the brand was perceived as a 'poor quality', 'technologically outdated', 'cheap', 'old fashioned' car for 'old fashioned people'. This image has been largely shed but there was some way to go yet.

- **Strength** – The company, prior to re-branding, had been in business for over 100 years, and had a skilled workforce and existing plants. It had full government backing for its re-branding and expansion plans. It enjoyed cheap labour; hence lower production costs than most Western car manufacturers.

- **Opportunity** – There was an opportunity for the company to create an alliance with VW of Germany in 1991 to improve the technology (the physical aspect of the brand) and also through association with VW, to improve the brand image (the emotional aspect) and to re-position the brand positively in the mind of the target audience. The economic growth in the UK and most Western economies in the 1990s was a further opportunity to pursue re-branding and expansion. Later, the company began to pursue opportunities to expand to Asia with production in India and China.

- **Threat** – Skoda was, and still is, threatened by competition from Korean car manufacturers, and by the slowly rising Russian brand Lada. Economic slow-down in Europe and rising fuel costs are further threats to Skoda. Finally, over-production of cars globally and environmentalist groups pose as threats.

Segmentation, targeting and buyer behaviour

Segmentation and targeting

Segmentaion is often the key to developing a sustainable competitive advantage, and refers to 'the identification of customer groups that respond differently from other groups to competitive offerings' (Aaker, 2005). Various criteria, often a combination of a number, are used for segmenting each market. Appropriate criteria for segmenting the car market are: performance, fuel economy, luxury or budget, level of technology, type of user (e.g. family), type of use (e.g. off road, commercial), etc. Skoda, prior to re-branding was targeted mainly at the budget segment consisting of individuals and families at the low-income end of the market, not so much interested in image, luxury or technology but interested in economy and low price. The aim of the re-branding was to keep the car aimed at the economy, individual and family segment but also to draw in the segment that is interested in luxury, technology and brand reputation. This was a strategy that was to increase sales at a time (1990s) when growing affluence had resulted in a decline for sales of 'mass market' cars but an increase for 'prestige' and 'budget' brands (www.archives.tcm). Skoda was to be seen as a top budget brand.

Consumer behaviour

Cars are durable consumer goods and often said to be the second biggest expenditure after a house purchase, with an average new car costing around £8-£12,000, and hence representing high involvement purchases. Cars are normally not changed frequently and a fair degree of perceived risk is involved in their purchase. Therefore, normally a reasonably high degree of information search is involved. In this market, brand reputation and image created through marketing communications and also through word of mouth are important deciding factors. Of course, a large percentage of cars in the UK are company fleet cars sold in bulk to companies for use by their staff. In this case, as well as the normal factors affecting sales and consumer/customer behaviour the relationship of the car manufacturer or dealer with business clients is also important. Renault UK, for example, have in the past won a prize for their fleet section's customer relationship management programme. This segment of the market seems to have been ignored by Skoda.

Positioning

Positioning is defined as 'the process of creating an image for a product in the minds of target customers' (Dibb et al., 2001) and is closely related to branding. It is achieved thorough the management of marketing communications and other elements of the marketing mix.

Communications strategy

Communications strategy refers to the means of achieving communications objectives. While without insider knowledge it is impossible to know what model of strategic planning Skoda would have used, it would have probably been something similar to STOP & SIT (Smith and Taylor, 2002); that is:

- **Segmentation** – Criteria would have been determined to divide the market. The relevant criteria were discussed earlier.

- **Targeting** – Relevant targets would have been chosen from the identified segments. The main target would have in all probability been determined as male, female, single or married, with or without children, social class B, C1, interested in economy, reliability, value for money and moderate level of luxury and technology.

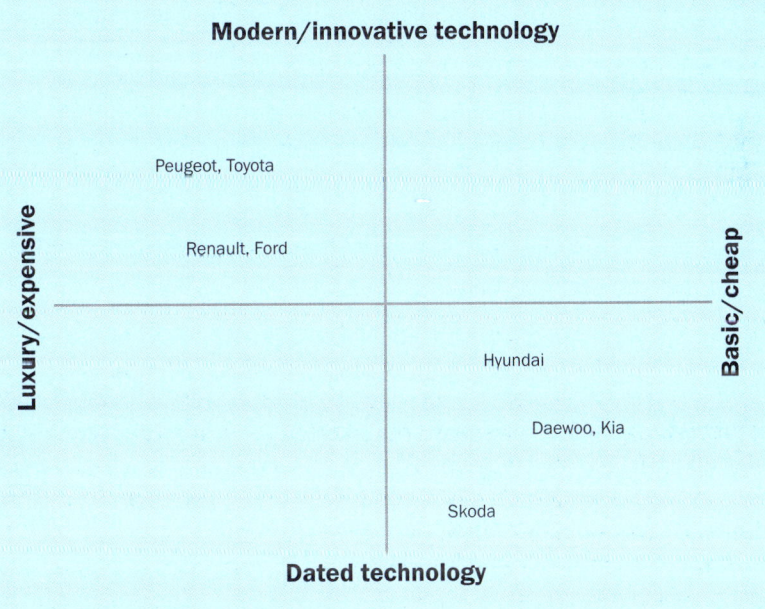

Figure 4.28 Perceptual positioning map of Skoda prior to re-branding

Unit 4: Contemporary issues in marketing

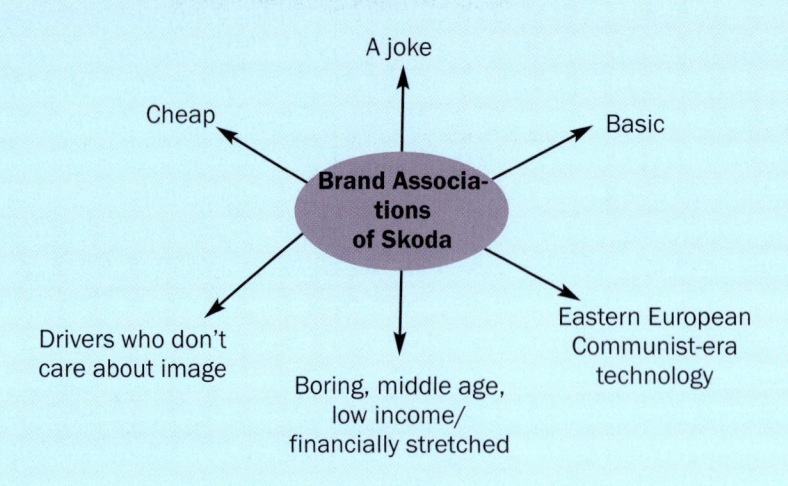

Figure 4.29 Brand associations of Skoda prior to re-branding

Objectives

Objectives would have been set after careful internal audit and environmental, competitor and consumer analysis. As discussed earlier, Skoda's problem was not lack of brand awareness but negative attitudes to the brand. Hence, the main objective was to change negative attitudes to positive ones and this was to be done through re-branding and re-positioning of the brand. The objective would have read something like: Reduce negative attitude or create positive attitude to the brand amongst the target audience by X per cent over Y period (i.e. a SMART objective). The objective if successfully achieved would improve the brand's image amongst the target audience. *Images surrounding brands enable consumers to form a mental vision of what and who brands stand for. Specific brands are selected when images they convey match the needs, values and lifestyles of consumers* (de Chernatony and McDonald, 1998).

Positioning

Positioning is a strategic, not a tactical activity that is concerned with managing perceptions (Temporal, 2000). Skoda would have aimed to re-position the brand closer to the more popular brands in the market on the criteria of technology and luxury features as well price. A perceptual map of Skoda prior to re-positioning is shown in Figure 4.28. The re-positioning, in my opinion, was to place Skoda closer to its European rivals as technologically competing with them and as value for money instead of a cheap brand.

Skoda's re-branding strategy

Skoda's branding strategy was to continue with its corporate branding, where each individual brand also carries the corporate name, e.g. Skoda Octavia. This is common in the car industry. It makes brand extension easy and builds on existing brand awareness, but one sub-brand's failure can affect all others.

Unit 4: Contemporary issues in marketing

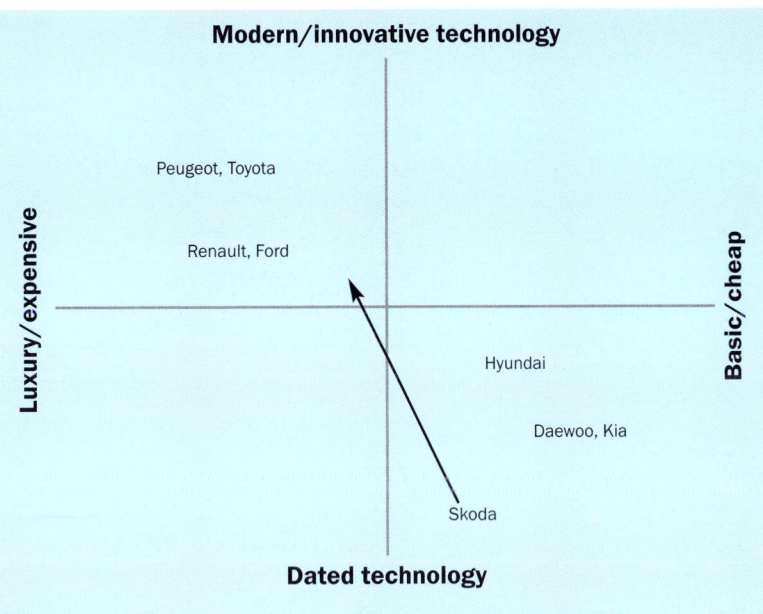

Figure 4.30 Positioning aimed for by Skoda shown by the arrow

(Perceptual map axes: Modern/innovative technology — Dated technology; Luxury/expensive — Basic/cheap. Brands plotted: Peugeot, Toyota; Renault, Ford; Hyundai; Daewoo, Kia; Skoda. Arrow points from Skoda's current position toward the Luxury/expensive–Modern/innovative quadrant.)

Below is an illustration of the desired brand associations aimed for by Skoda. These have been arrived at by a careful study of Skoda's advertising.

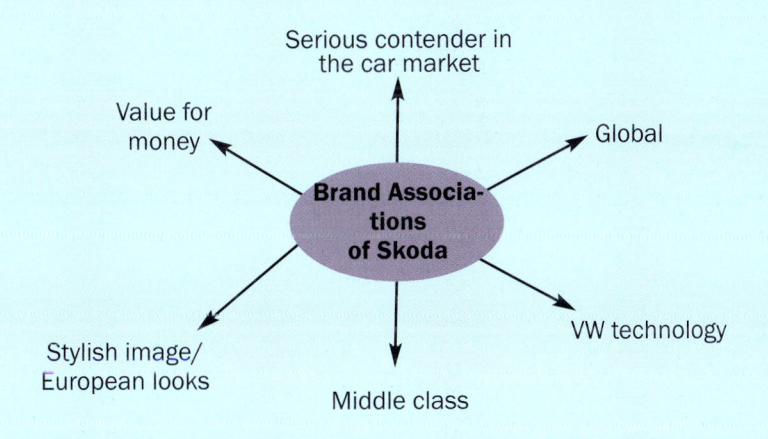

Brand Associations of Skoda:
- Serious contender in the car market
- Value for money
- Global
- VW technology
- Middle class
- Stylish image/European looks

Figure 4.31 Brand associations aimed at by Skoda in the re-branding communications strategy

Stages and integration

Skoda would have drawn up an implementation plan with clear actions and timetables to activate and carry out the strategic plan. They would have given serious thought to the integration of their various tactics so as to send out a clear and uniform signal to the target audience, reducing and eliminating any chance of confusion (noise).

Communications tools or tactics

Communications tools refer to the marketing communications tools that Skoda selected to use in re-positioning of the brand. It must be remembered that other marketing mix tools -- product, price and place -- would have played their role too in the re-branding, but the marketing communications tools that Skoda chose, initially for Fabia and later for other models, were TV and print as well as PR and direct mail campaigns.

The message in the adverts was one that lightly poked fun at customer perceptions: *so good you won't believe it's a Skoda*. Later adverts showed disbelieving customers running away from Skoda showrooms. The PR campaign was aimed at journalists and, as stated earlier, produced positive stories for Skoda. The direct mail was aimed at existing Skoda owners and improving Skoda's image with them.

Evaluation

The success of the campaign could be judged by the increasing sales of Skoda cars, which have continued to rise (www.archives.tcm), and also the fact that after the main thrust of the campaign was finished only 42 per cent of those questioned said they would not buy a Skoda (compared to 60 per cent prior to the campaign) (www.tutor2u.net).

The re-branding and re-positioning of Skoda continues. In 2005 Skoda added another tool of marketing communications to its armoury: sponsorship of the famous cycling event, Tour de France. This is to 'increase the company's profile in both European and global markets', as the event is watched by two billion TV viewers world-wide (www.archives.tcm).

Question

What further advice can you give to Skoda regarding its marketing communications strategy, focusing on enhancing its brand image?

References

Aaker, D.A. (2005) *Strategic Market Management, 7th edition*, Hoboken, NJ: John Wiley.

de Chernatony, L. McDonald, M. (1998) *Creating Powerful Brands in Consumer, Service and Industrial Markets*, Oxford: Butterworth Heinemann.

Dibb, S., Simkin, L., Pride, W. And Ferrell, O.C. (2001) *Marketing Concepts and Strategies, 4th edition*, Boston: Houghton Mifflin.

Smith, P.R. and Taylor, J. (2002) *Marketing Communications: An integrated approach, 3rd edition*, London: Kogan page.

Temporal, P. (2000) *Branding in Asia: The Creation, Development and Management of Brands for the Global Market*, London: John Wiley.

http://www.archives.tcm.ie.

http://www.tutor2u.net.

Source: Roxie Marandi

Case study: Argos

Argos operates within the so-called 'variety goods sector' in the UK and Ireland. Part of the Argos Retail Group is owned by Gus; Argos is the market leader in its field with over 500 high street and out-of-town catalogue showrooms. Argos's business proposition is that of delivering value and choice at locations that are convenient to customers. The latter visit the showrooms and order products from catalogues and collect within minutes after payment. Argos catalogues offer numerous goods: personal items, homeware, electric appliances, TV, hi-fi, sports and photographic equipment, computers and so on. Argos's closest competitor is Littlewoods Index. Argos with an annual turnover of approximately 3 billion pounds (Mintel, 2004) continued to expand the number of its showrooms in 2004 and retailers in the United Kingdom, including Argos, experienced a prosperous 2004, although Christmas sales figures were not as expected. Argos customers are now able to purchase products online or by telephone.

Briefly:

- Argos is the market leader of the non-food mixed goods retailer sector in the United Kingdom.
- Argos' core competencies include the successful operation of a multi-channel retailing network.
- Argos, while competing with a range of department and variety stores, only has one competitor in its strategic group, Littlewoods Index.
- Argos' experience of running the catalogue showroom format appears to be its main source of competitive advantage, ensuring its position as market leader.
- Argos' position in the industry enables it to purchase and retail strongly branded products with value-for-money as its primary trading proposition.

Physical and operational assets

- Over 500 catalogue showrooms.
- Twenty 'Call and Collect' stores.
- Major modern warehousing and distribution network, including Argos Direct Distribution Service and arrangements for delivery direct from manufacturers.
- State-of-the-art call centre facility.
- Argos has undertaken major investment in its operational assets including in its supply chain management, IT systems and warehousing.
- Interactive technologies and plasma screens being introduced to improve customer queuing.

Human resources

ARG has 49,000 employees in the United Kingdom and Europe (www.gusplc.co.uk).

Systems

- IBM Websphere software provides e-commerce infrastructure.
- New IT and software system investments in enterprise and resource planning.
- Software to facilitate management information systems and database analysis.

Marketing assets

- Stores in all major towns and shopping locations.
- Around 50 million catalogues distributed annually. Argos catalogues present in 70 per cent of households (www.4i.co.uk).
- Consumers are able to select from product lines at home, using telephone or use website to check availability and reserve products before travelling to stores.
- Argos is a well-recognized brand name in the United Kingdom and Ireland.
- Argos is the United Kingdom market leader in toys, jewellery, watches, portable audio, small kitchen appliances and is also the leading retailer of furniture and home furnishings.
- Multi-channel distribution network ensures rapid distribution of goods to customers through wide range of distribution channels.

Organizational competencies

Strategic:

- Argos has managed to stay ahead of its main rival Littlewoods/Index.

Functional skills:

- Marketing campaigns successful in terms of customer recall rates (over 75 per cent) (Grant, 2002); 'never out of stock' policy achieved on 500 key lines (accounting for 20 per cent of sales) (Mintel, 2002).
- Money-back guarantee to customers honoured within 16 days of purchase for any reason.

Operational:

- Argos has introduced a successful multi-channel retailing strategy. Its strength is in its experience of operating in the market, where location of stores and distribution network provide access to wide customer base.

Corporate level:

- In addition to achieving market leadership from sales in store, Argos has made innovation part of its strategy: Argos was the first chain to launch a satellite TV channel and became the first in the world to introduce a 'Text and Take Home' mobile phone stock check and reservation service (BBC, 2002).

SWOT analysis

- **Strengths** – Argos established as the UK's leading multi-channel retailer, achieving market leadership in many product lines.

- **Weaknesses** – Argos Additions clothing is currently loss making, and sales in mail order home shopping are declining.

- **Opportunities** – Improvement of customer in-store experience through introduction of modern technologies to improve waiting times; expansion of sales through the Internet.

- **Threats** – Loss of market share to large grocery retailers offering one-stop shopping; continued decline in mail order reducing overall group performance.

Value chain analysis

- Investment in latest technologies to improve customer experience in-store and to ensure purchases may be made in the most convenient way to individual consumers may be considered to be a key value-adding service to consumers.

- Continues to follow an aggressive offensive marketing strategy to ensure it remains the market leader of catalogue and multi-channel retailing in a market in which growth is expanding.

- Latest marketing and promotional campaigns have proved successful.

- Improved inbound logistics are expected to reap benefits of £50 million per year to further improve its sales position (www.argos.co.uk).

Industry analysis

The industry is one in which there is likely to be intense rivalry between competitors. Although goods sold are strongly branded and, therefore, suppliers have some control over prices, the size of the buyers, coupled with suppliers' needs for large distribution channels, gives buyers strength to squeeze suppliers to lower prices. There is growing danger of substitutes from Internet distributors.

Question

Using the information in this case study and any additional information you may be able to find, devise a three-year strategic marketing plan for Argos. Where information is not available make assumptions.

References

http://www.argos.co.uk.

http://gusplc.co.uk.

http://4i.co.uk/expertise.

Grant, J. (2002) Argos aims to broaden audience with 'rock star' theme, *Marketing*, September 5, p.20, London: Haymarket Publications.

> Mintel (2002) Department and Variety Store Retailing in the UK, February, Mintel International Group Ltd.
>
> Mintel (2004) Variety Stores – UK, August, Mintel International Group Ltd.
>
> BBC (2002) Argos Introduce Shopping by txt msg, BBC I News, October 23.
>
> *Source*: Reshma Ranchhod

Internal marketing

SMiP candidates should be aware of the growing importance of internal marketing as a subject area. Berry (1980) first used the term, defining it as 'the means of applying the philosophy and practice of marketing to people who serve external customers so that (i) the best possible people can be employed and retained and (ii) they will do the best possible work. This line of thinking implies a belief that 'to have satisfied customers, the firm must also have satisfied employees' (George, 1990) and that processes such as market research, segmentation, product modification and communication can be applied internally to the organization. Hence, internal marketing is an area where human resource management and marketing, arguably, overlap. Internal marketing is the process aimed at attracting, developing and retaining qualified employees. This is a philosophy that treats employees as customers and develops job products to fit their needs and wants.

The main reason behind proposing the adoption of an internal marketing strategy by those quoted above are the assumptions that motivated and satisfied staff will be more productive and more customer-oriented, providing a better service quality to customers. The suggestion is that internal marketing helps create an internal environment that supports customer orientation among the personnel. Other benefits of internal marketing have been highlighted as helping the alignment of the efforts of the various functions within an organization (Winter, 1985) and a crucial tool in the implementation of strategic change (Piercy, 2002). Ballantyne (2000) suggested that the generation and circulation of knowledge renewal is the main function of internal marketing. Finally, a number of authors, for example Winter (1985), have looked at internal marketing in a wider context and suggested that internal marketing can be used as a tool for motivating employees to help achieve organizational goals.

In summary, Rafique and Ahmed (2000) identify five main elements of internal marketing within the literature:

1. Employee motivation
2. Customer orientation and customer satisfaction
3. Inter-functional co-ordination and integration
4. Marketing-like approach to the above
5. Implementation of specific corporate or functional strategies

In the following paragraphs, the constituent elements of internal marketing will be highlighted.

Employee recruitment, training and empowerment

This refers to the hiring of suitably qualified staff and training them as customer-oriented employees at the same time as paying attention to their personal motivations and personal development needs. The role of employee empowerment is considered crucial in the successful implementation of internal marketing.

Internal application of the marketing concept

Going hand in hand with the above point, internal marketing requires researching employee needs and wants, segmenting them accordingly and helping them satisfy those needs and wants through appropriate staff development, promotion and remuneration.

Internal communication

Communication plays a vital role in internal marketing. Internal communication channels ought to be designed and operated in such a way that they facilitate interaction, exchange of ideas, awareness of organizational objectives and, importantly, feedback. Regular meetings, Intranet, in-house newsletters and magazines, suggestion boxes, away days, team building activities and so on all play a vital role in internal communications.

The debate surrounding internal marketing is concerned with whether it is a tool to be used by management in the pursuit of organizational objectives or whether the objectives and strategies should emerge as a consequence of dialogue with internal and external stakeholders.

References

Ballantyne, D. (2000) Internal relationship marketing: A strategy for knowledge renewal, *International Journal of Bank Marketing*, **16**(6): 274–286.

Berry, L. (1980) Services marketing is different, *Business*, May–June, 25–26.

George, W.R. (1990) Internal marketing and organizational behaviour: A partnership in developing customer-conscious employees at every level, *Journal of Business Research*, **20**: 63–70.

Piercy, N. (2002) *Market-led Strategic Change, a Guide to Transforming the Process of Going to Market*, Oxford: Butterworth-Heinemann.

Rafique, M. and Ahmed, P.K. (2000) Advances in the internal marketing concept: definition, synthesis and extension, *Journal of Services Marketing*, **24**(6): 449-462.

Winter, J. (1985) Getting your house in order with internal marketing, *Workforce*, **80**(5): 84–91.

Social marketing utilizing Internet marketing campaigns

Dr. Calin Gurau

Introduction

Nowadays, marketing has become an effective tool not only for business organizations but also for influencing and changing social behaviour. At the same time, the advent of the Internet as a flexible, dynamic and interactive channel of communication has opened new possibilities for communication and social interaction. Social marketing campaigns can take advantage of this new and increasingly popular medium, adapting the theoretical principles of behaviour change theories to the specificity of Internet communication.

Social campaigns represent a new field of marketing application, both in industrialized and developing countries. They are often prompted by the perception that some situation represents a social problem and merits social action.

As social problems are complex and interrelated, solutions need to be developed in the light of the specific socio-economic, historical, religious and cultural framework (Gray, 1996). Often, segments of society need to be identified who are particularly vulnerable or exposed to be able to develop a targeted campaign.

Some social campaigns are designed merely to help bring problem areas into the open and draw attention to their causes, which can often be a taboo subject. Although increasing the social awareness of a problem is indeed necessary, it is by no means sufficient for determining changes in societal attitudes and behaviours, as these are shaped by habits, interests, feelings and beliefs, among other factors (Novartis, 2001). For these reasons, social campaigns conceived only to educate or admonish often turn out to be relatively ineffective.

These limitations and the success of advertising techniques used in the commercial world provided the impetus for the development of social marketing. Introduced by Philip Kotler and Gerald Zalitrian in 1971, this concept combines traditional approaches to social change with commercial marketing and advertising techniques (Kotler and Andreasen, 1991; Kotler and Zalitrian, 1971). Its originators define social marketing as the design, implementation and control of programs aimed at increasing the acceptability of a social idea or practice in one or more groups of target adopters (Kotler, 1979; Kotler and Zalitrian, 1971).

Previous studies

In the last ten years, social marketing has become an important field of action and research (Lefebvre and Flora, 1988). The number of non-profit organizations and governmental agencies applying social marketing operations has increased substantially, and the operational effectiveness has been refined.

The specialists and practitioners have developed research about organization and ethics of strategic alliances in social marketing (Andreasen, 2000a), the transfer of knowledge concepts and tools from commercial to social marketing (Andreasen, 1984; 2000b), and the organization of specific social marketing campaigns (Andreasen, 2000b; Bang, 2000).

There is also an extensive literature available on the theories and models of behaviour change, which have a direct application in social marketing (Cooper, 1979; Frederiksen et al., 1984; Glanz et al., 1990; Kotler and Clarke, 1986; Rothschild, 1999).

The present paper attempts to respond to the demand formulated by specialists for a potential application of electronic commerce principles and tools to social marketing campaigns. In doing this, it fills a gap in the social marketing research and theory and opens the way for a better understanding of e-marketing techniques that can be applied in social marketing campaigns. Its objectives are both theoretical and practical:

1. To define the characteristics of the Internet tools used for social marketing campaigns.
2. To develop understanding regarding the elements of e-marketing that can increase the effectiveness of social marketing operations.
3. In the light of the theoretical principles identified, to analyse the structure of the websites presently used for social marketing campaigns.

Social marketing is distinguished by its emphasis on the so-called 'non-tangible products, ideas and practices', as opposed to the tangible products and services that are often the focus of commercial marketing (Andreasen, 1995). Considering this, the Internet should be considered as an attractive communication channel for social marketing. As most of the social marketing activities are focusing on changing beliefs, perceptions and attitudes, the ubiquity, flexibility and interactiveness of the Internet can offer important advantages for effective social marketing campaigns.

Social marketing activities are based on the theories and models of social change. If the Internet is ever to be used effectively for social marketing campaigns, the requirements and the elements of these theories have to be incorporated in the design, structure and content of the website.

Theories and models of social change

The correct understanding of the social change theories is paramount for the design, implementation and success of any social programme (Frederiksen et al., 1984; Glanz et al., 1990). Social marketing operations are no exception to this. Theories and models explain behaviour and suggest ways to change its undesirable aspects. They can also provide methods to identify and define the main target audiences and the most effective means to reach them.

When analysing the possibilities of the Internet to provide an effective channel for social marketing campaigns, it is important to identify and describe the specific implications of these theories/models in the digital environment.

Adopting an ecological perspective on social marketing

The ecological perspective provides two key ideas for identifying the individual and environmental leverage points for social marketing operations.

First, behaviour is viewed as being affected by, and affecting, multiple levels of influence. Five levels of influence for health-related behaviours and conditions have been identified.

They are: (1) intrapersonal or individual factors; (2) interpersonal factors; (3) institutional or organizational factors; (4) community factors; and (5) public policy factors (McLeroy et al., 1988).

The application of this principle to Internet campaigns results in the following propositions:

◆ **Proposition 1:** The online social marketing campaign has to integrate and to interact with the physical elements of the social marketing campaign (integration).

◆ **Proposition 2:** The online social marketing campaign should address and include, as much as possible, elements from all possible levels of influence (complexity).

The second key idea relates to the possibility of reciprocal causation between individuals and their environments; that is, behaviour both influences and is influenced by the social environment. From the Internet perspective, this principle has the following consequence:

◆ **Proposition 3:** The online social campaign has to influence and be influenced by the social environment (interactiveness and flexibility).

This multi-level, interactive perspective clearly shows the advantages of multi-level interventions, such as those that combine behavioural and environmental components.

Table 4.5 An ecological perspective: levels of influence

Concept	Definition
Intrapersonal factors	Individual characteristics that influence behaviour, such as knowledge, attitudes, beliefs and personality traits
Interpersonal factors	Interpersonal processes, and primary groups including family, friends, peers, that provide social identity, support and role definition
Institutional factors	Rules, regulations, policies and informal structures, which may constrain or promote recommended behaviours
Community factors	Social networks and norms, or standards, which exist as formal or informal among individuals, groups and organizations
Public policy	Local, state, federal policies and laws that regulate or support healthy actions and practices for disease prevention, early detection, control and management

Source: Adapted from National Cancer Institute (1995)

Cognitive behavioural models

Contemporary behaviour models at the individual and interpersonal levels usually fall within the broad category of cognitive behavioural theories (Bandura, 1977 and 1986; Fishbein and Azjen, 1975). Two main concepts are common to these theories (National Cancer Institute, 1995):

1. Behaviour is mediated through cognitions: what we know and think affects how we act.

2   Knowledge is necessary but not sufficient to produce behaviour change. Perceptions, motivation, skills and factors in the social environment also play important roles.

The application of these principles to Internet marketing operations imply the following:

◆   **Proposition 4:** The online social marketing campaign should try to influence/change knowledge (education).

Proposition 1 is reinforced.

The 'Stages of Change' model

The 'Stages of Change' model explains the behaviour change of individuals. The basic premise of this model, introduced by Prochaska and DiClemente (Prochaska et al., 1992), is that behaviour change is a process and not an event and that individuals have different levels of motivation, or readiness, to change. People at different points in the process of change can benefit from different interventions, matched to their stage at that time.

Five distinct stages are identified in the 'Stages of Change' model: pre-contemplation, contemplation, decision/determination, action and maintenance.

It is important to understand that this is a circular, not a linear, model. People do not go through the stages rigidly; they can enter and exit at any point and often recycle. Also, there appear to be differences in how the stages fit the situation for different problem areas. For example, with a problem that involves overt, easily recognized behaviour and includes a physical addiction component (e.g. alcoholism), the stages might have a different meaning than with a problem where target goals are not easily identified and where undesirable

Table 4.6 The 'Stages of Change' model

Concept	Definition	Application
Pre-contemplation	Unaware of problem, has not thought about change	Increase awareness of need for change, personalize information on risks and benefits
Contemplation	Thinking about change in the near future	Motivate, encourage to make specific plans
Decision/determination	Making a plan to change	Assist in developing concrete action plans, setting gradual goals
Action	Implementation of specific action plans	Assist with feedback, problem solving, social support, reinforcement
Maintenance	Continuation of desirable actions or repeating periodic recommended step(s)	Assist in coping, reminders, finding alternatives, avoiding slips/relapses

Source: Adapted from National Cancer Institute (1995)

habits may have been formed without physiological addiction (e.g. following a diet with no more than 30 per cent calories from fat).

The 'Stages of Change' model can be used both to understand (explain) why people are sensitive to different methods of behaviour change and to develop a better-targeted social marketing campaign. Translating these possibilities in the Internet environment, it can be said that:

◆ **Proposition 5:** The online social marketing campaign should be adapted to the specific problems targeted for change (circumstantial adaptation).

◆ **Proposition 6:** The online social marketing campaign should use appropriate messages targeted to different audiences (segmentation, targeting and customization).

The 'Health Belief' model

The 'Health Belief' model (HBM) can be useful in analysing these people's inaction or non-compliance. It was one of the first models that adapted theory from the behavioural sciences to health problems, and it remains one of the most widely recognized conceptual frameworks of health behaviour (National Cancer Institute, 1995). It was originally introduced in the 1950s by psychologists working in the US Public Health Service (Hochbaum, Rosenstock, Leventhal and Kegeles). They assumed that people feared diseases and that health actions were motivated in relation to the degree of fear (perceived threat) and ex-

Table 4.7 The 'Health Belief' model

Concept	Definition	Application
Perceived susceptibility	One's opinion of chances of getting a condition	Define population(s) at risk, risk levels; personalize risk based on a person's features or behaviour; heighten perceived susceptibility if too low
Perceived severity	One's opinion of how serious a condition and its sequelae are	Specify consequences of the risk and the condition
Perceived benefits	One's opinion of the efficacy of the advised action to reduce risk or seriousness of impact	Define action to take; how, where, when; clarify the positive effects to be expected
Perceived barriers	One's opinion of the tangible and psychological costs of the advised action	Identify and reduce barriers through reassurance, incentives, assistance
Cues to action	Strategies to activate 'readiness'	Provide how-to information, promote awareness, reminders
Self-efficacy	Confidence in one's ability to take action	Provide training, guidance in performing action

Source: Adapted from National Cancer Institute (1995).

pected fear-reduction potential of actions, as long as that potential outweighed practical and psychological obstacles to taking action (net benefits).

The HBM can be summarized in terms of four constructs representing the perceived threat and net benefits: perceived susceptibility, perceived severity, perceived benefits and perceived barriers (National Cancer Institute, 1995). These concepts were proposed as accounting for people's 'readiness to act'. An added concept, cues to action, would activate that readiness and stimulate overt behaviour. A recent addition to the HBM is the concept of self-efficacy, or one's confidence in the ability to successfully perform an action. This concept was added by Rosenstock et al. (1988) to help the HBM better fit the challenges of changing habitual unhealthy behaviours, such as being sedentary, smoking or overeating.

As in the case of the 'Stages of Change' model, the HBM can be used to explain people's behaviour and to design better social marketing strategies for behaviour change. From the Internet marketing perspective, this model directs towards the following:

◆ **Proposition 7.** The online social marketing campaign should emphasize the disadvantages of the present situation and the positive aspects of change, and minimize, or provide solutions regarding, the barriers to change (strategic approach).

Proposition 6 is reinforced.

Research methodology

To identify and define the characteristics of the websites used for online social marketing campaigns, 57 websites have been accessed and analysed. From these websites, 44 (77.2 per cent) were related with health problems (including smoking, drugs and alcohol consumption), 10 (17.5 per cent) were related with environmental issues (environmental protection) and 3 (5.3 per cent) with road safety.

Taking into consideration the propositions formulated in relation with the social change theories applied in social marketing, the survey attempted to identify the website elements in Table 4.8.

The survey approach was characterized by three main features, determined by the specificity of social marketing campaigns and by the complexity of research objects (websites):

1 **A focus on qualitative aspects** – As a simple quantitative analysis of online messages would have provided a limited perspective on the strategic design and effects of Internet social marketing campaigns, the survey has not only categorized the types of online information but also studied their capacity to segment and target different user segments, the strategic connection between different types of messages and their integration into the general website structure.

2 **Abstractization** – Starting from the specific features of every investigated website, the study attempted to identify and define the main characteristics of the Internet tools for social marketing campaigns and to describe the principles of their functioning.

3 **Critical perspective** – Considering the existing structure and use of the websites dedicated for social marketing campaigns, as well as the principles derived from the theories of social change, the study tried to provide recommendations for future improvements.

Unit 4: Contemporary issues in marketing

Table 4.8 The elements of websites and their corresponding function for social marketing campaigns

Elements	Function
Online information about site integration with the physical world social marketing campaign	Integration with other social marketing policies
Online messages addressing individual, interpersonal, institutional, community and public policy problems and factors	Capacity of the website in presenting different aspects of the same problem
Online possibilities for interaction between users, organization and community: • Interaction with the organization (telephone number, e-mail) • Interaction with the site (search, personalization tools) • Interaction with the community (discussion forums)	Capacity of the website to provide personalized interactive possibilities and to build a dynamic communication pattern
Time passed since last update	Flexibility and content relevance
Educational messages	Capacity of the website to educate its users
Site content, structure and design in relation with the subject presented	Capacity of the website to adapt to the social marketing topic
Online messages targeted to the users in different stages of the behaviour change process: • Pre-contemplation • Contemplation • Decision • Action • Maintenance	Capacity of the website to segment and target different audiences
Online messages that: • Emphasize – disadvantages of undesirable behaviour; positive aspects of behaviour change • Minimize – barriers to change • Provide solution for surpassing the barriers to change	Strategic approach of the online social marketing campaign

Research findings

1. The online social marketing campaigns are usually integrated with other marketing operations, but indirectly (as for example online messages about social marketing events). The connection is not clearly specified, and the website is often limited to the function of advertising channel.

2. The information presented by the websites addresses the social problems from different perspectives, including individual (online messages relevant for individual behaviour/situations), interpersonal (the effect of undesirable behaviour on friends, relatives and so on), institutional (organizations that support behaviour change and their specific policies), community (community events, social statistics, discussion forums) and social policy (regulations/legislation/initiatives relevant to the social problem addressed, the official opinion of government and other non-profit organizations) elements. It is important to note that the messages addressing various issues are also influenced by the characteristics of the social problem being addressed and by the strategic approach of the website.

3. The interactive possibilities of the studied website are extremely different. Usually, every site offers a very clear connection with the organization, providing the physical address, telephone numbers, e-mail connections or standardized feedback forms.

4. The second more frequent interactive feature is the existence of virtual communities that are connected through bulleting boards or discussion forums. The use intensity of these discussion forums varies a lot, ranging from less than 10 messages/month to more than 100 messages/month. The identification of factors that determine and influence the use intensity of discussion forums on social topics is a good subject for future research, because the capacity to provide social interaction and a sense of community between distant people is one of the major advantages offered by the Internet.

5. Another interesting feature of the discussion forums is their rather limited geographical reach. Most of the users are located regionally or nationally. Although this is understandable considering the local, regional or national character of the sponsor organizations, this limitation does not take advantage of the international dimension of the Internet network.

6. The capacity of websites to become personalized is quite low. Some sites offer a rudiment of personalization, asking the user to select a specific topic of interest. Usually, these are the sites that offer connections to multiple and various subjects.

7. The period of time passed since the last website update varies greatly, ranging from two years to two weeks. However, most of the studied sites (83 per cent) have been updated in the last three months. The necessity of frequent updates is given by the communication function of websites, many of them providing free newsletters and updated lists of relevant news and social events.

8. One of the main purpose of social marketing websites is to educate its users. This function is evident considering the large number of reports, social statistics, documents explaining the consequences of undesirable behaviour and the benefits of change, which are available online. The editing of these texts and their specified purpose is also demonstrating the strategic approach of online marketing campaigns and the circumstantial adaptation to the problem addressed. In some cases,

children are directly targeted by the educational messages displayed on social marketing websites, and there are attempts to create virtual communities of children (www.srsc.org.uk). Often, the sites provide lists of links to other similar sites created by international or foreign organizations, enhancing the interconnection and the international dimension of the social marketing educational sources.

9   The social marketing website show a high degree of circumstantial adaptation to the problem addressed. The content is highly relevant and in most cases frequently updated. The structure is complex, because most sites present a large amount of information. However, the existence of site maps and general contents lists provides a clear picture of information categories and eases the web navigation. The design is both appropriate for the subject of the website and for the profile of the main users:

- The sites targeting younger users (children and teenagers) are more colourful, dynamic, direct, surprising, involving.
- The sites targeting older users are more sober and structured; the accent is put on increased accessibility and ease of navigation.
- The health-related sites focus mainly on scientific facts, using these as powerful arguments for change; these are also supported by practical advice/procedures for health improvement or maintenance.

10   The capacity of social marketing websites to segment and target the users belonging to different stages of the behaviour change process is not very evident. The sites rely on the capacity of the users to segment themselves, by choosing from the information available, the topics of main interest. In many cases, the user is supported by mini search engines active within the site (67 per cent of the surveyed sites had a mini search engine available within the site). This strategy can be justified by the great diversity of people accessing the site and the limitations of personalization tools available. However, considering the common characteristics of the users from different stages of the behaviour change process, the online marketing sites should implement more active methods to segment the users and to differentiate their information offering. This is a necessary premise for increasing the effectiveness of online social campaigns and for saving the time of Internet users.

11   Most sites (93 per cent of the surveyed websites) adopt a strategic approach. The information provided addresses both the negative aspects of the undesired behaviour and the possible benefits of behaviour change. In many cases, the barriers to change are identified, explained (reports, FAQ, personalized communication and discussion forums) and practical solutions are provided for their resolution or avoidance (www.ash.org.uk).

Online social marketing – a theoretical framework

The theoretical principles of online social marketing derived from the research findings can be considered on two different levels:

1   A content level
2   A functional level

This classification corresponds to the specific characteristics of a website that can be defined through the categories of contents hosted and by the multiple functionalities provided:

1. At the content level, the research findings have demonstrated a close connection between the message categories, the strategic approach and the circumstantial adaptation of the website. However, these three dimensions seem to lack a close connection with the segmentation of different categories of audience.

   The implementation of a better segmentation approach at the early stages of website access can provide the basis for better targeting and customization of online information. For example, a number of website alternatives can be designed to target the specific needs of the users in pre-contemplation, contemplation, decision, action and maintenance stages and then connected with a practical method to characterize each individual user (such as a short online questionnaire). Once the new user has completed the questionnaire, the software can automatically identify his/her needs and make a connection to the most appropriate website alternative.

   The content is not internationally adapted. The context of the problems debated, the organizations involved and the contact numbers are all local, regional or national. The Canadian sites investigated are bilingual (English and French), providing a possible international dimension and a language-based segmentation of the users. However, the alternative sites are identical in content, structure and design, which shows that the cultural differences between these communities are not considered for specific site adaptation.

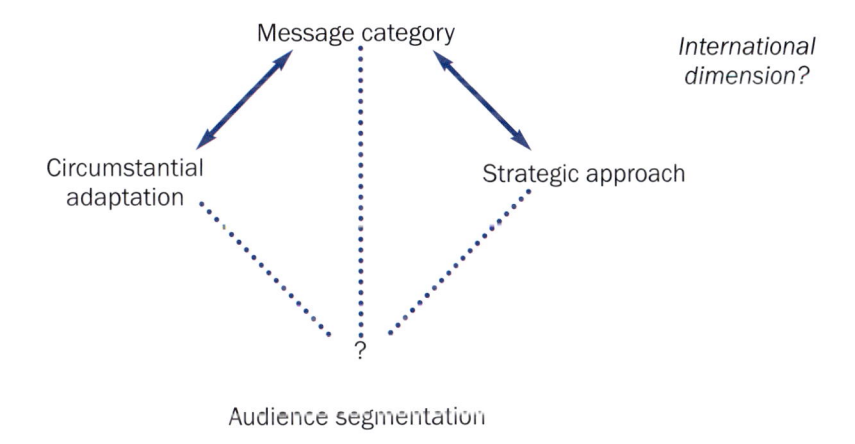

Figure 4.32 The 'diamond' of content dimensions of a social marketing website

2. At functional level, the social marketing online campaigns fulfil well the three main functions of a website:
   - Interactiveness
   - Education
   - Flexibility

Unfortunately, the integration of the online campaign with other social marketing operations is vague and indirect, when it exists. Every web function should aim to be integrated in a complex network of digital and physical events and processes, which can enhance the effectiveness of the whole campaign. For example, the education provided on the web can be connected with open-day seminars organized within local communities, when the representatives of the social marketing organization can meet, discuss and interact with the Internet users.

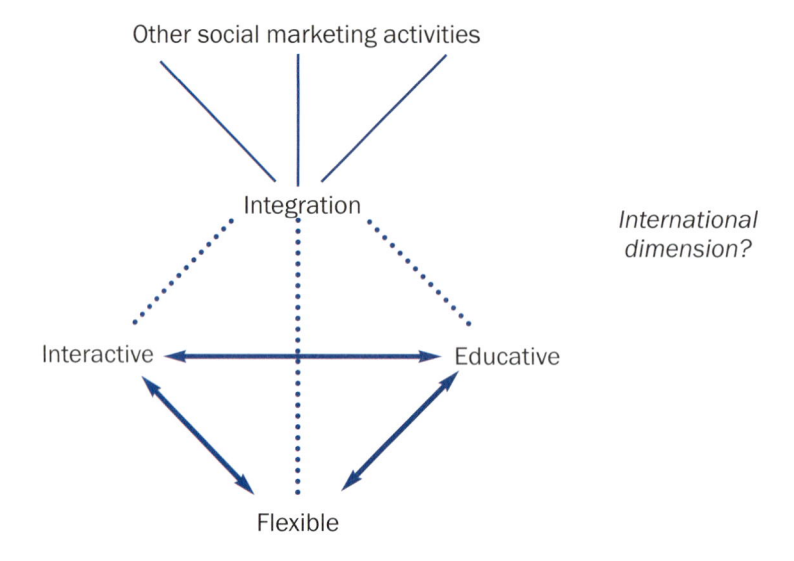

Figure 4.33 The 'diamond' of functional dimensions of a social marketing website

The improvement of these connections at content and functional levels will improve the overall effectiveness of the Internet social marketing campaigns. In fact, the recommendations for improving these two levels are inter-related: a better segmentation of the Internet users will help the integration of the online campaign with the appropriate social marketing events. This way, specially targeted environments will be designed to address the specific needs of people, both in the digital and in the physical universe. The effectiveness of the campaign will be further enhanced through the application of life-cycle theories of behaviour change and by the complex combination of Internet information and social events.

The integration can also enhance the international dimension of the online social marketing campaign. Connections with global institutions and events can increase the scope of the campaign and the reach of its influence.

Concluding remarks

Social marketing is most successful when it is implemented as a systematic, continuous process, which is driven at every step by decision-based research used as feedback to adjust the program. A clear, workable marketing process includes six stages: analysis, planning, development of plan elements, implementation, assessment of in-market effectiveness and feedback to the first stage. There is constant research-based feedback and planning within each stage as well.

To change the consumer's behaviour, one must first understand both what drives and maintains current behaviour and what 'levers' in the consumer's life and environment might drive and maintain the new behaviour. To create and run an effective program, one must also understand the characteristics and the constant evolution of potential intermediaries, channels of distribution and communication.

The Internet has changed the rules of the classical models of communication. If previously the one-to-one communication (e.g. telephone conversation) and one-to-many communication (e.g. TV broadcast) offered little feedback and interaction between the sender and the receiver(s), the Internet has created a complex communication model, in which one-to-one, one-to-many and many-to-many communication can be dynamically conducted between distant people. The medium itself has become an active element of the interaction: the communicators can create content within the medium, shaping a communicational universe in permanent evolution and expansion.

The Internet allows social interaction without limitations of space and time and instantaneously segments and aggregates audiences around specific interests. The profile of Internet users has become more diverse in the last two years, the web space being shared and used by people of different ages, levels of income and education. Because of these characteristics, the Internet becomes a primary channel for implementing social marketing campaigns.

Despite its specific advantages (flexibility, interactiveness and dynamism), the Internet remains, however, only a communication channel. The type and the format of the information transmitted online is extremely varied, but to be effective, the online social marketing campaigns have to fulfil the same objectives (change of undesirable behaviour), using the same theoretical principles (the theories of behavioural change).

This paper has presented the principles of online social marketing campaigns (integration, complexity, interactiveness and flexibility, education, circumstantial adaptation, segmentation, targeting and customization and strategic approach), interpreting the theories of behaviour change applied by social marketing from a specific Internet perspective. These theoretical principles have then been verified through the survey of social marketing websites.

The findings have shown that:

1. Most of the social marketing websites are well designed, applying the principles of behaviour change theories and providing a wealth of useful information.
2. The interactiveness of the social marketing websites is usually good; the sites offering possibilities for one-to-one, one-to-many and many-to-many interaction. However, the interactiveness is limited to local, regional or national communities, the online campaigns not taking full advantage of the international dimension of the Internet.

3   The flexibility of the websites is quite limited to simple choices of topics. Most of the sites are often updated, offering regular digital newsletters and lists of social events.

4   The segmentation of users is not very sophisticated, the organizations relying on the users to select themselves the topics of their interest. A future study should investigate if the sponsor organizations do receive any form of feedback from the users, regarding their interest priorities, and if they transform the websites accordingly (e.g. direct connection to the pages of high interest priority, more information about the topics of high interest). A better segmentation and targeting (applying the principles of behaviour change theories) of different categories of users would increase the effectiveness and the popularity of these websites.

5   The integration of the online campaign with other social marketing operations is not clearly defined.

The triangles of relationships created at the content and functional levels of these websites have to be transformed into diamonds, to combine efficiently the advantages of Internet communication with the objectives of social marketing campaigns. These transformations should always be based on a continuous process of analysis, planning, feedback and evaluation, whose conclusions can direct the evolution of websites towards a better adaptation to users' needs.

The importance of web design for social marketing campaigns is demonstrated by the initiative of some sponsor organizations to publish online checklists for website planning (Health Canada, 2000; www.helping.org:80/nonprofit/).

The present study has a number of limitations determined by the restrictions of the research methodology applied. The number of websites investigated was not very large, and the sponsor organizations have not been directly contacted to provide primary information about their Internet marketing strategies. The future studies should fill these gaps, creating a more complete picture of the Internet social marketing campaigns. The importance of creating a comprehensive model of Internet-enabled social marketing is paramount, because the importance and the popularity of Internet communication and interaction will increase in the future.

References

Andreasen, A.R. (1984) A power potential approach to middlemen strategies in social marketing, *European Journal of Marketing*, **18**(4): 56–71.

Andreasen, A.R. (1995) *Marketing Social Change,* San Francisco: Jossey-Bass.

Andreasen, A.R. (2000a) Alliances and ethics in social marketing, *Ethics in Social Marketing,* Washington: Georgetown University Press.

Andreasen, A.R. (2000b), Intersector transfer of marketing knowledge, Paul N. Bloom and Gregory T. Gundlach, *Handbook of Marketing and Society,* Thousand Oaks: Sage Publications.

Bandura, A. (1977) *Social Learning Theory*, Englewood Cliffs, New Jersey: Prentice-Hall.

Bandura, A. (1986) *Social Foundations of Thought and Action,* Englewood Cliffs, New Jersey: Prentice-Hall.

Bang, H.-K. (2000) Misplaced marketing, *Journal of Consumer Marketing,* **17**(6): 479–480.

Cooper, P.D. (1979) *Health Care Marketing: Issues and Trends,* Germantown: Aspens Systems Corporation.

Fishbein, M., Azjen, I. (1975) *Belief, Attitude, Intention, and Behavior: An Introduction to Theory and Research,* Massachusetts: Addison-Wesley Publishing, Reading.

Frederiksen, L.W., Solomon, L.J., Brehony, K.A. (1984) *Marketing Health Behavior: Principles, Techniques, and Applications,* New York: Plenum Press.

Glanz, K., Lewis, F.M., Rimer, B.K. (1990) *Health Behavior and Health Education Theory, Research, and Practice*, San Francisco: Jossey-Bass, Inc.

Gray, R. (1996) Making an impact on society, *Marketing,* **15**: 26–28 August.

Health Canada (2000) Needs Assessment Checklist, http://www.hc-sc.gc.ca/hppb/get-wcb ready/checklists/needsassessment.html.

Kotler, P. (1979) Strategies for introducing marketing into nonprofit organizations, *Journal of Marketing,* **43**(1): 37–44.

Kotler, P., Andreasen, A.R. (1991) *Strategic Marketing for Nonprofit Organizations,* Englewood Cliffs, Prentice-Hall, 4th edition.

Kotler, P., Clarke, R.N. (1986) *Marketing for Health Care Organizations,* Englewood Cliffs: Prentice-Hall.

Kotler, P., Zalitrian, G. (1971) Social marketing: An approach to planned social change, *Journal of Marketing,* **35**: 3–12.

Lefebvre, R.C., Flora, J.A. (1988) Social marketing and public health intervention, *Health Education Quarterly,* **15**(3): 299–315.

McLeroy, K.R., Bibeau, D., Steckler, A., Glanz, K. (1988) An ecological perspective on health promotion programs, *Health Education Quarterly,* **15**: 351–377.

National Cancer Institute (1995) Theory at a glance, http://oc.nci.nih.gov/services/Theory_at_glance/HOME.html.

Novartis (2001) A Short Course in Social Marketing, www.foundation.novartis.com/social_marketing.htm.

Prochaska, J.O., DiClemente, C.C., Norcross, J.C. (1992) In search of how people change: Applications to addictive behaviors, *American Psychologist,* **47**(9): 1102–1112.

Rosenstock, I.M., Strecher, V.J., Becker, M.H. (1988) Social learning theory and the health belief model, *Health Education Quarterly,* **15**: 175–183.

Rothschild, M.L. (1999) Carrots, sticks and promises: A conceptual framework for the management of public health and social issues behaviors, *Journal of Marketing,* **63**: 24–37, October.

www.ash.org.uk.

www.helping.org:80/nonprofit.

www.srsc.org.uk.

Contemporary issue in the context of the case study

This unit highlights some of the major issues surrounding company organization and development in an ever-diminishing energy base within a competitive world. Issues of sustainability, branding, corporate identity and responsibility as well as customer loyalty are becoming extremely important for developing marketing strategies. These topics are now at the forefront of many company decisions. Students should become well versed in these contemporary issues.

Unit 5 Effective customer orientation

Learning objectives

In this unit you will:

- Formulate and present a creative, customer focused and innovative competitive customer strategy for any given context, incorporating relevant investment decisions, appropriate control aspects and contingency plans.
- Promote and facilitate the adoption and maintenance of a strong market and customer orientation with measurable marketing metrics.

This unit will build on the concept of relationship marketing within the customer context as already discussed in the previous unit:

1. Market orientation and customer orientation
2. Details of financial analysis and marketing metrics as control mechanisms
3. Discussion and formulation of contingency plans

Introduction

Being customer-focused is becoming an important plank of many organizations' marketing strategies. Being customer-focused largely results from well-developed customer orientation strategies.

Market and customer orientation

For many years, there have been discussions about market orientation and its meaning to organizations when producing marketing strategies. Market orientation has as its main constructs:

- Intelligence gathering
- Intelligence dissemination
- Competitor analysis
- Customer analysis

Unit 5: Effective customer orientation

In addition to the above, companies face turbulent environments moderating the strategies they adopt for both customers and competitors. It could be argued that a truly market-oriented company is one that organizes its activities, products and services towards the needs of its customers, in a better manner than its competitors.

However, the essence of all the arguments lies in the following:

1. **Information generation** – This is the generation of customer, market and competitor-related information as a result of a company's intelligence gathering activities. The information is either from internal or external sources.

2. **Information dissemination** – Having obtained the necessary information, a company needs to disseminate this information effectively to all the individuals operating within its confines. If information dissemination is poor, it can be difficult for a company to develop the correct strategy for a given market or set of customers.

3. **Implementation and response to the information received** – A company needs to act on the information received, and it needs to act in a clear and precise manner. Therefore, the *type* of information gathered and the *speed* with which it is disseminated within a company play an important role in determining marketing strategies and the implementation of those strategies.

Figure 5.1 encapsulates the key components of market orientation and how they affect the success of a company in the market-place. In general, there are three main themes that relate to the marketing concept: *Customer focus* – information generation pertaining to customers; *Competitor focus* and *Responsiveness* – dissemination of information obtained pertaining to customers across the functional departments. This would be with a view to meeting customer needs as quickly as possible by having good inter-functional co-ordination within the departments.

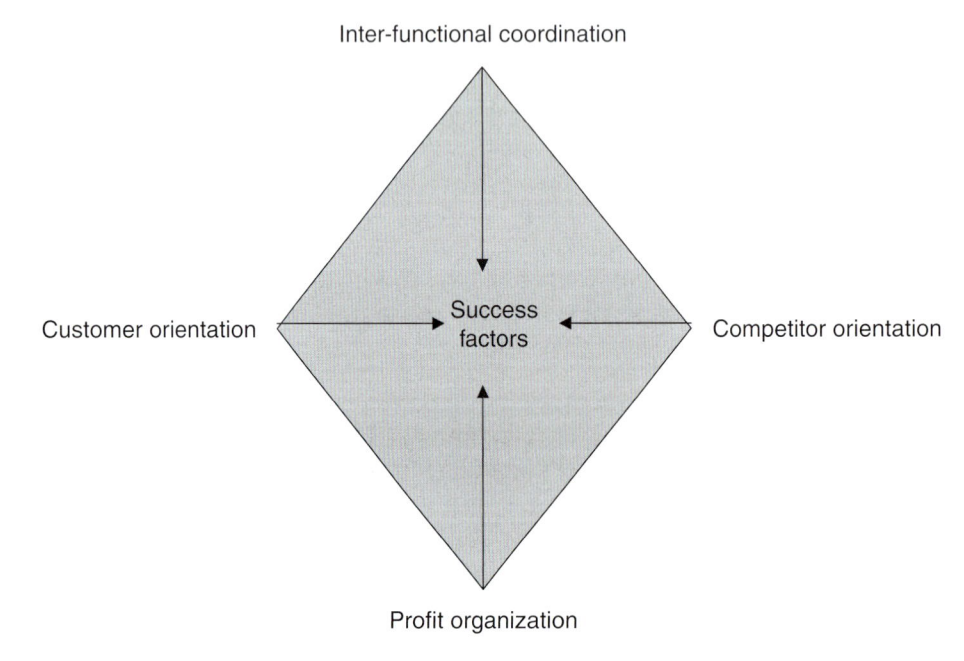

Figure 5.1 Components of market orientation
Source: After Deng and Dart (1994)

Unit 5: Effective customer orientation

Case study: Leica Microsystems increases market orientation

Leica Microsystems has announced sweeping restructuring measures all along the value-added chain to improve customer orientation and therefore enhance the market impact and competitiveness of the globally-operating company. 'In view of the growing customer demand for integrated digital application solutions for the display and analysis of microscopic structures,' says the manager of the Business Area Microscopy Systems, Dr Roland Zarske, 'we have decided to restructure our Business Units. Instead of the four Business Units we have at the moment, there will be just two: "Compound Systems", where the main emphasis will be on Life Science, and "Stereo Systems", which will continue to make most of its turnover in industry.' Both units integrate various technologies as well as software development, which was previously independent. The aim of this measure is to enhance the intelligence of system developments and make the new units particularly efficient, as an integrated customer solution can only be provided by offering automated microscopes together with digital application solutions. At the same time, the company plans to move capacities from German locations to its factories in Asia for reasons of cost efficiency or to transfer to business partners.

Simultaneously, Leica Microsystems is to set up a pan-European sales organization reflecting the market segments. This will allow the European Selling Units to market their innovative all-round applications in the segments Research (Life Science), Clinical, Industry, Surgery and Sample Preparation in a more targeted, co-ordinated and customer-oriented way. Additionally, Leica's presence all over Europe will be consolidated by expanding the existing dealer network, whereas the teams already existing in each country will continue to provide local after-sales service. 'Through greater customer orientation we can accelerate sales growth and increase profitability, which are key elements of our business strategy,' explains the manager of the European Sales Organization, Dr David Martyr. With centralized organizations, functions such as Marketing and Technical After-Sales Service will be able to operate more powerfully on a European scale.

'With the new structures, we will be able to focus our competences even more accurately on the benefit of the customer and enhance our competitiveness,' says CEO Dr Wolf-Otto Reuter. 'In conjunction with improvements in efficiency, this will enable us to intensify investing in further innovations and assets to safeguard our future.'

Source: http://www.light-microscopy.com/WebSite/SC_MQM.nsf?opendatabase&path=/website/pressrelease.nsf/(All IDs)/BD14834D6BDC0CB8C1256E3200522025

Question

Think of an organization you know, perhaps as an employee or customer. Suggest ways in which that organization can become more customer-orientated.

The above example indicates how companies are starting to become more customer-oriented in their approach. Customer-centric planning is becoming more and more useful as many companies compete within an increasingly competitive market-place.

Unit 5: Effective customer orientation

There is now considerable interest in trying to understand how companies can become customer-centric. Every organization, whether it is profit-oriented or not, has to be able to satisfy its customers. Figure 5.2 shows the gradual evolution in marketing towards customer orientation. To be customer-centric, marketers need to be able to assess each customer individually and satisfy their needs either directly or through a third party.

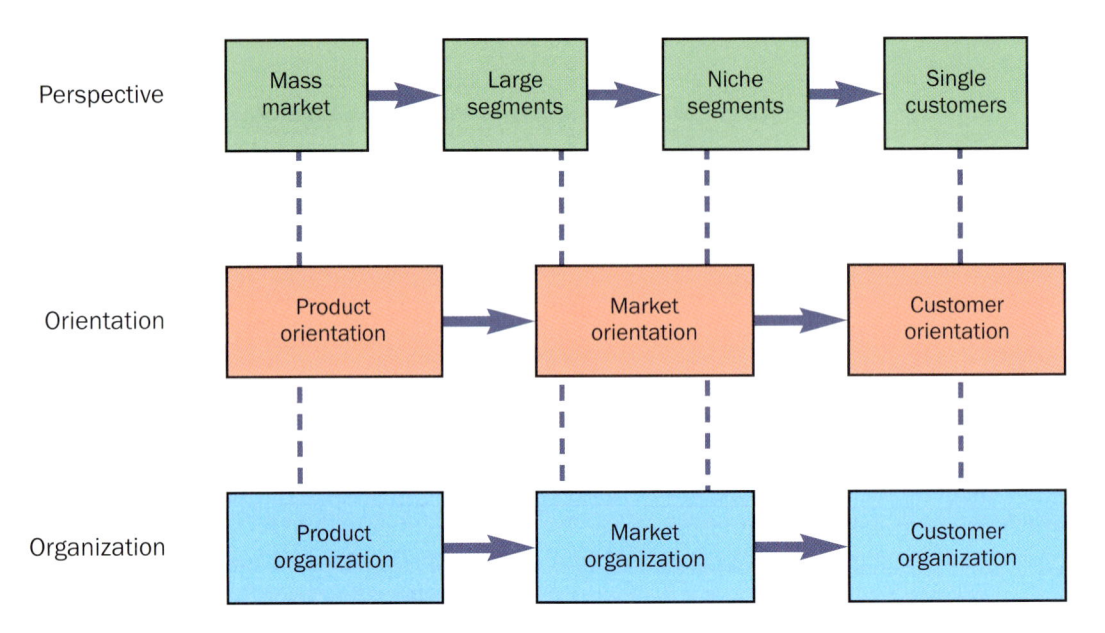

Perspective	Mass market	→	Large segments	→	Niche segments	→	Single customers
Orientation	Product orientation	→	Market orientation	→		→	Customer orientation
Organization	Product organization	→	Market organization	→		→	Customer organization

Figure 5.2 Growth of customer-centric marketing
Source: Sheth et al. (2000)

In addition to this, technology is rapidly changing the way in which relationships are managed. Customers are able to contact companies through various channels, and these need to be understood and managed by an organization. These are shown in Figure 5.3.

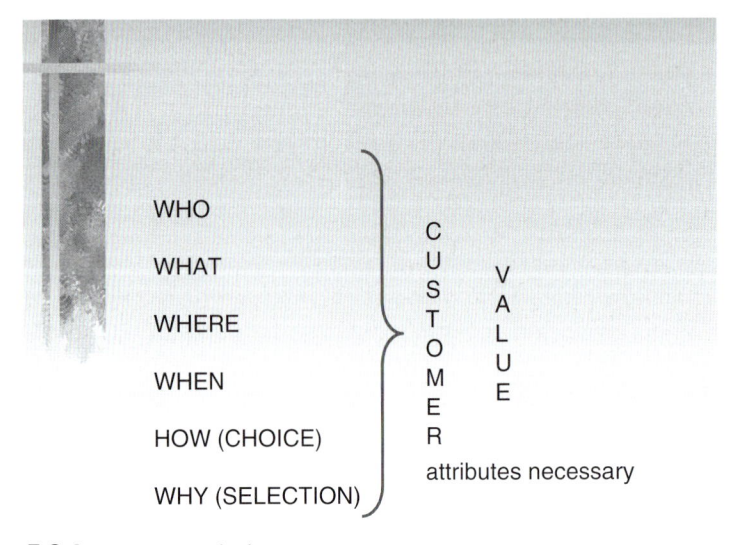

```
WHO        ⎫
WHAT       ⎪  C
WHERE      ⎬  U  V
WHEN       ⎪  S  A
HOW (CHOICE)  T  L
WHY (SELECTION) O  U
           ⎭  M  E
              E
              R
              attributes necessary
```

Figure 5.3 Customer analysis

Valuing customers

In calculating customer profitability, most methods start from the customer lifetime value (CLV). CLV is a controversial concept among the business specialists (Ranchhod and Gurau, 2003). Some consider it as 'an elaborate fiction of presumed precision' (Jackson, 1992), whereas other analysts declare that companies should abandon lifetime value theories and take care of the customers now (Ambler, 2001).

In mathematical terms, the CLV consists of taking into account the total financial contribution – that is, revenues minus costs – of a customer over his or her entire life of a business relationship with the company. Despite its simplicity, the measurement of CLV requires great care. All cash flows involved in the process have to be identified and measured on a very detailed level and allocated precisely to each customer or type of customer. Figure 5.4 represents a concise seven-step approach to measure CLV (Bacuvier et al., 2001).

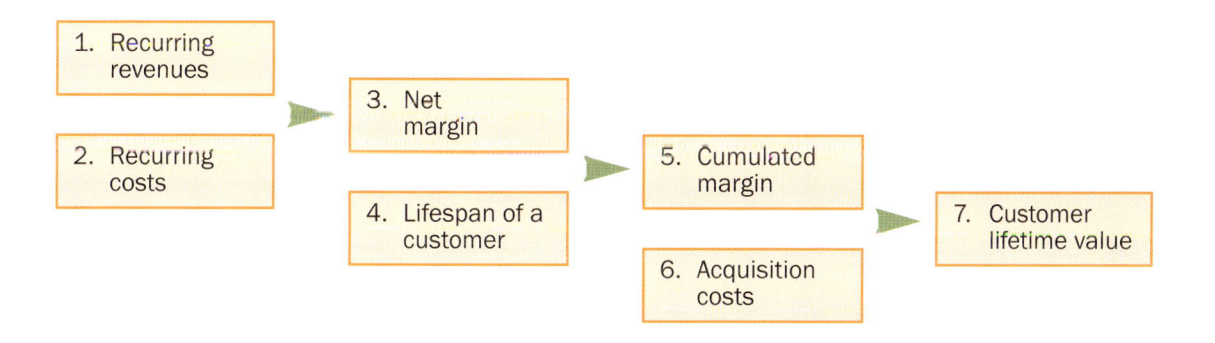

Figure 5.4 Seven-step process to measure CLV

Translating Figure 5.4 into mathematical formulas, we obtain:

CLV – Customer lifetime value (Profitability)
RR – Recurring revenues
RC – Recurring costs
Y – Lifespan of a customer or number of transactions
AC – Acquisition costs
P – Total profits
C – Number of customers

$$CLV = (RR - RC) Y - AC \quad (5.1)$$
$$P = CLV \times C \quad (5.2)$$
$$P = [(RR - RC) \times Y - AC] \times C \quad (5.3)$$

Unit 5: Effective customer orientation

The mathematical expression of the CLV can represent a sound basis for analysing the existing situation and for identifying the possible strategies to increase customer profitability. Analysing equation 5.3, five levers of customer value creation can be identified (Bacuvier et al., 2001). These strategies represent only the starting point of a company-wide operational effort. Table 5.1 shows the complexity of implementing customer-oriented strategies based on the analysis of the CLV.

Table 5.1 The operational requirements for implementing customer-oriented strategies based on CLV analysis

Strategy	Tactics	Operation	Requirements
Conquer – increase C – the number of customers	Improve the existing offer to attract the potential customers close to the existing customer segments	Improve: – Product – Price – Distribution – Promotion	Research Segmentation Investment
	Diversify the offer to attract new segments of customers	Increase the product/service portfolio	Research Segmentation Investment
Increase RR – recurring revenues	Increase the volume of sales	Diversification Stimulate the demand	Research Segmentation Investment
	Increase the value of sales	Upgrade the offer	Research Segmentation Investment
	Increase both the volume and the value of sales	Diversification Stimulate the demand Upgrade the offer	Research Segmentation Investment
Reduce RC – recurring costs	Reduce general costs (administration, maintenance, etc.)	Increased efficiency	Research Segmentation
	Reduce cost of: – Product/service – Distribution – Communication	Cheaper supplies Cheaper outsourcing Increased efficiency	Research Segmentation Investment
Retain – increase Y – lifespan of a customer	Increase customers' loyalty, maintaining and/or increasing customer satisfaction	Improve present offer Better targeting Score better than competition	Research Segmentation Investment
Reduce AC – acquisition costs	Better targeting of potential customers	Improve offer Improve targeting Use the same resources more efficiently	Research Segmentation Investment

Problems in calculating the CLV

The calculation of the CLV is not problem-free. However, most of these problems can be successfully solved taking into consideration two main issues:

1. The company applying this method has to define clearly from the beginning the purpose of using CLV analysis and the expected benefits.

2. The problems raised by the CLV analysis are often industry- and company-specific; as a result, the company has to select the most appropriate way to apply this concept in its particular situation.

Defining a 'customer'

The first challenge is to define the customer unit (Ness et al., 2001). Is it an individual, an account, a household or a business address? A second challenge is linking customer information into a single customer record when they leave and return multiple times during their lifetime.

The answer to these questions is industry-specific. The business organization has to identify the characteristics of its customer relationship and, on this basis, to define the customer unit and the customer lifetime cycle. In the present market-place, a company can be confronted with the following situations.

Table 5.2 The characteristics of customer relationships in different industrial markets

Number of customers	Number of transactions	Level of involvement
Large	Large	High
Medium	Medium	Medium
Small	Small	Low

Table 5.2 shows the possible combinations of customer relationship characteristics, different among industrial sectors and even among companies within the same industry. For example, a company with a small number of customers, which makes a small number of transactions that require a high level of company-customer involvement, will probably define the customer unit as being single customers (individuals or organizations) and the customer lifecycle depending on the business cycles specific for the industry (production cycle, investment cycles, consumption cycles). On the contrary, for a company dealing with a large number of clients, with large numbers of transactions and low involvement, it might be more appropriate to aggregate the individual customers into particular segments with homogeneous profiles and behaviour. This type of segmentation helps a company to become more customer-focused in a sensible, profitable manner (Figure 5.5 illustrates this). It also helps a company to develop feedback loops and a chance to develop contingency plans in case a given situation does not materialize.

Unit 5: Effective customer orientation

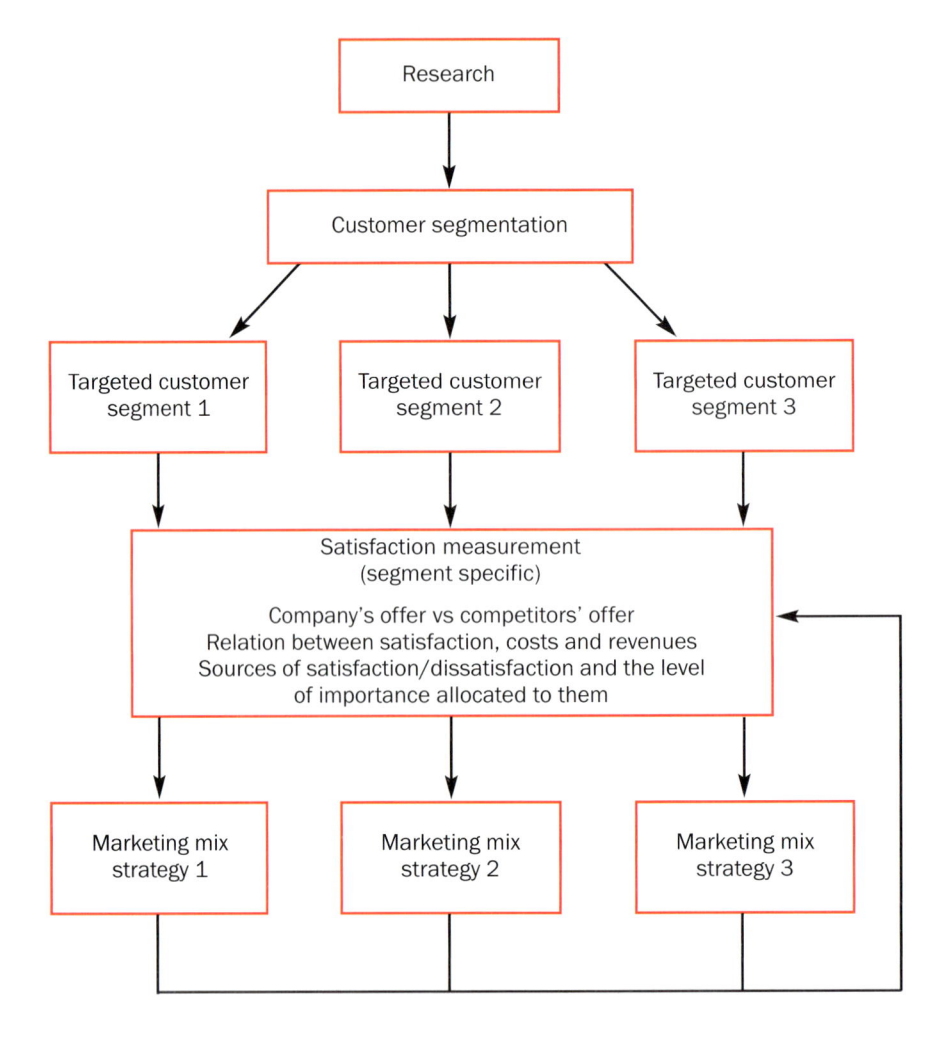

Figure 5.5 The use of customer segmentation and customer satisfaction measurement for designing and implementing targeted marketing mix strategies

Financial analysis and marketing measures

Introduction

Cases are based on real companies that have financial reporting systems. Usually, for the purposes of disseminating information to shareholders and stakeholders, companies produce annual accounts explaining financial flows, profits and losses and balance sheets. Many accounts also contain information on market shares, geographical segmentation and regional segmentation. Recently, there has been considerable interest generated in understanding the use of particular sets of data pertaining to marketing. These can be measurement of brand equity, customer satisfaction, loyalty/retention, share of voice and marketing spend. Some of these measures are shown in Table 5.3 (see page 172).

Interestingly, not many companies actually utilize the full range of marketing metrics for measuring their marketing performance. Often we are only left with the age-old financial measures. These measures do help in understanding the position of a company. Quite often, they are used by senior managers to gauge trends, especially if data for previous years are available in the same format. In most cases, the analyses are based on financial ratios. These accounting ratios are used in the interpretation of financial statements. Usually, these ratios are at their most useful when compared to ratios for different time periods. This can be helpful in identifying trends and understanding strengths and weaknesses. If, for instance, inventory levels are high in a balance sheet, does it imply that there is a peak, where the company is anticipating a surge in demand for products, or does it imply falling sales? The section below outlines the key ratios that are useful for analysing company performance.

In addition to this, companies have to be able to understand measures that are about marketing performance. Some of these measures may link up to financial performance and indeed may be the key to the success or failure of a company's marketing strategy. Such measures could be customer satisfaction, information dissemination capability within an organization, IT sophistication, market share and customer retention, amongst others.

Profit ratios

Profit ratios measure the management's overall effectiveness in generating profits from the available resources. If a company is highly efficient in its markets, then it should exhibit a high level of profitability. It is useful to compare a company's profitability against that of its major competitors in its industry. Such a comparison tells whether the company is operating more or less efficiently than its rivals. Over a period of time any changes in profit ratios will indicate whether a company is improving its performance or not:

1. **Gross profit margin** – The gross profit margin is obtained by deducting variable production expenses from the general sales. The amount remaining can then be allocated to cover general and administrative expenses and other operating costs. It is defined as follows:

$$\text{Gross profit margin} = \frac{\text{Sales revenue} - \text{Cost of goods sold}}{\text{Sales revenue}}$$

2. **Net profit margin** – This is based on the net profits obtained after taxes, loan interest and administration expenses have been paid. This net income is then divided by the sales revenue to obtain the net profit margin. Net profits are important because companies need to make profits to survive and also invest in the future to develop and grow markets.

$$\text{Net profit margin} = \frac{\text{Net income}}{\text{Sales revenue}}$$

Unit 5: Effective customer orientation

3   **Return on total asset** – This ratio measures the profit earned on the employment of assets. It is defined as follows:

$$\text{Return on total assets} = \frac{\text{Net income}}{\text{Total assets}}$$

4   **Net income** – This is the profit after preferred dividends (those set by contract) have been paid. Total assets include both current and fixed assets.

5   **Return on shareholders' equity** – This ratio measures the percentage of profit earned on the shares held within the company. Companies attractive to shareholders are those that can maximize this ratio. The greater the return, the greater the amount of money that can be distributed to individual shareholders. It is defined as follows:

$$\text{Return on shareholders' equity} = \frac{\text{Profits after taxes}}{\text{Total equity}}$$

6   **Liquidity** – The amount of liquidity refers to ready cash that may be available to a company for immediate use. The lower the liquidity, the greater the danger of a company not being able to meet its immediate cash commitments or tactical marketing requirements:

a $$\text{Current ratio} = \frac{\text{Current assets}}{\text{Current liabilities}}$$

b $$\text{Quick ratio} = \frac{\text{Total assets}}{\text{Total liabilities}}$$

c $$\text{Inventory to net working capital} = \frac{\text{Inventory}}{\text{Current assets} - \text{current liabilities}}$$

7   **Leverage** – If a company has borrowed little money, then it is possible for it to increase the amount of money it can raise in the market-place, through either loans or

share issues. The money can enable further investments in marketing or new product development:

a $$\text{Debt to assets ratio} = \frac{\text{Total debt}}{\text{Total assets}}$$

b $$\text{Debt to equity ratio} = \frac{\text{Total debt}}{\text{Total equity}}$$

c $$\text{Long-term debt to equity ratio} = \frac{\text{Long-term debt}}{\text{Total equity}}$$

8 **Activity** – This reflects the efficiency with which the company is dealing in the market-place. High inventory levels could signify flagging sales, indicating poor distribution, lack of advertising or sales efforts:

a $$\text{Inventory turnover} = \frac{\text{Sales}}{\text{Inventory}}$$

b $$\text{Fixed asset turnover} = \frac{\text{Sales}}{\text{Fixed assets}}$$

c $$\text{Average collection period} = \frac{\text{Accounts receivable}}{\text{Average daily sales}}$$

Marketing metrics

These will vary from one company to another. The key points to consider are: 'Who are the main users of company reports, and how important are they as data sources?'

Shareholders will be interested in profitability and long-term growth. On the contrary, directors and employees will be interested in issues such as market share, growth in the client base, profitability per customer, distribution costs, customer satisfaction and so on. Thus, information usage is very dependent on the functions within an organization.

Unit 5: Effective customer orientation

Corporate Goal

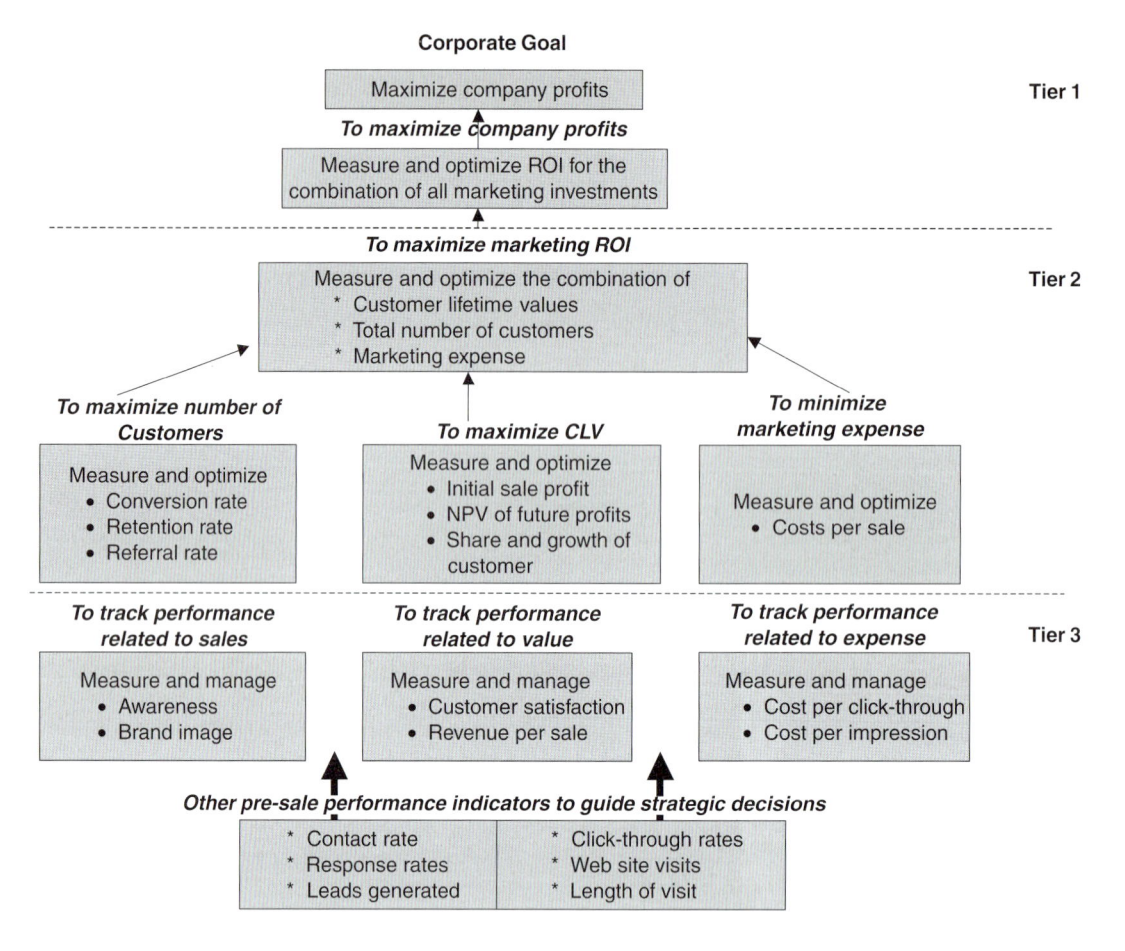

Tier 1
- Maximize company profits

To maximize company profits
- Measure and optimize ROI for the combination of all marketing investments

To maximize marketing ROI

Tier 2
- Measure and optimize the combination of
  * Customer lifetime values
  * Total number of customers
  * Marketing expense

To maximize number of Customers
- Measure and optimize
  - Conversion rate
  - Retention rate
  - Referral rate

To maximize CLV
- Measure and optimize
  - Initial sale profit
  - NPV of future profits
  - Share and growth of customer

To minimize marketing expense
- Measure and optimize
  - Costs per sale

Tier 3

To track performance related to sales
- Measure and manage
  - Awareness
  - Brand image

To track performance related to value
- Measure and manage
  - Customer satisfaction
  - Revenue per sale

To track performance related to expense
- Measure and manage
  - Cost per click-through
  - Cost per impression

Other pre-sale performance indicators to guide strategic decisions
* Contact rate
* Response rates
* Leads generated
* Click-through rates
* Web site visits
* Length of visit

Figure 5.6 Corporate goal

Marketing metrics have become a point for serious consideration for many organizations that are looking for the best ways in which performance can be measured. Performance varies according to the company characteristics and according to the sector in which it operates. Having standard metrics for all organizations is difficult, so it is useful to consider how metrics models can be developed for each organization. Figure 5.7 offers an idea of how some general marketing measures could be developed for an organization. However, there are many other issues to consider such as:

- Brand equity measures
- Environmental measures
- Customer satisfaction measures
- Customer loyalty measures
- Customer profitability measures
- New product success measures

There is also a range of others. In all cases, it is useful to categorize the measures according to their acceptability, suitability or feasibility for adoption by a particular organization (Ranchhod, 2004). Table 5.3 indicates the types of metrics that could be considered by companies.

Unit 5: Effective customer orientation

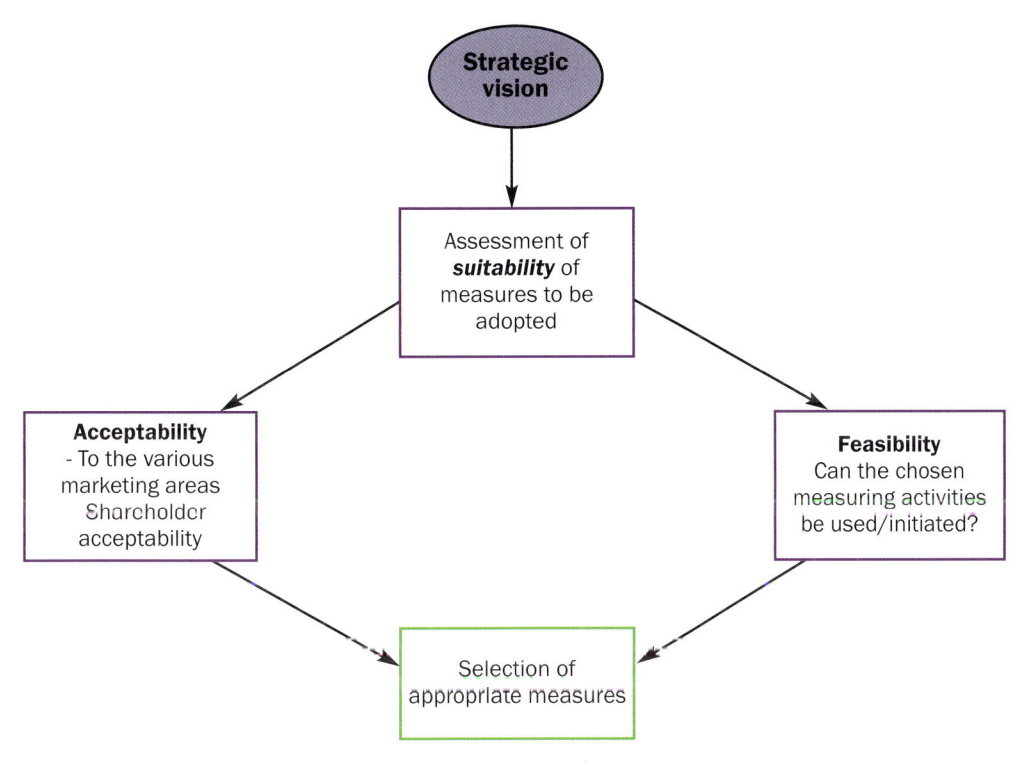

Figure 5.7 A framework for selecting marketing measures
Source: Ranchhod, 2004

Suitability

This provides an assessment of the most suitable measures that could be adopted for a particular company. This is likely to depend on the following:

- Industry sector.
- Service or product orientation of the organization.
- Not-for-profit or a non-governmental organization (NGOs).
- The level of technology used for automatic measurement. For instance, on the Internet, transactions can be recorded automatically. When loyalty cards are used, the customer transactions are recorded in a database. These records can then be subsequently used for data mining.
- The strategic vision of the company. For some companies, there may be an emphasis on rates of return; on others such as NGOs, the emphasis could be on the rates of consumer awareness or the level of funds generated.
- Is the measure chosen likely to be valuable in the long run and can trends be ascertained?
- Can the measures chosen be used to benchmark against competitors?

These measures can then be screened by considering the following criteria.

Unit 5: Effective customer orientation

Table 5.3 Marketing metrics for possible use in company reporting

Market data	Market size	Market trend
Relative market performance	• Unit volume trend • Market share (volume) • Market share by mix by major market segment (value)	• Relative price levels and trends • Sales by major brand (value) • Major brand trends (value) • Channel (value)
Customer performance	• Number of customers • Customer loyalty • Customer complaints • Relative quality • Relative value	• Customer service levels • Customer satisfaction • Consumption per capita (value) • Would recommend company or brands to friend
Innovation	• Activity calendar (past year) • New product/service review • New products/services launched in past 5 years as percentage of this year's sales	• Statement of future opportunities and objectives • Partnerships, acquisitions, licences
Efficiency	• Capacity utilization • R&D productivity	• Awards
People and competency	• Percentage of employee turnover • Percentage of employees participating in share purchase or profit-sharing	• Training activities, and training spend • Spend as % of sales • Employee satisfaction • Intellectual property
Investment	• R&D priorities and spend as percentage of sales • Capital expenditure activity and spend as percentage of sales • Advertising spend as percentage of sales	• Total marketing spend as percentage of sales • Technical support to customers
Branding	• Preference • Purchase intent • Brand value • Brand strength	• Awareness • Image • Perceived differential • Brand positioning
Distribution	• Level • Trend	• Channel mix • Channel trend

Acceptability

Are these measures acceptable to the various stakeholders? Do they make sense and do they actually measure the right areas/issues? There are instances where measures have been adopted but have really not been acceptable to the individuals developing the strategies. This, then, results in fudged or anomalous results. The measures would also have to demonstrate something tangible to the various stakeholders and be in line with their expectations. Measures such as brand equity are often undertaken by advertising agencies and as such need to be acceptable and meaningful to marketing personnel.

Feasibility

This tests whether the chosen measures can be usefully adopted. For instance, does the organization have the correct software to measure customer contact automatically, especially if they are introducing CRM strategies? Has the company enough resources to carry out brand equity research through an agency? Does it have systems in place with retailers to obtain details of revenues generated at point of sale through Electronic Point of Sale (EPOS) systems?

Some common measures

Usually in marketing, there are some measures that are used commonly by organizations. These measures are:

- Customer satisfaction – Measurement can be complex and depend on attributes measured – possible internal barriers to measurement.

- Customer loyalty – A measure of good marketing? Brand purchase measures? Financial performance also affects the situation/'lifetime value' of customers in the base.

- Brand equity – Many academics and managers believe that a powerful brand is probably among the greatest marketing assets a firm can have.

These measures can:

- Allow firms to charge price premiums over unbranded or poorly branded products.
- Can be used to extend the company's business into other product categories.
- Reduce perceived risk to customers (and investors?)

The measures could be behavioural, looking at perceptions or purchase patterns. They could also indicate knowledge of the brand and show the effectiveness of brand marketing within a complex portfolio. Another important measure could be the financial value of the brand to a company's investors. Such measures may be long-term rather than short-term in nature.

Unit 5: Effective customer orientation

Case study: Understanding online metrics

Online companies spent £150 million on advertising last year. Did it work? Oliver Rowe reports on the business of getting your dot-com company recognized in the real world.

It is one of the most important questions you have to face. You are setting up an Internet business. Everybody tells you that marketing and advertising the site will make or break you. There is no point having a good idea if nobody hears about it. So, you siphon off a large part of your launch budget for the purposes of building your brand. Domination of your market is what you seek. And to achieve that, you pay advertising companies lots of money to tell the world that you have arrived. But does it work? Advertising and media agencies up and down the country have certainly enjoyed a windfall over the past few months. But new figures revealed here show that many companies, whatever they spend on advertising their wares, are not getting the immediate brand recognition they crave. As we all know, brand is king. 'The only effective barrier to entry in e-commerce is branding,' says Simon Murdoch of Amazon. David Taylor, head of digital branding at the Added Value Company, a leading brand consultancy, concurs. 'Dot-com companies have a real need to develop a clear positioning and identity to survive and prosper in the long run.' Data from ACNielsen MMS, which records advertising expenditure, show that online companies spent in excess of £150 million on advertising in 1999 – not including direct mail, sponsorship or promotions. This has all been spent advertising online brands in the real world of traditional media. It represents a threefold increase in what was spent in 1998. However, the issue now is whether these companies are getting value for money.

This should cause some alarm for online companies because what naturally preoccupies all advertisers is how effective their advertising spend actually is. One key measure of advertising effectiveness is awareness of the brand amongst the public. Research undertaken in the last two weeks by CIA MediaLab as part of its Sensor study has analysed what the UK's major online companies spend on advertisers and compared it to people's awareness of the brand. What is clear from this analysis is that the public's awareness of your brand and the amount you actually spend on advertising are certainly related. But, more worryingly for those spending precious resources telling the public 'We're here!', some brands have got more recognition bang for their advertising buck.

Let's look at the figures. Four major brands, AOL, Yahoo!, Freeserve and BT, all achieve awareness of over 40 per cent amongst the UK adult population. The amount each has spent on advertising differs hugely, raising the question: who has the most effective advertising? Of course the level of recognition also reflects other factors such as the time since each launched and the amount of press coverage they have received. Looking specifically at Internet service providers (ISPs), we find that AOL has only been outspent by Freeserve. The two have very similar awareness levels, although AOL has been around much longer than Freeserve. AOL's recent merger with Time Warner will certainly have helped general awareness levels. What is clear is that Freeserve has been more aggressively going after market share, but AOL has decided to fight back with a spend of around £1.4 million in the past two months.

It should be made clear that advertising needs to play a different role in the marketing mix as the brand moves through its cycle from an initial launch to a growth to maturity. These ISPs are still growing but are using advertising to help attract both existing and new Internet users. The fascinating part of all this is not only trying to work out why differing levels of advertising spend have delivered different results but also why so many companies are spending so much on advertising. The perception is that there is currently an opportunity to build online brands, and thus market share, more quickly and easily (and cheaply) than in a year or two's time when the Internet will be a bigger place. When a market is being launched it is cheaper to buy a share while it is still small than try and steal it off competitors once the market has matured. It is for this reason that venture capitalists are keen to give promising young Internet start-ups large sums of money to spend advertising their brand before someone else gets into that sector of the market.

A prime example of the advantage of being first to market can be seen in the differences in awareness levels and advertising spend between Amazon and BOL. Despite spending nearly £3.7 million on advertising in the last 12 months, BOL only has an awareness of 27 per cent amongst people who used the Internet in the past month. This compares to a significantly higher awareness of 75 per cent for Amazon from a slightly smaller spend. Maintaining awareness is an easier job than gaining it in the first place. Also, the amount BOL has spent on advertising does not compare favourably to other online brands such as Lastminute, which has a 29 per cent awareness from a £1 million spend. Meanwhile, online retailer Boo has spent more than £750,000 in the past two months and has failed to show any significant change in awareness amongst CIA's sample.

To be fair, asking people whether they are aware of a brand at a particular moment in time is a relatively crude measure of advertising effectiveness. However, doing it amongst a pre-defined target audience that has been agreed by the brand owners and the media agency is a good place to start, but media agencies do get judged by the awareness they deliver. Even so, as for AOL and Freeserve, achieving awareness may only be the first part of the advertising process. As well as achieving awareness, advertising needs to communicate some brand values that should help drive share and loyalty. The temptation for brands is to launch with a fanfare to the world, but without any budget left, they cannot follow it up. The result is that brand awareness will quickly decay. It could be argued that some brands should use their advertising budget more wisely.

Media agencies could more accurately target the right consumers, possibly using other media and over a longer period of time, thus satisfying the joint media requirements of frequency of advertising exposure and recency. But does this excite investors, or the MD, as much as blowing the annual budget on a few weeks of high-profile TV advertising?

One sector that is moving wholeheartedly online is banking, and its experience with advertising and brand building holds some important lessons. As yet unreleased research by CIA shows that amongst those that have already opened an online bank account or who intend to open one in the next year, 89 per cent of those aware of Egg say it appeals to them as a brand. This compares to only 60 per cent for the parent brand Prudential. The Smile brand appeals to 70 per cent of those aware of it in this target audience compared to 58 per cent for parent Co-operative Bank. Smile has shown impressive awareness growth in the last two months on the back of a £1.2 million advertising budget.

Advertising is clearly establishing new values for a new brand while trying not to cannibalize the existing customer base of the parent. As the Internet audience grows, then so the amount brands will be encouraged to spend on advertising will increase until those that cannot afford to play the spend game drop out or get bought up. Make sure your brand works. Spend money on advertising. But make sure it works.

Note: Oliver Rowe is operations manager at CIA MediaLab, ORowe@cia-group.com.

The above article demonstrates the use of marketing metrics within the context of the Internet and the difficulties of determining the effectiveness of online advertising.

Source: The Guardian, Monday, 6 March 2000.

Question

With reference to the above case study evaluate the increasing importance of public relations as an alternative to advertising in improving public awareness of brands and companies.

Contingencies

With an increasing uncertain and risky environment, the need for developing contingency plans is becoming increasingly important. Unfortunately, often companies develop budgets for marketing plans, with little thought given to 'what if' scenarios. Sometimes, subjective assessments of potential growth in market share are made, and risks are discounted. Contingency is described as an allowance for unforeseen expenditures or revenues. Contingency, if not applied reasonably, might destroy an otherwise good plan, and if not applied adequately, might create financial problems.

As Figure 5.8 shows, the control aspects are important, and contingency plans can be taken into account in Figure 5.9. Metrics can help to understand the deviations from given plans and situations. However, when the strategies do not go according to plan, the contingencies come into play. These contingencies can be quite variable in nature:

- Greater than expected growth in sales or vice versa
- Greater expenditure on advertising because of failure of set campaigns
- Supply chain cost variations
- Price pressures resulting from customer actions
- Variations in product quality/quality recall
- Poor or good publicity for the company affecting sales
- Changes in economic conditions, for example rise in interest rates
- Changes in technology rendering the current product range obsolete
- Internal production delays affecting sales

Unit 5: Effective customer orientation

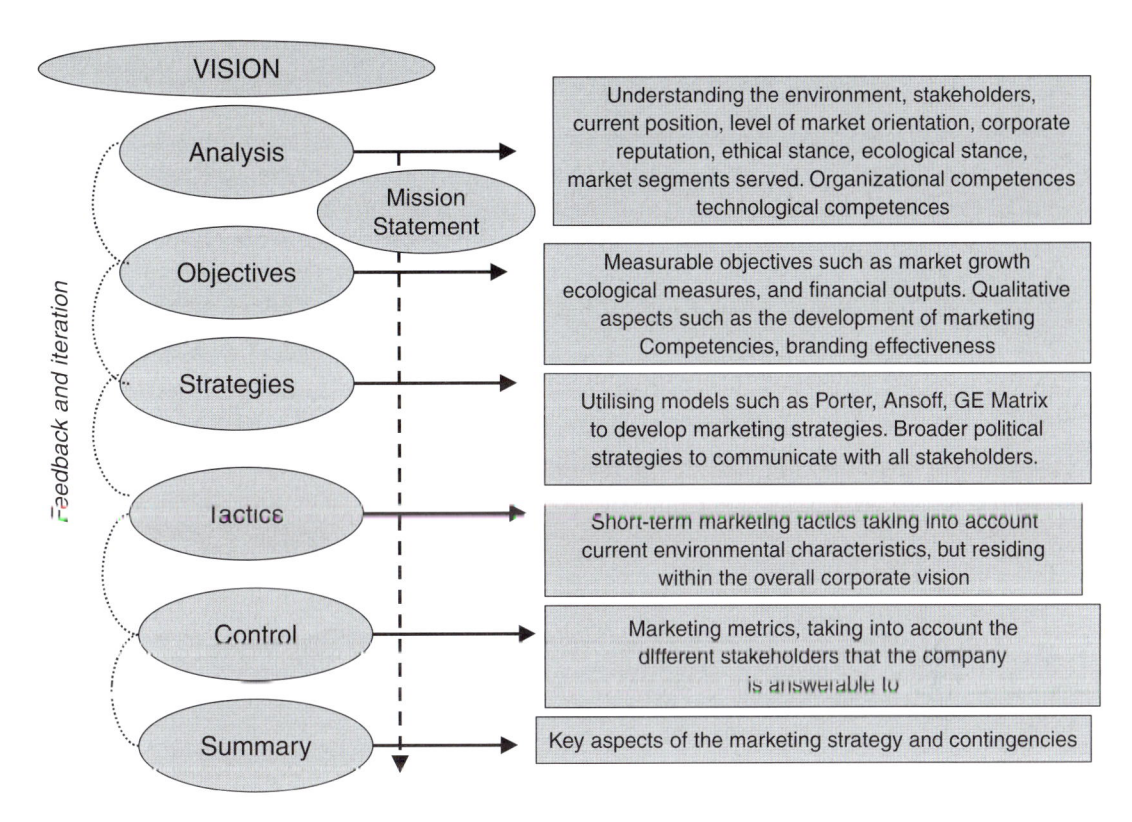

Figure 5.8 Strategic marketing model for the 21st century

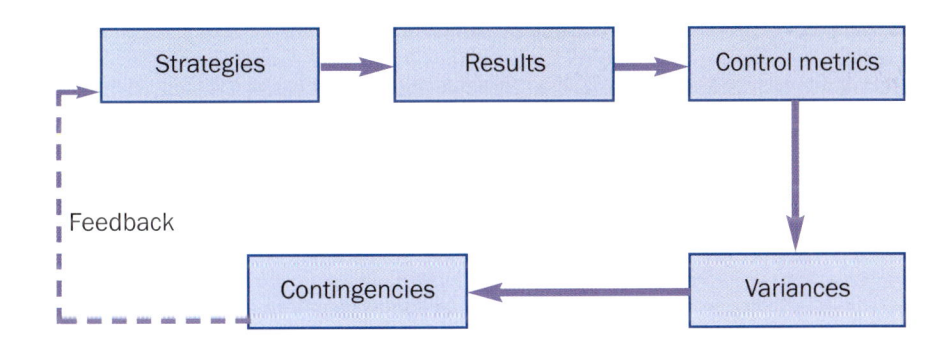

Figure 5.9 Contingencies and control

There are many others, depending on the nature of the business and the sector in which it operates.

Summary

This unit demonstrates the usefulness of understanding customer-related issues when developing marketing strategies. It also shows the importance of developing strategies that take into account measures that are useful and meaningful within the context of the company under consideration. Every organization, in every sector, has its own key issues that it needs to take into account. These key issues then translate into effective control measures based on their suitability, acceptability and feasibility for adoption. Finally, every plan needs to incorporate contingencies that come into play as a result of the detection of variances within the determined control metrics.

References

Ambler, T. (2001) Abandon lifetime value theories and take care of customers now, *Marketing,* **18**, July 12.

Bacuvier, G., Peladeau, P., Trichet, A., Zerbib, P. (2001) *Customer lifetime value: Powerful insights into a Company's Business and Activities*, http://www.bah.com/viewpoints/insights/cmt_clv_2.html.

Jackson, D.R. (1992) In quest of the grail: Breaking the barriers to customer valuation, *Direct Marketing,* **54**(11): 44–48.

Ness, J.A., Schroeck, M.J., Letendre, R.A., Douglas, W.J. (2001) *The role of ABM in measuring customer value,* www.mamag.com/strategicfinance/2001/03f.htm.

Ranchhod, A. (2004) *Marketing Strategies: A 21st Century Approach,* Pearson Education FT Knowledge.

Sheth, J.N., Sisodia, R.S., Sharma, A. (2000) The antecedents and consequences of customer-centric marketing, *Journal of the Academy of Marketing Science,* **28**(1): 55–66.

Unit 6: The examination

Learning objectives

In this unit you will:

◆ Put everything together:
   1. How to analyse case studies and formulate good analyses in line with the new requirements of SMiP.
   2. How to apply and use analyses in the closed-book examination.
   3. What the examiners will be looking for.

The examination

The examiners, when looking at answers to examination questions based on the case study, look for the qualities described below.

Analytical and critical thinking

The case study is based on real organizations, and we expect candidates to critically analyse it utilizing a range of techniques. The case study is sent to students four weeks before the date of the examination. As this is a closed-book examination and we are looking for pre-prepared analyses, it is important that in the weeks before the examination, time is spent on understanding and analysing the case. The purpose of a case is to develop the following:

◆ Analysis and critical thinking
◆ Decision-making
◆ Judging between courses of action
◆ Handling assumptions and inferences
◆ Presenting a point of view
◆ Listening to and understanding others
◆ Relating theory to practice

185

Unit 6: The examination

Candidates should be able to analyse each case and comprehend the other areas of the Professional Postgraduate Diploma syllabi from where they may need to draw their underpinning knowledge. Although candidates need to demonstrate their underpinning knowledge in the context of the case study, it is important that they show some creative flair and innovation in their answers. Candidates will also be expected to show an understanding of contemporary marketing issues. Examples of these are given in Unit 4.

The examiners are looking for the candidates to demonstrate analytical ability, interpretive skills, insight, innovation and creativity in answering questions. They are also looking for candidates to take clear and sensible decisions within the context of the case study. A critical awareness of the specific issues involved, relevant theoretical underpinning, attention to detail, coherence and justification of strategies (within the context of the questions set) adopted will also be assessed.

Answering questions within the set context

The SMiP paper asks for special understanding of the case within the context of the question set. As this is a closed-book examination, the only material allowed in the examination will be the pre-prepared analysis. The title of the paper SMiP means that we are looking for an understanding of strategic issues involved in developing specific strategies within a company. The candidates need to be competent enough to analyse problems within a marketing context and subsequently take appropriate decisions to implement marketing strategies for an organization. To achieve competence in this area, prospective candidates will need to be conversant with all aspects of marketing, as strategic marketing problems do not come in neat packages. A comprehensive grasp of the basic subjects at the Certificate and Advanced Certificate levels together with the syllabi for the Professional Postgraduate Diploma modules, is needed. Decisions made have to reflect the fact that candidates have thoroughly understood the key marketing issues impinging on the case. They have to make decisions that are realistic and justifiable and above all actionable within the given constraints.

Judging between courses of action

When analysing a case study, it would be surprising if only one course of action was possible. Often there are several alternatives to a problem, and a company has to weigh up the chances of success and pursue a particular course of action. As an examination candidate, you are expected to pursue courses of action that are possible, realistic and sustainable. The examiners are not looking for right or wrong answers; they are searching for solutions that will work within the given scenario of the case study.

Handling assumptions and inferences

All cases are based on real-life information that may have gaps within it. No company works in a perfect environment or with perfect information. This would not only be impossible but also be outside the capability of any human being. The result is that we all create an image of the way in which a company is operating. In creating that image and understanding it, there may be gaps that need filling. These can be done by the projection of trends or by making certain assumptions about market demand or product suitability. In most cases, students will need to make certain assumptions. As long as these are not wildly off the mark and help to augment the case and your arguments, they are perfectly acceptable. In some cases, candidates may wish to point out that further market research is necessary.

Presenting a point of view

All cases are about presenting a point of view. Examiners expect student answers to vary. It is therefore important, when preparing for the case, that you do not get hung up on thinking that your friend or colleague has the right answer. If you have analysed the case thoroughly and you feel that you have a clear view of the strategies that should be adopted by the company, then you should put these forward. At all times, you should consider the detail, coherence and strategic aspects of arguments, justifying them fully.

Relating theory to practice and vice versa

To be a good practising marketing manager, you need to be able to seamlessly knit marketing theory to practical solutions. I see this as a symbiotic process. Too often, we see managers who only emphasize the practical aspects and, by doing that, deny their companies the benefit of marketing frameworks and any new knowledge that may be available. By the same token, simply propounding theoretical frameworks, with little or no thought given to the practical application of these frameworks to real problems is also unacceptable. To formulate sensible solutions to cases, you will need to be knowledgeable about both practical marketing aspects and theoretical issues, and contemporary marketing thinking.

How to pass the case study paper

In general, candidates are expected to allocate some study time at a centre to prepare for the case study. The notional study time is 45 hours over a period of 10–12 weeks. Roughly half of this time should be allocated for work on previous cases and the rest for developing analyses and scenarios for the new case and preparing for the examination that candidates will be sitting.

The paper

The SMiP paper is the culmination of all the marketing subjects covered at all levels, but especially the Diploma and the Advanced Diploma. For this reason, there is no specific syllabus for this paper. This type of expertise will be needed to tackle the case study paper. It is also clear that it will not be possible to tackle the case study without a clear grasp of the fundamentals of Analysis and Evaluation, Strategic Marketing Decisions and Managing Marketing Performance. In this sense, for all students, the case study is a culmination of the application of all the marketing knowledge that you have gained over several years.

Closed-book examination

For all the students, the SMiP paper is a *closed-book* examination. This means that candidates are only allowed to take their pre-prepared analyses into the examination. Used judiciously, this material can be useful for referencing when answering questions. Fifteen marks are also allocated for the *application* of the analyses to the question set. Many candidates think that excellent analyses with poor answers will enable a pass. This is misguided as, no matter how good the analyses are, they have to be applied within the context of the case. Skimpy answers relying on analyses will almost certainly fail. It is, therefore, important for candidates to spend time developing good answers and using the analyses to augment these answers.

It is highly important that a considerable amount of time is spent on developing tables, undertaking detailed analyses, producing diagrams and assembling this information on six A4 sides. This is helpful for quick referencing during the examination. It also leaves candidates free to think about which bits of information may be useful to use in framing answers.

Allocation of marks

The marks will be allocated in the following manner:

    Marks for analysis: 10

    Marks for the application of the analysis: 15

This methodology:

- Rewards students for work done in the four weeks between the release of the case and the day of the examination.
- Enables students to concentrate on the case and utilize the analyses effectively in their answers.

Candidates should note the following advice (repeated from Unit 1):

1. Write or print pre-prepared analysis on six single-sided pages of A4. Examiners will be looking for tables, diagrams and key issues. Tables such as SWOT, though helpful, do not show deep analytical thought.
2. If candidates use the available sheets for writing 'crib' material, such as models or plans, they will penalize themselves as there will be less space for good analysis that counts towards the final marks.
3. The diagrams should be clearly visible and the writing should be legible. Typing should be no less than font size 11.
4. Data given within the case should be analysed clearly and effectively.
5. All the work should be on CIM paper, which will be issued two weeks before the examination.
6. Please note that it will be totally unacceptable for students to present standardized group analysis/appendices, and they will therefore be penalized accordingly.

During the examination:

1. The answers should reflect the use of the pre-prepared material as necessary. Candidates, when writing answers, should cross-reference the work to guide the examiner to a particular table or chart or piece of analysis.
2. Examiners do not expect students to use *all* the pre-prepared material to augment their answers. Obviously, they should only use whatever is necessary for answering the questions as set.
3. Candidates should attach the pre-prepared work as an appendix. All papers must be hole punched and include the student registration and centre number.
4. Please note that 15 marks are allocated *for the application* of the pre-prepared work.

Unit 6: The examination

5 Only the pre-prepared analysis can be taken into the examination room; therefore, no textbooks, journals or other pre-prepared work will be allowed.

6 You will be allowed to bring an annotated copy of the case study into the examination hall.

Notes to candidates

These notes are modified from time to time, depending on the context within which the cases are set. The following is an example of what was used in the June 2003 case study.

Extending knowledge

Notes to candidates, June 2003

The examiners will be marking your scripts on the basis of questions put to you in the examination room. Candidates are advised to pay particular attention to the *mark allocation on the examination paper and budget their time accordingly*.

Your role is outlined in the candidates' brief, and you will be required to recommend clear courses of action.

You will be awarded marks for analysis, but poor application may mean the difference between a pass and a failure. The analyses should have been undertaken before the examination day in preparation for meeting the tasks that will be specified in the examination paper.

Candidates are advised not to waste valuable time collecting unnecessary data. The cases are based on real-life situations. No useful purpose will therefore be served by contacting companies in this industry and candidates are *strictly instructed not to do so* as it would simply cause unnecessary confusion.

As in real life, anomalies will be found in this case situation. Please simply state assumptions where necessary when answering questions. The CIM is not in a position to answer queries on case data. Candidates are tested on their overall understanding of the case and in key issues, not on minor details. There are no catch questions or hidden agendas. In addition, for this particular case, the CIM is not prepared to answer any financial queries.

Additional information will be introduced in the examination paper itself, which candidates must take into account when answering the questions set.

Acquaint yourself thoroughly with the case study and be prepared to follow closely the instructions given to you on the examination day. To answer examination questions effectively, candidates must adopt a report format.

The copying of pre-prepared 'group' analyses written by consultants/tutors is strictly forbidden and will be penalized. The questions will demand analysis in the examination itself, and individually composed answers are required to pass.

From case to case, there may be minor modifications to the candidates' notes depending on the type and style of case.

The candidate's brief

This brief is an integral part of the case study. It gives some idea of the role you are expected to play in solving the case study. The candidate's brief gives individuals a position either as an external consultant or an internal manager. On the day of the examination, they are expected to answer the question set from the point of view of the role that has been allocated. The brief is likely to contain the following:

- A brief analysis of the company situation
- Some idea of the deliberations within the company
- An attempt to place you at the centre of the action, asking you to prepare reports on some critical strategic issues/problems facing the organization
- Some statement on incorporating any contemporary issues of your choice into the answers that you propose

The use of additional information

Cases will vary in nature and, from time to time, additional information may be provided. It is important therefore for you to incorporate this material in your answers, as and when it is needed.

The additional information is something that you should take into consideration when answering the question set, as it is likely to have some bearing on the market conditions or on some areas of the case. The additional information will not invalidate all the work that has been undertaken over the four weeks. The additional information is introduced to test the ability of candidates to be flexible in their thinking and to test the ability to assimilate and effectively incorporate new material into the development of their strategies.

Gauging performance

To perform well on the paper, candidates will have to exhibit the following:

- A need to concentrate on the strategic aspects of marketing underpinned by the necessary detail
- The ability to identify 'gaps' in the case study and to outline the assumptions made
- The ability to critically apply relevant models for case analysis
- The ability to draw and synthesize from any of the diploma subject areas as relevant
- Concentration on the question set rather than just the pre-prepared analysis
- The ability to answer in the report format with comprehensive sentences rather than providing simplistic lists
- The judicious use of diagrams for illustrative purposes
- The ability to draw disparate links together and give coherent answers
- The use of interesting and useful articles from journals in their answers
- Developing strategic ideas, centred around contemporary marketing issues
- Innovation and creativity in answering the questions

Unit 6: The examination

- Demonstration of practical applications of marketing knowledge
- Sensible use of time and an ability to plan the answers within the set time
- A good understanding of the case study set

The best way to prepare for the case would entail the following considerations:

- Practice on previous examination papers
- Reading and digesting the senior examiner's report
- Reading books, newspapers, relevant marketing and academic journals
- For each examination case, ascertaining the relevant knowledge base that will be required
- Being flexible and critical when using analytical models instead of being prescriptive
- Depending on the case study, utilizing a range of different analytical models and tools appropriate to the context of the case (see Figure 6.1 for an illustrative schedule for preparing for the examination)

In addition to the above, candidates should also be prepared to undertake the following:

- The use of relevant models for the sector in which the case study is based
- The use of each candidate's practical and business experience using any illustrative examples
- The use of diagrams
- A thorough marketing and financial analysis of each case study within the given context of the case study
- An awareness and application of strategic marketing ideas and solutions
- Revisiting relevant syllabi from the Diploma and Advanced Diploma within the given context of the case study

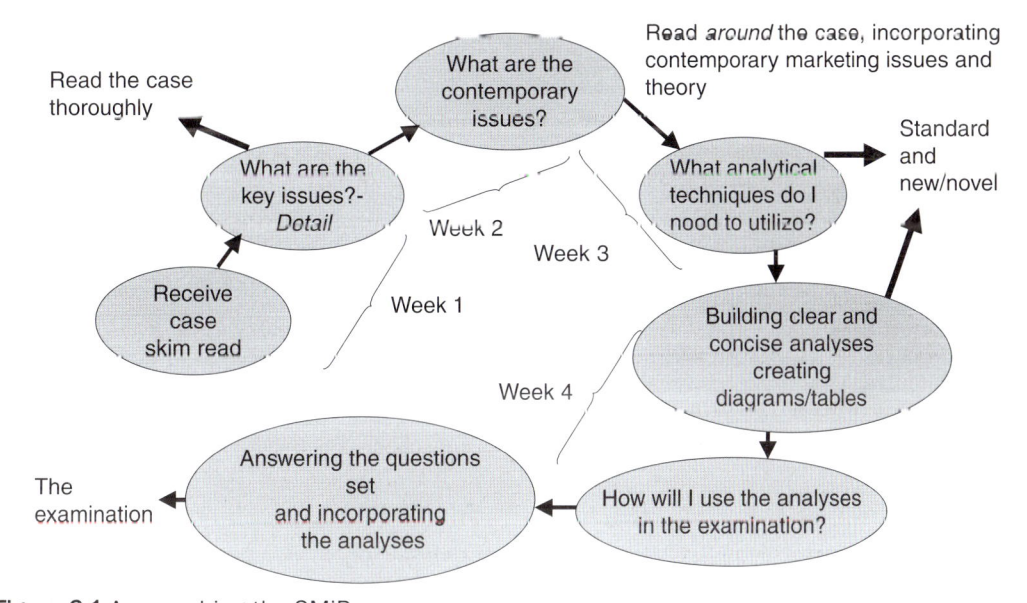

Figure 6.1 Approaching the SMiP case

Unit 6: The examination

An examiner's point of view

It would be of help if candidates would briefly wear an examiner's hat when preparing for the exam and imagine their scripts and answers as perceived from the other side. This section has been written by an experienced A & D, and now SMIP, examiner and feedback writer for failed scripts. It provides very useful advice for candidates.

Presentation

It is a fact that most of us are forgetting the skill of handwriting. Although no CIM examiner expects or rewards beautiful handwriting, it is expected that he/she must be able to read what the candidate has written. Unfortunately, increasingly examiners are confronted with truly awful handwritings that are difficult, and sometimes impossible, to read. If your handwriting is bad, try to practice handwriting large amounts of work without a break, as in the exam situation.

Another problem with many scripts, sometimes in addition to bad handwriting, is the number of words or lines crossed out, or parts of an answer written on one page with additional parts on another with instructions to the examiner where to find the missing parts. Messy presentation does not help you. Some scripts contain diagrams/illustrations with so many tiny words written in bad handwriting that even a magnifying glass is not enough to make sense of what is presented. Then, there are those answers that last several pages without a paragraph break, with no, or very few, sub-headings.

All of the above makes an examiner's job difficult, and although it is the duty of all examiners to read the scripts carefully and reward candidates for correct answers, there is also an onus on the candidates to present their work in such a way that it can be marked with reasonable effort and within a reasonable period of time. Make sure your handwriting is legible, and use headings, sub-headings and paragraphs. Leave a reasonable gap between different answers and mark each answer clearly. Underline sub-headings, if you wish, and use highlighters too to make important words, terms or figures stand out, but do not overdo it.

Read the question

This may sound too obvious to mention but experience shows otherwise. Candidates must read each question several times and break each question into its constituent parts. Some candidates see a familiar word or two and start answering the question right away. For example, the Senior Examiner can ask dozens of different questions on branding. Seeing the word 'branding' in the question and starting the answer is dangerous. You must make it clear to yourself what exactly the question wants you to do. This is closely linked with another type of answer, which examiners are sometimes confronted with. That is, candidates writing everything they know about a concept either hoping to impress the examiner or hoping the examiner, somewhere in the long answer, will be able to find parts that relate to the question.

Read each question carefully, understand what it requires and give a concise and to the point answer. The examiner will be more impressed with a compact and precise answer that is three to four pages long than with one that is a whole answer book long but not relevant for the most part.

Messages to examiners

Examiners will mark the answer that is in front of them. They will ignore your messages about running out of time and so on. Do not write messages and, as in the case of a recent candidate, please do not mark your script either!

Prepared answers

Some of the answers from a number of centres are often very similar, if not identical. Although themes and ideas may be discussed in advance, and may be similar, the actual answers are not expected to mirror each other. The candidates are expected to write answers individually during the exam. There is a consensus amongst examiners for SMiP that in future very similar/identical answers may be penalized.

Another form of prepared answer is where candidates guess what the questions will be and rehearse or prepare answers, which they then include in their scripts, sometimes clearly giving the wrong answer because they have guessed incorrectly. This approach became common with some centres taking the A & D paper and has partly been responsible to the changes made to the SMiP paper, where advance guessing of questions will be more difficult.

Prepare for different scenarios but do not limit yourself by guessing the questions exactly

Understanding of marketing theory and its application

The SMiP paper requires a demonstration of both academic theory and application of that theory to real life situations. Unbalanced answers stand to lose marks. Although you are not required to engage in pure theoretical discussion, you should use definitions, and particularly models and theories in your answers, where appropriate. Sometimes, such models are included in the case study – use them! The answer to a question requiring a marketing plan does not require any theoretical discussion at all, but even there theoretical models -- for example Boston Matrix, Porter's Five Forces -- should be included when relevant.

The SMiP paper will require an understanding of contemporary issues in marketing, as well as questions on branding, internationalization and communication that A & D candidates came to expect. It would be useful to keep abreast of contemporary issues in marketing. Contemporary issues, by their nature, are subject to change, but currently, it may be suggested, include corporate social responsibility, relationship marketing/CRM, mobile and e-marketing, corporate identity, public relations and added value.

The importance of analysis and justification

The marking scheme for the SMiP paper allocates a significant portion of the total mark to analysis and application. Good recommendations can only be based on a thorough analysis, with the latter helping the justification of the former. Where the relevant analysis is included in the appendices, make clear references, in your answer, to the relevant diagram/table/illustration, giving page number and title. Remember that the maximum number of pages you are allowed to attach to your script is six (and no more). These must be single sided.

Unit 6: The examination

Additionally, always justify your recommendations/opinions. Although bullet points are allowed in answers, those that are so short as not to mean much will not gain you any marks.

Finally, remember that analysis means breaking down the given information and making sense of it or determining its significance. Merely repeating what is in the case study does not equate to analysis and does not get any marks.

Summary

When working on the case and in the examination, do not repeat in summary form large pieces of factual information from the case. The examiners are fully aware of the case. It is better to use the information in the case to illustrate your statements, to defend your arguments or to make salient points. Beyond the brief introduction to the company, you must avoid being descriptive; instead, you must be analytical.

You will need to ensure that the sections and sub-sections of your discussion flow logically and smoothly from one part to the next. Try to build on what has gone before, so that each analysis builds on the previous one. A piecemeal approach to analysis results in fragmented writing lacking coherence. This is because the parts do not flow from one to the next, and this becomes apparent to the examiners. Sometimes this happens when intensive group and individual approaches are put together.

It is important to write in a report format using clear English, avoiding grammatical and spelling errors. Clarity of approach and the judicious use of diagrams help examiners to follow your arguments easily.

Finally:

- Practice on previous cases and see how you would have approached the case differently from the specimen answers given.
- Read and digest the Senior Examiner's reports.
- Read books, newspapers and relevant marketing and academic journals.

Be flexible and critical when utilizing analytical models and steer away from being prescriptive in your approach. More practice will result in better insights and help you being creative and innovative when framing your answers.

Index

A

Advantage – competitive 24
Agenda – business 2
Aims and outcomes for Strategic Marketing in Practice 9
Alliances 62
Analyses 20
  product market 22
  PESTLE 20
  SPACE 23
  SWOT 21
Analysing a case study 20
Analytical thinking 185
Answering questions 186

B

Benefits of customer loyalty 63
Biological boomerang 95
Brand development strategies 137
Brand loyalty and its measurement 65
Brand positioning 138
Brand re-positioning 138
Brand revitalization 137
Branding 135
Business agenda 2
Business intelligence 38
Buyer behaviour 140

C

Case study – analysing 20
Chemicals 95
Chemicals policy 104
Chemicals practice 104
Climate 94
Closed-book examination 187
Cognitive behaviour models 152
Commerce 95
Communication tactics 144
Communication tools 144
Communications 71
  importance 88
  internal 149
  role 134
Communications strategy 141
Competitive advantage (CA) 24
Constraints 14
  company 27
Consumer behaviour 140
Consumer protection legislation 62
Contemporary marketing issues 15
Contexts – marketing 4
Contingencies 182
Control 15
Control systems 27
Core products 61
Corporate identity 132
  defining 134
  graphic design approach 132
  integrated communication approach 132
  synthesis approach 134
Corporate image 134
Corporate personality 134
Critical thinking 185
Cross-functional co-ordination 88
Customer awareness 62
Customer lifetime value 169
  problems in calculating 171
Customer loyalty 62, 64
  benefits 63
  limitations 67
  types 64
Customer orientation 165
Customer satisfaction 64
Customers
  defining 171
  valuing 169

Index

D

Development of sector 20
Development of the company 20
Discarded products 105
Double-loop learning 50

E

Early-KAM 78
Ecological footprint 92
Ecological prospective on social marketing 151
Effective qualitative primary market research 42
Employee recruitment 149
Empowerment 149
Energy 94
Environmental marketing 93
Environmental stability (ES) 25
Evaluation 144
  SWOT 21
Evolution of population 92
Examination 185
Examples of mission statements 52

F

Financial analysis 172
Financial issues 15
Financial strength (FS) 24
Foreign market entry strategies 55

G

Globalization 14, 56, 61
  responses 57
Green consumer behaviour 117
Green marketing strategies 120

H

Health Belief model 154
Household consumption 92

I

Implementation 15
Industry strength (IS) 25
Information technology – role 47
Integration 143
Intelligence – business 38
Internal communications 149

Internal marketing 148
International trade 61
Internationalization process of firms 53
Issues of implementation and control 15

K

Key account development cycle 78
  implications 79
  stages 78
Key account management (KAM) 75
  activities 76, 82
  contemporary issues 90
  rationale 77
  synergistic 79
  uncoupling 79
  infrastructure 84
Key account management system – type 84
Key account manager
  role 86
  skills 86
Key account team 87
Key accounts 79
  adding value 82
  communication 83
  conflict resolution 83
  customization 83
  ease of replacement 80
  information sharing 83
  problem-solving 83
  profitability 80
  quality improvement 82
  relationship history 80
  resource sharing 83
  resources synergies 81
  selection criteria 79
  status 80
  strategic compatibility 81
  volume 80
Key historical events 20
Key issues 28
Key supplier, criteria 81
Knowledge and skill requirements for Strategic Marketing in Practice 11
Knowledge of contemporary marketing issues 15

Index

L

Learning
  double-loop 50
  single-loop 49
Learning organization 48
Life cycle analysis (LCA) concept 104
Life cycle thinking 104
Limitations of customer loyalty 67
Links to strategic marketing 22
Long-term orientation 71
Loyalty 64
  brand 65
  customer 62, 64

M

Market orientation 165
Market research 42
Market-based learning 48
Marketing concept 149
Marketing contexts 4
Marketing issues 15
Marketing measures 172
Marketing metrics 175
  acceptability 179
  common measures 179
  feasibility 179
  suitability 177
Marketing paradigm 62
Marketing
  internal 148
  models 3
  strategic activities 5
Mergers 62
Mid-KAM 78
Mission statements 52
Models of marketing 3
Mutual objectives 71

O

Objectives 142
Oceans 95
Online social marketing 158
Organizational issues 14
Organizations
  implications of environment 113
  learning 48
  market-based learning 48

P

PESTLE analysis 20
Planning processes 5
Plans and planning processes 5
Population – evolution 92
Portfolio analysis 34
Positioning 141, 142
  brand 138
Potential strategies 34
Potential strategies emanating from
    portfolio analysis 34
Pre-KAM 78
Primary research 42
Producer responsibility 105
Product market analyses 22
Products
  core 61
  discarded 105
Profit ratios 173
Public image 134

R

Recruitment 149
Recycling 105
Relationship marketing 68
  misconceptions 68
  specific application 88
Relevance of KAM to relationship marketing
    88
Research
  primary 42
  secondary 46
Research findings 157
Research methodology 155
Responses to globalization 57
Revitalization – brand 137
Role of communications 134
Role of information technology 47
Role of strategic marketing 6

S

Secondary research 46
Segmentation 140
Senior management support 88
Single-loop learning 49
Skill requirements 11
Social change – theories and models 151

197

Social marketing 151
  online 158
SPACE analysis 23
Stability – environmental 25
Stages of Change model 153
Strategic marketing activities 5
Strategic Marketing in Practice
  aims and outcomes 9
  knowledge and skills requirements 11
  links with other syllabi 12
Strategic marketing
  links 22
  role 6
Strategies – foreign market entry 55
Strategy 91
Strength
  financial 24
  industry 25

Structural features 27
Sustainability 14, 91
SWOT analysis and its evaluation 21
Synergistic KAM 79

T

Takeovers 62
Targeting 140
Training 149
Types of customer loyalty 64

U

Uncoupling KAM 79

V

Value creation 66
Valuing customers 169